THE ZULUS
AT WAR

T0056800

Also by Adrian Greaves

Flight of Colour, Debinair, 2000

Isandlwana, Cassell, 2001

A Review of the South Africa Campaign, Debinair, 2001

Curling Letters of the Zulu War, (co-author with Brian Best), Pen & Sword, 2001

Rorke's Drift, Cassell, 2002

David Rattray Guide to the Battlefields of Zululand,
(co-author with David Rattray, and editor), Pen & Sword, 2003

Redcoats & Zulus, Pen & Sword, 2004

Crossing the Buffalo, Cassell, 2005

Who's Who of the Anglo-Zulu War, 2 Volumes,
(co-author with Ian Knight), Pen & Sword, 2007

Lawrence of Arabia – Mirage of a Desert War, Cassell, 2011

Isandlwana – How the Zulus Humbled the British Empire, Pen & Sword, 2011

Forgotten Battles of the Zulu War, Pen & Sword, 2012

THE ZULUS AT WAR

THE HISTORY, RISE, AND FALL OF THE TRIBE THAT WASHED ITS SPEARS

ADRIAN GREAVES & XOLANI MKHIZE

FOREWORD BY IAN KNIGHT

Skyhorse Publishing

Copyright © 2013 by Adrian Greaves and Xolani Mkhize

FIRST NORTH AMERICAN EDITION 2014
FIRST SKYHORSE PUBLISHING EDITION 2014

All rights to any and all materials in copyright owned by the publisher are strictly reserved by the publisher.

First published in Great Britain in 2013 by Pen & Sword Military, an imprint of Pen & Sword Books Ltd

All rights reserved. No part of this book may be reproduced in any manner without the express written consent of the publisher, except in the case of brief excerpts in critical reviews or articles. All inquiries should be addressed to Skyhorse Publishing, 307 West 36th Street, 11th Floor, New York, NY 10018.

Skyhorse Publishing books may be purchased in bulk at special discounts for sales promotion, corporate gifts, fund-raising, or educational purposes. Special editions can also be created to specifications. For details, contact the Special Sales Department, Skyhorse Publishing, 307 West 36th Street, 11th Floor, New York, NY 10018 or info@skyhorsepublishing.com.

Skyhorse® and Skyhorse Publishing® are registered trademarks of Skyhorse Publishing, Inc.®, a Delaware corporation.

Visit our website at www.skyhorsepublishing.com.

Typeset in Palatino Light by CHIC GRAPHICS

10 9 8 7 6 5 4 3 2

Library of Congress Cataloging-in-Publication Data is available on file.

Cover design by Jon Wilkinson

Print ISBN: 978-1-5107-2283-5
Ebook ISBN: 978-1-5107-2285-9

Printed in China

Contents

CONTENTS

Acknowledgments

I would like to acknowledge a number of people who have rendered valuable assistance to me in the preparation of this book.

I owe a huge debt to my wife Debbie for her unfailing patience and assistance while I was conducting the necessary research and putting the book together. Our lovely house was strewn with papers, photographs and maps, and whilst I always claimed to know where everything was, she didn't, and the temptation to tidy up was almost too much.

I will always thank Consultant Surgeon Cliff Stossell and his wife Katie, his operating theatre sister, for saving my life in 1986 following a road traffic accident, and for their care and skill during the many operations that followed over the years. It was my greatest pleasure, eventually, to accompany them around the stunning battlefields of Zululand and introduce them to my many South African and Zulu friends.

I especially thank all my long-standing Zulu friends at Rorke's Drift, especially Xolani Mkhize and the Reverend Wilfred Mbatha, who showed me some of the secret places of Zululand and who sought out and provided me with local material and interpretations of Zulu folklore that would have been impossible for me to access without their support. Xolani volunteered to be my co-author and he provided the interpretations of Zulu folklore. He was always a delight to work with.

Ian Knight was, as ever, hugely supportive and his willingness to comment, especially on the later Zulu kings, was always appreciated. Dr David Payne generously volunteered the impressive volumes of Charlie Harford's papers, which enabled me to fill many gaps in my research. I have relied on some material previously unseen by researchers and while this is referenced, any interpretation is mine and mine alone. This is my final book, due to *anno domini*, and I have used my twenty-five years of walking the battlefields of Zululand to try to understand and explain the Anglo-Zulu War, its participants and their descendents. I have been privileged to accompany some remarkable people while exploring these fascinating and desolate battlefields. They include, in no particular order, Xolani Mkhize and Reverend Wilfred Mbatha of Rorke's Drift, Chelmsford Ntanze from Isandlwana, David Rattray, Dave Charles, Ian Knight, Ian Castle, Dr David

Payne, George Chadwick, Paddy Ashdown MP, Prof John Laband, Ray Heron, Isobel Swan, Ron Lock – and all the guests from Holt's Battlefield Tours who, over many years, so politely listened to me at all those haunting battlefield sites.

I am also eternally grateful to David and Nicky Rattray for their generosity in accommodating me at their magnificent Fugitives' Drift Lodge during my numerous visits to Zululand. I first met David at Rorke's Drift nearly twenty-four years ago while I was accompanying some tourists to the graves of British soldiers. David was supervising the groundwork of his proposed lodge and innocently asked me, 'Do you think people will pay to come here?' The following year I took the first tourist coach the 20 miles along a bumpy dirt road to the new lodge for Holt's Battlefield Tours; other tourists, regal and otherwise, soon followed. While staying at the lodge, I was privileged to experience numerous 'walkabouts' with David to explore some of his special locations and talk over the finer points of Zululand's rich history. David's savage murder was an inconsolable loss to his family and friends and I am grateful to Nicky for enabling my association with her lodge to continue.

Hala gachle!

Adrian Greaves
Tenterden

Photographs are from Adrian Greaves' collection unless otherwise stated.

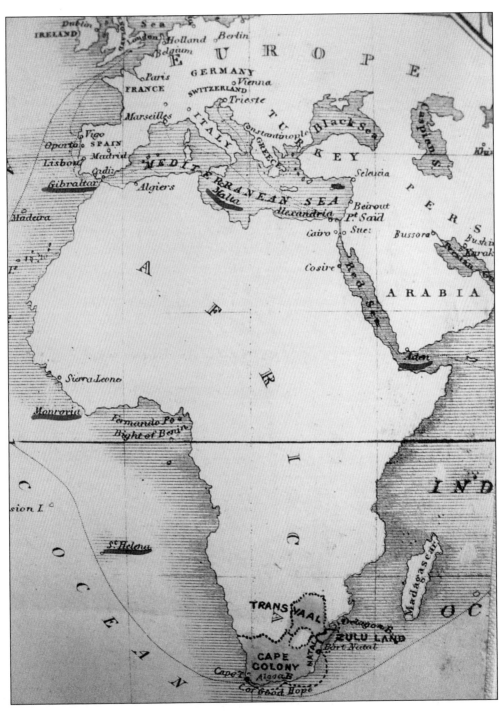

1870s map with the location of Zululand.

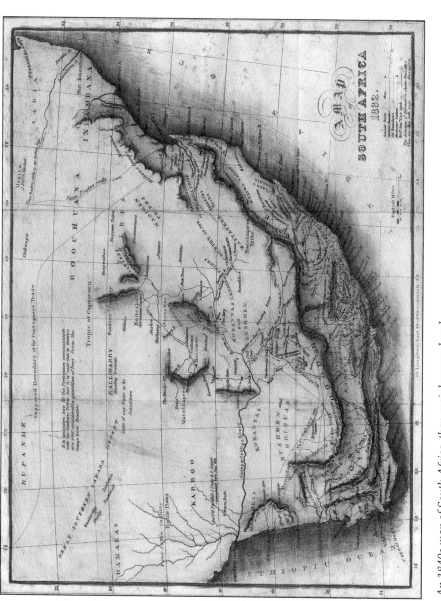

An 1840s map of South Africa, then mainly unexplored.

An original and rare 1879 map of Zululand, with pre-invasion British positions.

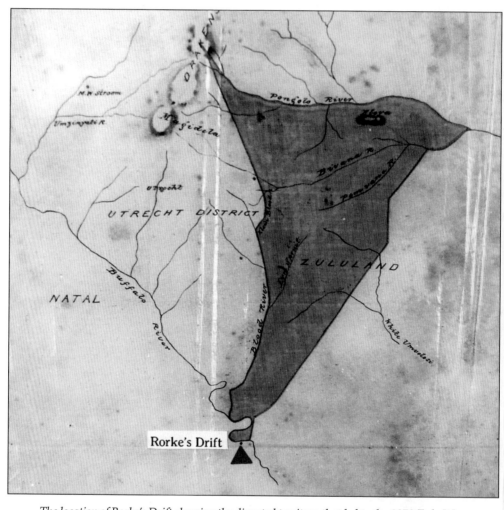

The location of Rorke's Drift showing the disputed territory that led to the 1879 Zulu War.

A Zululand map showing the disputed territory and battlefields.

Foreword

I first met Adrian Greaves in 1992 at Fugitives' Drift Lodge where I was then working for the late David Rattray as a guide. Adrian had phoned before departing Durban to check directions and I had given him details of the route to the Lodge, only for one of us to have mixed up our lefts and rights. Adrian duly arrived three hours late, having forged his way, with his young family, in an old Mercedes across 60 miles of rarely-used dirt tracks, crossing the Thukela River on a planked bridge and negotiating numerous hill ranges and two dense forests. Drinks at the bar and a few laughs quickly resulted in the beginning of a long friendship – to this day we are still unsure of the route by which he actually got there.

In the years since, Adrian has extensively broadened the reading public's awareness of Zululand and its travails, both through his books and through the Anglo Zulu War Historical Society, which he founded in 1997, and whose journal he edits. His books have proved very popular and his investigative style has unearthed some startling material from participants in the Zulu War of 1879. These range from the diaries and papers of Lieutenant Henry Curling RA, the only regular British officer who held a front-line command at Isandlwana to survive the battle, the papers of Henry Harford, the officer who led the first attack of the war and who later conducted King Cetshwayo into exile, the journals and drawings of Sister Janet Wells, who nursed hundreds of wounded British soldiers at the front-line hospital at Utrecht and who finished her Zulu War duties at Rorke's Drift, to the letters of August Hammar, who was a Swedish visitor at Rorke's Drift just as the Zulus attacked.

His latest work reviews the struggle of the Zulu people from the time of the first Boer incursions into their territory through to the present time and is sure to appeal, as always, to his many followers.

Ian Knight
Chichester

Zulu Names

There are many ways of spelling Zulu names and words; the art of correct orthography has been the result of many years of trial and error – and errors abound. Among the Zulu people, their history is generally oral; what is written is usually the work of European historians making their own spelling assumptions. The first records of the Zulus' history were made by Europeans, resulting in mixed spellings. Many Zulu spellings reflect the silent 'h' and the number 6 to replace the letter 'b'. There are many twists to the language, similar to the English trick of making 'ph' sound like an 'f'. Except when quoting, I have avoided these nuances in my text to make certain Zulu words easier to comprehend – otherwise the pronunciation of Zulu words would be as difficult for an Englishman to follow as English is for a Zulu reader.

This book refers to many names that are commonly known and abbreviated. I have used these spellings as they are in common usage and frequently easier on the European ear than the full Zulu name. For example, King Cetshwayo's name was presented in a variety of forms and spellings that I have standardized for ease of reading. It has been Zulu custom for a man to add after his own name those of his ancestors, back as far as his clan's founder. For example, Senzangakhona is used throughout, while I acknowledge his correct and full name was *Senzangakhona ka Jama ka Ndaba ka Punga ka Mageba ka Zulu*. Likewise, Shaka is the spelling according to modern orthography but early accounts spell his name as *Chaka*, itself a variation of *Tshaka*, previously *Utskaka*, although his full name was *Tshaka ka Senzangakhona ka Jama ka Punga ka Mageba ka Zulu* (*ka* means 'son of').

For those interested in a list of Zulu kings, I quote from King Cetshwayo's own 'death-bed' request, with contemporary spelling, for his assessment of the Zulu royal line to be passed to the British authorities. Full details can be found in British Parliamentary Papers, C.4037:44 Encl. 1.

Mageba
Punga
Undaba
Jama

ZULU NAMES

Senzangakhona
Chaka
Dingane
Umpande
Cetywayo
Dinizulu

When referring to Zulu kings by name, the title of king is used for the first mention in each chapter; thereafter, the king is referred to by name only, except where to emphasize his position.

Modern European usage is also used throughout when referring to towns, rivers and geographical locations, unless in quoted form. Likewise, imperial distances are used, as these were used at the time and feature in all contemporary documents and maps. To avoid ambiguity, I have referred to participants from Britain as the British; I have avoided specifying whether they were English or otherwise, except in direct speech. Throughout the period under consideration the term to denote British nationality, in both official and personal papers, was always 'English'. Where a unit or a named individual was from a colony or a colonial unit, the term 'colonial' is used.

Timeline of Events Significant to the Zulu People

1816	Shaka succeeds his father, *inkosi* Senzangakhona.
1824	British settlers establish Port Natal.
1826	Port Natal settlers support Zulus in Battle of iziNdolowane against the Ndwandwe.
1827	Shaka defeats Bheje tribe.
1828	(24 September) Shaka assassinated by Dingane.
1834	Great Trek and Boer-Zulu War.
1838	(6 February) Dingane murders Piet Retief and party.
	(16-19 February) Zulus massacre Boer Voortrekkers.
	(end April) Zulus ravage Port Natal.
	(16 December) Battle of Blood River.
1839	Peace treaty between Zulus and Boers.
	(September) Mpande flees to Boer Republic of Natalia.
1840	Mpande and Boers defeat Dingane.
	(10 February) Mpande made king by Boers. Cedes part of Zululand to Boers.
	(March-April) Dingane murdered.
1856	Battle of Ndondakusuka – Cetshwayo defeats Mbuyazi.
1872	(October) King Mpande dies.
1873	King Cetshwayo crowned.
1877	Bulwer offers mediation in border dispute.
1878	Boundary Commission meet at Rorke's Drift.
	(28 July) Sihayo incident.
	(mid-September) Smith and Deighton incident.
	(11 December) British ultimatum to Zulus.
1879	(6-11 January) British invasion of Zululand.
	(4 July) British defeat Zulus at Ulundi.
	(28 August) King Cetshwayo captured in Ngome Forest.
	(1 September) Wolseley partitions Zululand.
1880	(May) first unsuccessful Zulu request restoration of King Cetshwayo.

1882	(April) second unsuccessful Zulu request restoration of King Cetshwayo.
	(August) King Cetshwayo travels to London to plead his case.
1883	(10 January) King Cetshwayo returns to Zululand.
	(30 March) Zibhebhu routs king's Usuthu in northern Zululand.
	(21 July) King Cetshwayo defeated at Ulundi by rival chiefs, Zibhebhu and Hamu.
	(15 October) King Cetshwayo seeks refuge with British at Eshowe.
1884	(8 February) King Cetshwayo dies – probably poisoned by his own people.
	(April-May) internecine warfare continues.
	(2 May) Dinizulu and Boers form alliance.
	(21 May) Boers crown Dinizulu in exchange for 3 million acres of northern Zululand.
1888	(March-April) Dinizulu musters supporters on Ceza Mountain.
	(May) Usuthu under Dinizulu join abaQulusi and raid loyalists.
	(2 June) British repulsed by Dinizulu at Ceza.
	(24 June) British abandon northern Zululand.
	(2 July) British restore authority across northern Zululand.
	(6 August) Dinizulu disbands Usuthu and seeks refuge with ZAR.
	(15 November) Dinizulu surrenders to British – placed under arrest.
1889	(February-April) Dinizulu tried and then banished to St Helena.
1897	(30 December) Colony of Zululand annexed by British and becomes a province of Natal.
1898	(January) Dinizulu returned to Zululand in an attempt to restore stability.
1903	All parts of Zululand brought under control of Natal authorities.
1906	(January) White farmers and settlers authorized to occupy Zululand.
	(February-August) Zulu uprising commences (Bambatha Rebellion).
1910	(31 May) Natal becomes a province of the Union of South Africa.
1913	Dinizulu dies.
1923	Inkatha kaZulu formed.
1925	(June) Prince Solomon meets with the British heir apparent, Edward, Prince of Wales.
1933	(4 March) King Solomon dies.

TIMELINE OF EVENTS SIGNIFICANT TO THE ZULU PEOPLE

1952	Prince Cyprian recognized as king by the British Government.
1953	Prince Mangosuthu Buthelezi elected to the tribal constituency of Mahlabatini.
1955	(October) Zululand re-established and its lands returned to the Zulus.
1968	(September) King Cyprian dies.
1971	(4 December) Goodwill Zwelithini crowned king.
1975	Prime Minister Buthelezi founds a new version of Inkatha – later the Inkatha Freedom Party.

Glossary of Terms

(Zulu words in italics)

abathakathi	evil spirits.
abelungu	drowned European shipwrecked sailors that were occasionally found washed up on the shores.
amabandla mhlope	regiments that had been allowed to marry but were still required to muster regularly.
amadlozi	the spirits (or shades) of ancestors.
amakholwa	Christian converts.
amalala	menial workers.
amanhlwenga	destitutes.
amaviyo	companies of warriors.
assegai	a flat-bladed spear named after the African tree of the same name. Shaka was frustrated with conventional spears, which, when thrown, were lost to the enemy or, when used during the rigours of close combat, tended to snap at the shaft.
Bantu	the European term for the ancient black native *abaNtu*, which means 'people'.
Bastaards	early Dutch term used around the Cape denoting the children of mixed blood.
battle names	battles of the Zulu War are usually named by the British after a local hill or river – the Zulus name these battles after the nearest homestead or settlement. To the Zulus, the Battle of Ulundi is known as Nodwengu, although the place of Ulundi, or oNdini, means 'The Heights', a Zulu

GLOSSARY OF TERMS

	name for the Drakensberg mountain range. Eshowe is named by the Zulus 'Tshowe', to sound like a sneeze – as Eshowe overlooks the low-lying coastal plain and is occasionally subjected to cool breezes.
Boer	mainly Dutch-speaking white settlers, with some French, German and other Europeans, originating from the Cape of Good Hope.
column	the main British invading columns were known variously as the Coastal or No. 1 Column; the Centre or No. 3 Column; the Northern or No. 4 Column. Lieutenant Colonel Durnford and Rowlands' Reserve Columns were the 2nd and 5th respectively.
donga	a rift in the ground caused by heavy rain and in depths of between 2 and 50 feet – the bane of early travellers in Zululand; usually occurring when least expected and frequently involving a detour of many miles.
drift	a shallow river crossing point.
ebuto	company of young warriors under sixteen years.
ezibuto	carriers of provisions for the Zulu army.
giya	(ukugiya) a show of individual prowess during a Zulu war dance; opposing sides would confront each other at a distance of about 100 yards with shouted taunts and abuse; some spears would occasionally be thrown. Giya would last an hour or two and enabled inter-tribal disputes to be resolved by a theatrical 'letting off of steam' without causing serious damage. Victory went to the most impressive side.
Helpmakaar (b)	(a) is colloquial; (b) is the British spelling.
Helpmekaar (a)	(adaptation) a tiny hamlet atop a hill 15 miles from Rorke's Drift used by the British as their advance

base for the invasion of Zululand. Known by the soldiers as 'Help-my-cart-up'.

Hottentot first recorded in the seventeenth century referring to the Khoikhoi. Believed to be from the German *hotteren-totteren* – to stutter – referring to their clicking sound when speaking.

ibutho (pl. *amabutho*) a guild or regiment of age-graded Zulu warriors. Collectively, they were a form of national service.

ikhanda (pl. *amakhanda*) a homestead belonging to the king or a state barracks where amabutho were quartered when in the king's service.

iklwa (pl. *amaklwa*) a stabbing spear.

impi a fighting body of Zulu warriors, usually of regimental strength.

Impondo Zankhomo an encircling technique of attack, translated as 'horns of the bull'.

induku a stick or club.

inDuna (pl. *izinDuna*) a sub-chief, adviser or councillor, an officer appointed by the king.

inkosi chief.

inkwebane males under sixteen years of age.

intelezi medicines used by war doctors – *inyanga*.

inyanga war doctor (s.).

iphathi gathering of men to drink beer – probably from the English 'to party'. *See also ukudla.*

isibongo honorific names.

isiGodlo the royal enclosure quartering the women of the king's household; often misrepresented to be a

harem. These young women were a ready source of
wives and concubines but were, principally, young
women presented to a chief or king as a tribute – for
him to dispose of in marriage in return for a high
lobola, or bride wealth.

isiJula   (pl. *iziJula*) a throwing-spear.

iziendane   those with unusual hairstyles.

izikhulu   senior advisers.

izinyanga   war doctors (pl.)

kaffir   only used in the historical context due to the
sensitivity of the word. Commonly believed to be
the Arabic word for 'infidel' or 'non-believer', which
is curious as the word is not found elsewhere in
Africa where the Arab traders flourished. The
original usage of the word in South Africa could
also have come from the following Zulu and Bantu
sources, including:
a. *kafulwa*, the Bantu name for the early shipwreck
survivors 'washed up' along the Cape to Natal coast.
b. following the umfecane, those refugees fleeing to
the protection of the British Crown were known as
the *abakafula*, the 'washed out' or dispossessed.
c. *kafula* also has a modern usage, to denote the
'washing away' of an unhappy memory or washing
away a bad taste.
d. see *Through the Zulu Country* (Griggs, Durban,
1883) by Bertrand Mitford, who wrote that 'non
Zulu blacks were known as *Amakafula*', which is
only a short step from *kaffir*. Similarly, the
AmaFengu people later became known as *Fingoes*.

knobkerrie   a short stick with a knobbed head, used as a
weapon by South African tribesmen.

kop   or koppie – a small hill.

GLOSSARY OF TERMS

kraal	an enclosure for cattle; not to be confused with a Zulu homestead or *umuzi*. It is an old Dutch term that signified a 'beast fold', which early colonialists contemptuously designated all native towns and villages.
laager	a number of wagons formed into a circle to form a defensive perimeter.
lobola	(or *lobolo*) the bride price, or dowry, normally involving cattle.
maihlome	the order to take up arms.
mealie	maize.
Mfecane	or 'crushing'; denotes the period of internecine clan fighting pre-1825.
muti	magical medicine.
NCO	non-commissioned officer.
nek	a saddle between two hills.
Nguni	there were two major divisions of the southerly migrating Bantu peoples, the Sotho and Nguni. The term Nguni is used to denote those speaking the same language. The Zulu people originate from the Nguni.
NNC	Natal Native Contigent.
pont	a flat-bottomed punt or boat made of barrels.
qaqa	the act of disembowelling a fallen enemy.
sangoma	a Zulu diviner.
spruit	a small stream or tributary.
uDibi	(pl. *izinDibi*) a Zulu boy between the age of twelve and sixteen who supported older relatives on the march or in other military tasks.

GLOSSARY OF TERMS

ukudabuka bkwegoda	the symbolic rope, wrapped in a python skin, that held the Zulu nation together.
ukudla	group of beer-drinking men. *See also iphathi.*
ukugwanjiswa kwempi	to spiritually prepare the army.
ukuhlobonga	a form of external intercourse.
umhlaho	the public naming of an offender.
umKhosi	The annual gathering before the king to review the army and to usher in the new harvest, often referred to as the first fruits ceremony.
umkumbi	warriors formed into a circle for application of *muti*.
umnumzana	a local headman.
umnyama	communicating with both ancestors and evil spirits.
umthakathi	the act of detecting *umthakathi*, people or animals who secretly used magic.
umutcha	a shawl of leopard skin and tails, with lions' teeth and claw charms worn around the neck.
umuzi	(pl. *imizi*) a Zulu homestead – often mis-named as a *kraal*.
Umvelingqangi	God.
Unkulunkulu	the name of the first Zulu god.
Usuthu	the political party of King Cetshwayo – the term was the popular Zulu war cry during the 1879 war.
uxoxa impi	where deeds of bravery or cowardice were passionately discussed by Zulu warriors.
veghekke	wooden gates lashed to Boer wagons against Zulu attacks.

Introduction

A very remarkable people, the Zulu.[1]

Following the 1879 defeat of her army in South Africa, Queen Victoria asked 'Who are these Zulus?'[2] It was one question being asked across Britain that could not readily be answered and it is still difficult to answer today. Modern perception of the Zulus is of a warlike nation, as indeed they were for fifty years – a relatively short span of time. The complexity of the Zulu people, their culture and their many wars remain little understood by those outside the field of Zulu culture and history. Yet the history of these people is as remarkable as it is poignant. From the very founding of the Zulu nation, its effect on British and colonial history could never have been imagined by those first white traders bravely venturing into unexplored Zululand in the 1820s. From then on, the history of the Zulu people is as short as it is tragic; their development was as savage as its warriors were brave in battle. Their history carries us from the 1820s, when they existed as disparate clans living together in relative peace, to the formation of a powerful and warmongering nation. Inevitably, its very success led it to confrontation with the British, who were busy developing their own commercial interests around the Cape. Worldwide interest in the Zulus progressively developed following the appalling and mournful events of the crushing British invasion of Zululand in 1879. It was an unnecessary and brutal war, which resulted in the Zulus' defeat and subsequent humiliation. They were then powerless to stop their country being divided into thirteen kingdoms by the victorious British administrators in South Africa; the Zulus thereafter lived their lives in abject despair. 1906 saw their despair turn to an overflowing anger when they unsuccessfully rebelled against British rule, their defeat resulting in their country being further weakened by partitioning.

A brief review of the past will, perhaps, make order and sense of these dramatic events but at no point do I pretend to fully cover the subject. Examining Zulu history has been a difficult journey for every researcher and the 1920s' observation by the noted South African historian Dr A.T. Bryant, who produced one of the very first sociological works on the Zulus, soon rang in my ears. He wrote:

INTRODUCTION

> So far as we know, no public fund or South African government, be it of the Union or of Natal, has ever considered the systematic collection and preservation of Zulu history as worth the outlay of one brass farthing or the expenditure of one hour's labour – a grim reflection of the white man's consistent and deliberate neglect of Native interests.[3]

Notwithstanding these difficulties, I will attempt to unravel the complexities of Zulu history by considering the origins and culture of the Zulu people, by analysing their leaders and the many campaigns they fought and, equally importantly, by considering the influence and effect on the Zulus of white settlement and its political power, often supported by crushing military force. This examination of events will be, as far as is possible, from the Zulu perspective – for which I am indebted to my Zulu friend of more than twenty-five years, Xolani Mkhize, the manager of the Zulu Village at Rorke's Drift in Zululand. His family roots at Rorke's Drift can be traced to before the infamous British invasion of Zululand in 1879. His ancestors were of the Mkhize tribe, who lived to the north of Rorke's Drift, thereby making him well placed to provide a Zulu perspective to this account. His and other Zulus' explanations of so many aspects of the various Zulu military campaigns have been faithfully handed down, according to Zulu custom, across the generations through the art of storytelling, and these renditions, invariably consistent even in small detail, are frequently at variance with accepted British accounts. These differences will be examined. Even with a strong Zulu contribution and twenty-five years of personal research I acknowledge that I have understated the Zulu case.

Further into this project, the reader may wonder why I have seemingly gone into so much detail about the resultant and ongoing cost and loss to the Zulus following the British invasion of Zululand in 1879. It is worth remembering that Zululand had suffered many upheavals before the British invaded. They had suffered epidemic tribal wars but the scale of death and disruption caused by the British invasion dwarfed anything that had happened earlier. It left the Zulu nation bereft and bewildered.

Since their foundation, even as a tribe but especially as a nation, the Zulus have been a challenge to the white man, be he the most highly educated administrator, an army general or the British red-coated soldier tasked with fighting a formidable foe, usually in impossible conditions,

INTRODUCTION

somewhere in the far-flung fringes of the British Empire. Such was the challenge because early Zulu victories in the war of 1879 brought failure to Britain's generals and politicians in South Africa by out-smarting them. Due to a powerful succession of Zulu kings, the Zulu nation had grown and prospered, but by their very success they inevitably faced ultimate defeat at the hands of Britain, a nation itself well honed to the cult of war and used to the delights and profit of conquest and domination. Yet the Zulus survived, just. Their glory and place in history is founded on their spirit of resistance to the overwhelming force used against them when the British invaded in 1879, and by the bloody nose they inflicted on the imperial invaders. Thereafter, the Zulus have willingly fulfilled the expectations of the 'first world' for a number of reasons; by being fierce warriors, ruthless savages, a people in dire need of missionaries or for being subject to their witch doctors' skill at evoking the 'spirits' of their forefathers. Their reputation is deserved; fighting is in their blood. Even in modern times, local 'faction fighting' at weekends is widespread and commonplace. Statistics are difficult to find although research conducted during my brief spell with the Durban Police revealed that seven out of every nine murders in their city could be attributed to Zulus fighting each other; and these same statistics would probably still apply today. Medical statistics are impossible to collate as most Zulu wounded treat their own injuries, especially in rural areas. I have seen very unpleasant machete and bullet wounds, and broken bones that have remained untreated either due to the lack of medical facilities or a wish to avoid 'trouble' with the authorities. Perhaps it is a legacy from Shaka that requires them to fight each other. When asked if the Zulu nation had any regrets for fighting the British in 1879, Xolani Mkhize replied, 'We know how to fight – we could do it again if the need ever arose,' but he added, reassuringly, that modern Zulus see the British as their friends.

To answer Queen Victoria's question, one must first consider the origin of the Zulu tribe, which is well documented thanks to a number of early explorers' accounts recorded in the early 1820s, such as that written by Reverend Kay and by the work of 1920s' historians such as A.T. Bryant and James Stuart. Zulus know that their power had waxed until 1879, when every vestige of their nation's military and civil administration was then crushed by the military might of the British Empire, the greatest empire the world had ever seen. The Zulus had been a most formidable nation for a relatively short period of time, a mere 100 years. Their ancestry is not disputed; they originated as a breakaway group from the largest migrating black Bantu tribe, whose absolute anthropological origins are conversely relatively unknown. The term 'Bantu' is the European adoption of the ancient black native *abaNtu*, which means 'people'. Modern archaeological discoveries and reasoned supposition suggest that, over several thousand years, the progressively migrating native Bantus' lives were exclusively centred on cattle, making them adept at nomadic life. They had departed from the equatorial west coast of Africa, perhaps via the Congo, and then gradually spread laterally across central Africa. They then headed south and east around the wastes of the Kalahari Desert towards the area known as the Transvaal and Natal, until eventually reaching the east coast, probably in the early sixteenth century.[4] The main Bantu migration did not reach the far south of the African continent for another 1,000 years but the eventual arrival of this cattle-owning society had an inevitably destructive impact on the original people living in the area. The sparsely populated indigenous people were made up of the hunting and food-gathering Bushmen and the pastoralist Khoikhoi, who subsisted on their sheep and cattle. These two ancient groups, with their own distinctive language and culture, had peacefully shared possession of the most southern reaches of the African continent. They were remarkably different from the forceful Bantu approaching from the north, and were therefore highly vulnerable.[5]

This spreading pattern of overland human settlement to the north-west of the Cape was already well established by 1486. It was at this crucial point in time that the first Europeans, led by the Portuguese explorer Bartholomew Diaz, landed at the Cape while searching for a southerly route to the East Indies. For the emerging European empires of Holland, Spain and Portugal, it was the newly discovered Americas and the East Indies that were the lands of opportunity and commercial development. Ten years later, Vasco da Gama landed at the Cape but only to replenish his water supplies. He then sailed further north along the lush coastline, far beyond the point previously reached by Diaz, and on Christmas Day he named the spray-swept coast Terra Natalis before sailing on to cross the Indian Ocean.

While the landmass of southern Africa was being progressively settled by the creeping occupation of the southerly migrating Bantu, one group of these people detached themselves from the Bantu and entered the previously unexplored coastal area on the eastern side of the Drakensberg Mountains bordering the Indian Ocean. This area measured a mere 40 by 100 miles and became settled by this group consisting of some 200 clan groups, one of which would later become the Zulus. This relatively insignificant area was beyond the main migration path southwards but very attractive to these cattle-orientated people who discovered its well-watered and lush pastures were much to their liking. This independent tribe became known as the Nguni people, differentiating them from the onward migrating peoples who became known as the Xhosa. Most of the Nguni settled in small clans to the north of the Tugela River and, as the land was virtually uninhabited, they quickly prospered being isolated from the outside world. Their lives were unaffected by the fierce inter-clan or clan-settler conflicts developing to the south.

The Xhosa were well established to the north, along the banks of the Great Kei River, by around 1670-75. Even though the ongoing Xhosa migration had consisted of one homogenous mass of like-minded tribes, its rapidly growing population soon began suffering the relentless pressure of a population faced with decreasing resources, a typical Malthusian philosophy.[6] This pressure was worsened by marauding clans seeking their own survival; clans that had themselves suffered the process of defeat and assimilation. These displaced people, usually starving and homeless, then fell upon their neighbours. The ongoing process became known as the *Mfecane* or 'crushing', an explosive pattern that was to wreak havoc and cause misery across southern Africa, later to be made worse during the period dominated by the Zulu king, Shaka. (See Appendix A for additional material relating to the *Mfecane*.)

Problems abound dating the Bantu migration and *Mfecane* with any accuracy. There are no documents and so this history was not properly formalized until after the publication of *African Researches* in 1834 by Dr Stephen Kay, based in part on his own experiences and partly on the diaries of Captain B. Stout following the loss of his ship *Hercules* 'on the coast of Caffraria', the south-western Cape in 1796. Curiously, Stout recommended that the whole area be colonized by the Americans but his proposal was rejected by the President of the United States, John Adams. The most extensive research work followed in the early 1920s by Bryant and Stuart. Prior to these historians' definitive works, African history was based on their oral tradition, which has to be respected and treated with care, especially where there is no empirical evidence. When questioning Zulus about historical events, any question from a European itself raises further complexities with the inevitable unspoken question: 'What does he want me to answer?' When trying to get to the bottom of a matter, especially where inconsistencies abound or beliefs differ, many historians of the Zulu wars have discovered that out of cultural politeness, Zulus have tended to offer pleasing answers, which can skew history.[7]

It was not until 1769 that the Cape whites explored to the north-east and made their first contact with the advancing Xhosa people approaching from the Eastern Cape area. To the Boers' surprise, their own large migration from the Cape had progressed only 500 miles to the north-east when they unexpectedly came face to face with the Xhosa spearhead moving in even greater numbers south-west. Both sides met on opposing banks of the Great Fish River in 1769. It is ironic and a coincidence that a migration of such magnitude, and over such a long span of time, should have failed to reach the nearby Cape and that Europeans should fill that vacuum at exactly the same point in time. But for a few years, the Xhosa could have been the first people to have reached the Cape, and had they done so it is reasonable to hypothesize that African history would now be very different.

This initial contact with the cattle-owning white settlers and the Xhosa, whose propensity was to take others' cattle, would soon result in tumult and conflict. To the white explorers, these people had features more Arabic than Negroid. They were cattle people with ancient traditions, intricate clan systems and fine adornments. To the Khoza, gold, silver and precious stones were meaningless, 'mere dross' was Kay's description, although colourful beads and brass wire were common and popular. The people's wealth was measured solely in cattle, in which the encroaching Boers were abundant. The personal possession of property was not an issue except where, traditionally, tribal clashes invariably occurred and would involve the seizure of a defeated clan's cattle. Kay wrote that the colonists:

> came upon and drove them out in a manner the most barbarous ... being armed and mounted they found no difficulty in making themselves sole lords of the manor.

Then, in 1806, the Cape Colony was seized by Britain. To keep the peace, an attempt was made to drive a wedge between the Boer settlers and the encroaching Xhosa. Twenty thousand Xhosa were forcibly moved from their territory northwards. It was a policy doomed to failure and a number of chiefs were later permitted to return their clans to the neutral buffer zone, subject to their 'good behaviour'.

Two hundred miles to the north the Nguni tribe was unaffected by these early disturbances. They were best known for tobacco trading; they controlled their own territories, which were known to the first white adventurers and traders as the 'Territory of the Zoola' or 'Vatwa Nation', later known as Zululand. With the inevitability of passing time, their clans also began to experience a growing lack of economic resources. As populations increased, the pressure of limited resources already being experienced across great swathes of southern Africa crept into the previously unaffected area controlled by the Nguni. Disputes inevitably led to violence, which, in turn, led to inter-clan war.

These pressures left the survivors of this creeping warfare, and those seeking to avoid conflict, no choice. Where such fighting occurred, survivors of a defeated people had no option but to be slaughtered out of hand or flee. When the effects of the *Mfecane* reached the Nguni, the process of expansion by force accelerated when one group, the Ndwandwe clan under Chief Zwide, violently drove the Ngwane clan, under Chief Sobhuza, from their tribal area, forcing them to flee west and then north to Swaziland. In their flight, they in turn fell upon their neighbours. The process involved killing the male warriors of the vanquished and the victors would absorb any surviving women and children into their own tribes. In a relatively short space of time, the *Mfecane*, with its multiple causes, forced uncountable thousands of refugees, especially from Natal, southwards into the unknown area of Pondoland between the Umzimkulu and Umzimvubu rivers. This area was originally named No-Man's-Land by the first white explorers, who were horrified by what they saw, describing the countryside as populated by 'starving and despairing skeletal people'.[8]

Within Zululand, the ongoing destructive conflicts eventually left just two notable protagonist chiefs, Zwide and Dingiswayo. The one significant difference between the two tribes was that Dingiswayo had influence over the much smaller Zulu clan, ruled by Chief Senzangakhona, whose warrior son was known as Shaka, soon to be given command of the fledgling Zulu army. When Senzangakhona died in 1816, Shaka assumed the mantle of chief with virtual total control of a kingdom ever increasing in size and strength – and with no viable opposition. In 1818 the two armies of Zwide and Dingiswayo, with Shaka in support of Dingiswayo, went to war, finally meeting at Gqokoli Hill. The battle resulted in defeat for Zwide and the subsequent merciless slaughter of many of his civil population. Zwide escaped but within days his followers captured and executed Dingiswayo, leaving Shaka as the only viable opposition to Zwide. It is still believed by the Zulus that Shaka deliberately held back while Dingiswayo led his army into battle, only for Dingiswayo to be captured and beheaded, creating the vacancy for Shaka.

Over the following decades the Zulus came to dominate their neighbours and, as their sphere of influence increased, they exerted total control over vast tracts of country south of the Tugela River formally known as Natal, today as KwaZulu-Natal. Before the emergence of the Zulu nation, the area was populated by a patchwork of independent but minor Nguni chiefdoms that broadly spoke the same Nguni language and followed the same cultural practices. The growing success of the developing Zulu clan was due to a powerful combination of astute diplomacy, ruthless military force and a willingness of the Zulu population to participate and share in the spoils of war.

By 1824 the first British traders had arrived at the coast on the periphery of Zululand. It was a land described by the explorer Reverend Kay as:

> beautiful beyond description, the meadows being carpeted with luxuriant herbage, and watered every few hundred yards by copious rivulets, whose banks are level with the prairies through which they meander; rivers abounding with fish, hippopotami, and alligators; plains and hills there covered with woods of gigantic forest trees, attaining the height of seventy or eighty feet; and enlivened with herds of elephants. Vegetation was rich beyond anything seen; the coast was abundantly supplied with oysters.

Within months these traders made contact with Shaka, who granted them land around the bay of Port Natal – the region's only viable landing point. It was from this embryonic settlement that all future British claims in the region would stem. Within a few years the Zulus abandoned their claims to Natal as it was too far beyond their main sphere of influence, as was the Cape district, where the British colony was slowly developing. When in 1838 the first Boer settlers crossed the Drakensberg Mountains into the Zulu area of northern Natal, a particularly brutal war broke out between them and Shaka's successor, King Dingane. In the ensuing campaigns, the Zulu army swept into Natal twice, once massacring Boer civilians in the foothills of the inland mountains, and once sacking the settlement at Port Natal itself. Although there were no further significant clashes between Natal and the

Zulu kingdom between the years 1840 and 1879, Zulu history was about to change.

This book will firstly consider the rise of the Zulu nation until the Anglo-Zulu War of 1879 and its destructive aftermath for the Zulu people. Attention will then be given to the totalitarian post-war settlements imposed upon the defeated Zulus on the direct order of Sir Garnet Wolseley, the British High Commissioner for South East Africa. This astute soldier/politician was determined to eradicate every hint of resistance to British rule in South Africa and, due to the nature of his severe and punitive measures, this author suspects there was a strong element in his blueprint to revenge the earlier British defeat at Isandlwana. Further, by sending King Cetshwayo into exile in 1879, Wolseley's settlement put Zulu against Zulu, tribe against tribe, and brought about a vicious civil war thus 'consummating the [British] military victory without further cost or responsibility,' a policy that effectively destroyed the Zulus as a nation.[9] The Afrikaner historian J.C. Voight wrote scathingly of events:

> The bones of the black and white victims of the cupidity and greed of a cattle annexing association of financiers and speculators, ruled and directed by a Privy Councillor of the British Crown. Hark! The bells are tolling their warning in the great echoing belfry of the temple of History. Is it only a warning? Or are they sounding the death knell of an Empire?[10]

Chapter 1

The Emergence of the Zulus

Settlement of the area known as Zululand and Natal predates the formation of the Zulu kingdom in the late 1700s by several thousand years. Archaeologists have discovered evidence of African Bronze Age settlements in the Tugela River Valley and sites in KwaZulu-Natal, which suggest on the limited evidence available that Khoikhoi communities were already established in the region by AD 300. Historians believe the pastoral black African people, the Bantu, were relatively recent incomers to southern Africa but from whence these people came is, by and large, unknown. The Bantu movement southwards was the greatest known migration ever witnessed in African history; it probably commenced in the first millennium AD and its timings and route remain something of a mystery. Its cause was most likely a combined process of pressure from expansion, colonization and conflict in their original homelands. Why this Bantu migration occurred is a matter of conjecture. It is possible that they were driven from their distant lands in the north by a stronger tribe, leaving their property and cattle to the victors. Perhaps they had little choice but, because Bantu lives had always been based upon cattle, it appears they were well suited to a nomadic life.

This slow but progressive migration over some 3,000 miles lasted more than half a millennium and took the route from the arid lands sub-Sahara, south-east around the wastes of the Kalahari Desert, after which they passed by the verdant coastline of the Indian Ocean before expanding further south towards the Cape. During this migration the growing population naturally began to experience land pressure, which invariably led to inter-tribal conflicts and the search for more peaceful lands. Being pastoralists and with cattle forming the greater part of their life, they would have been able to make good their losses from weaker clans on their progression south.

1

THE ZULUS AT WAR

The migrating Bantu people were recognizably similar to the main cultural and linguistic groups who inhabit the area today: the Xhosa to the south, the Sotho and Tswana in the interior, and the Nguni on the north-eastern coastal strip adjoining the Indian Ocean. The Bantu, the Xhosa tribe, were still on their journey south, soon to reach the Great Fish River, the limit of Boer scouting, in 1769.

The eventual arrival of this aggressive cattle-owning society to the north-east of the Cape had an inevitably destructive impact on the two indigenous populations. The pastoral Khoi avoided conflict by moving further south while the hunter-gathering San, a branch of the Khoi, were gradually forced to abandon their costal area in favour of the more marginal environments of the Qahlamba Mountains, later named 'Drakensberg' by the Boers. Due to persecution by white and black alike for being diminutive, large numbers of the San crossed the Qahlamba to seek sanctuary in the only area left uninhabited, the inhospitable and arid Kalahari Desert. The survivors became known as 'Bushmen'.

During this period of progressive migration and population growth, clans large and small naturally expanded and then split into smaller clans, which, as they grew, then had to repeat the cycle of competing against each other for increasingly scarce resources, such as land for cattle and crops. By this process, the Hlubi clan under *inkosi* Bhungane became the dominant tribe in northern Natal, extending its sphere of influence by subjugating lesser groupings until it dominated an area of 3,000 square miles.

While the main migration was still moving south, one comparatively small Nguni tribe, the Mtethwa (estimates suggest between 150 and 200 clans), split away and headed east towards the coast. One such clan would become the Zulus. The beginnings of Nguni development in the area known as Zululand can be identified as circa 1790-1830, just as the main Xhosa migration reached a point a mere 500 miles from the Cape. Unbeknown to the Xhosa, the land they were approaching to the south-west was already in the process of being colonized by the Dutch. But for a few years, the Xhosa could have been the first people to reach the Cape and African history would have turned out be very different.

Meanwhile, the breakaway Mtethwa tribe and its clans, all speaking a particular dialect and walking in step with their customs, began settling the lush land between the Drakensberg and the Indian Ocean. Due to the richness of their land the social development and wealth of the Mtethwa steadily expanded, even though they were quick to resort to force when necessary. One of these clans included an insignificantly small group of between 100 and 200 people who had settled themselves along the banks of the White Mfolozi River and in sight of the Indian Ocean. Their chief, Mandalela, had a son, Zulu, who eventually succeeded him and under whose chieftaincy the small group thrived. According to Zulu folklore, the clan adopted the title 'Zulu'. Chief Zulu was followed by Mageba; Ndaba followed Mageba, who was followed by Jama. During this embryonic stage of Nguni development, the Mtethwa clan had grown in size to more than 1,000 people and by the end of the eighteenth century probably amounted to 3,000 or 4,000 living under the aged chieftaincy of Jobe. Jobe had a number of sons, including Godongwana and Utana, who were over-eager to assume the mantle of chief. Apprehensive for his own safety, Jobe dispatched loyal warriors to kill his two ambitious sons but Godongwana escaped, severely wounded, to take refuge with the Hlubi clan near the Drakensberg Mountains while Utana died suddenly of a mysterious illness. In order to avoid detection from his vengeful father, Godongwana changed his name to Dingiswayo (meaning 'one in distress'). Dingiswayo remained with the Hlubi until his father died and then returned home to find another brother, Mawewe, on the throne. Meanwhile, Dingiswayo had acquired both a gun and a horse from a white trader – items that were unknown to the Mthethwa. Mawewe fled in fear for his life but he was tracked down by Dingiswayo and killed. In the midst of this turmoil, the chief of a fledgling Zulu clan, Senzangakhona, unwittingly started a chain of events that would dramatically affect southern Africa.

In 1787, Senzangakhona dallied with the daughter of an eLangeni chief, in itself a relatively insignificant event but one that would have major implications for the future of the Zulu people. The unfortunate girl, Nandi, soon fell pregnant, but marriage was impossible because she was a not a Zulu. After Nandi gave birth to a son, the eLangeni banished the disgraced Nandi and her child, which morally forced Senzangakhona to appoint Nandi as his 'unofficial' third wife. She was unable to get her son recognized or named by his father, so in defiance Nandi named him 'iShaka' after a common intestinal beetle. Nandi also bore Senzangakhona a daughter but the family lived a lonely and unpopular life until her equally despised son, Shaka, now in his early teens, lost some goats belonging to Senzangakhona. Such was the chief's anger at this youthful carelessness that Nandi and her children were evicted back to the unwelcoming eLangeni, who delighted in making life for the outcasts even more miserable.

By 1802, the starving eLangeni could no longer tolerate Nandi and her family so banished them into destitution at a time when the whole land was suffering widespread famine. Nandi fled to the Qwabe clan, where she had once given birth to a son by a Qwabe warrior named Gendeyana. Under Gendeyana's guidance, Shaka developed into such an excellent warrior that Senzangakhona sought the return of this fine young combatant, whether to develop his skills or, more likely, to murder him is unclear. Nandi's suspicions led her to move her family to the protection of yet another clan in order to protect Shaka from his father.

At the very beginning of the 1800s, Dingiswayo assumed the mantle of chief of the Mtethwa tribe and immediately set about training his force of 400 warriors and, by a sustained policy of subjugation and making threats of annihilation, he gradually assimilated the surrounding tribes. He became a politically astute leader who replaced recalcitrant chiefs with his own kind, usually favoured and trusted sons from his several hundred wives. It was Dingiswayo who first developed a liking for European goods and began trading elephant tusks for trinkets with the passing Portuguese traders from their Delagoa Bay settlement 200 miles to the north.

Within the clans, especially the growing Zulu clan, they developed complex social structures. They were competent cattle farmers with no concept of money, aspirations or worries; nature provided everything. They were able to make implements out of metal, the very best of which was virtually equal to steel. One of these items, the throwing spear, would soon ensure their ascendancy over their neighbours and any San and Khoikhoi they encountered, and would soon seriously inconvenience the encroaching whites.

Their social structure valued a form of marriage – a concept orientated more towards property than the values of conventional European marriage. Its complex system of dowry payments for a wife, known as *lobola*, ensured that a man could not marry until he was established in society and possessed sufficient cattle, the Zulu currency, to pay the required *lobola*. The more cattle a man had, the more wives he could buy. Most Zulu men had only two, or at the most, three, wives, to whom fell the hard physical work of planting and raising crops, while the task of tending cattle was the exclusive preserve of the youths, on behalf of the men. Under the emergence of the extended Zulu kingdom early in the nineteenth century, cattle seized from outsiders were regarded as property of the state for the king to dispose of as a reward, or to farm out to district chiefs who would care for them. It was this Zulu dependency on cattle for the vital *lobola* for social prestige and their subsequent wealth that was soon to bring the Zulus into permanent conflict with the surrounding Nguni tribes and, in due course, the advancing Boer trekkers.

Administratively, power was devolved from the tribal leader with diminishing power to each Zulu homestead chief and thence to all the scattered homesteads within their boundary. From the chief to the farmer and his family, all recognized themselves as part of a wider clan, a self-sufficient group living in a classless society. Zulus would explain their origin from the collective belief that they could trace themselves back to a common ancestor, real or imagined, who had two sons, Qwabe and Zulu. Each brother struck out on his own to establish his personal following. These two groups duly became known after their founding father, Zulu, the people calling themselves *amaZulu* (people of Zulu). Zulu means 'the heaven' or 'the sky'. Their beliefs were their means of explaining the reason for their existence and this belief is still widely acknowledged.

Each clan had its dominant lineage within the families, and it was from such that the male line of hereditary chiefs was drawn. Several small neighbouring clans, linked by ties of kinship, would form a chiefdom; the chief of the dominant clan in the area would have been the overall leader. This chief controlled the political and administrative life of the clan by heeding the advice of his 'inner council', although his decision in any dispute or clan matter was final.

A clan or homestead, the *umuzi*, would be largely self-sufficient with each homestead producing sufficient crops and managing their cattle to support themselves. Their domestic and farming tools were made within each *umuzi*; the only essential product not made at home was iron, which was necessary for the production of hoes and spear blades. Even this seems to have been readily available. One clan was renowned as metal workers – the Cube people, who lived in the Nkandla Forest, north of the Tugela River. As was common among African cultures, the Zulus regarded the forging of iron with superstition, and the smiths, keen to maintain the mystique of their trade, lived and worked away from ordinary dwellings. Ritual was an essential ingredient in the process, and it was widely believed that the most successful spear-blades were tempered with magical herbs and human fat to increase their efficacy.

Zululand was superb cattle country with freshly watered grasslands producing a succulent range of sweet and sour grasses. These pastures allowed the Zulu people to raise their stock without migrating any great distance and the relative absence of tsetse fly and other parasitic pests kept bovine mortality levels to a minimum. It was fortuitous that the Zulus were competent cattle farmers as their survival and prosperity depended on their cattle; cattle were not only an important source of food – although rarely for their meat except for special occasions and sacrifices. Their milk was drunk and curds, or *amasi*, formed an important part of their staple diet. The cattle provided hides for shields and garments, tails were a component of festive dress, and horns were used as containers for medicines or gunpowder. The ritual sacrifice of cattle to the ancestors was a common ingredient of a number of ceremonies, either pre-battle or to ensure harmony with the dead.

Such was the importance and value of their cattle that the physical layout of the *umuzi* was traditionally arranged in a circle around a central cattle pen. At the lowest level of Zulu society, a typical *umuzi* probably consisted of no more than four or five huts of a family unit, the married man together with his immediate family and any dependants. Within a particular clan, usually inter-related, one homestead would be close to the next with several on one hillside, usually overlooking a river or stream. All *umuzi* across Zululand were built along the same lines, and can still be seen today across rural Zululand. If the *umuzi* headman, the *umnumzana*, was sufficiently wealthy he would have his personal hut at the furthest end of the *umuzi*. Next in line was the hut of the principal wife, with the huts of lesser wives arranged in descending order of seniority. At the furthest point of the *umuzi* from the *umnumzana's* hut were the huts of unmarried dependants. In an ordinary *umuzi* the hut of the chief wife was his main place of abode although he would, at whim, visit the huts of his lesser wives.

Across Zululand the reeded thatched huts were all traditionally dome-shaped and circular, with a low arched door to defend or politely force a visiting guest to bend in homage. (Genuflection has always been part of Zulu culture.) The design ensured that the hut was cool in summer and warm in winter and consisted of a rounded framework of bent-over saplings with the ends bound together where they criss-crossed. If the hut was of any size, a large pole would be used to support the interior. The thatch would last for several years before needing to be replaced. The floor area was smeared with cow dung, which was then polished with stones to produce a rock-hard dark glaze. A raised dais in the centre served as a hearth but, without a chimney, smoke would have hung in the thatch, which had the advantage of keeping the huts pest-free. Each *umuzi* was self-contained and, by necessity, self-supporting. Work around the *umuzi* was clearly delineated. The men were the artisans and pastoralists who provided and maintained the huts and tended their cattle. Women were the housekeepers and agriculturalists, the growers, gatherers of food, water and wood, and the *umuzi* cooks. Until more recent times, fish had not been an acceptable source of food among the Zulus. As long ago as 1820, the Reverend Kay wrote:

> They have as great an antipathy to fish as to swine's flesh; and would as soon think of sitting down to a dish of snakes as to partake of any of the inhabitants of the deep.[2]

To the south, the situation changed between 1816 and 1824; the Cape Frontier Wars were fought between blacks and whites, both keen to extend their area of domination. While the more northerly Nguni chiefdoms were immune from the effects of these ongoing conflicts, the Nguni people were not immune from the growing pressure created by their own expanding populations. With resources being limited, internecine violence, later known as the *Mfecane*, resulted.

Chapter 2

Shaka and the Second *Mfecane*

The brutality of the *Mfecane,* a Zulu word for 'disturbance during the rise of the Zulu people', brought with it unremitting pressure for clans to expand and survive the growing incidence of inter-tribal rivalries. It was a long drawn-out process that took effect over 150 years. Under the Zulus it became a process of creeping domination.[1] The term could also be a neologism[2] from the Sotho word *Difaqane* (the scattering) and the Tswana *Lifaqane* (time of migration).[3] The two words are sometimes seen as interchangeable.[4] The term *Mfecane* is generally applied to the whole of southern Africa, or sometimes just to the eastern coastal regions, whereas the term *Difaqane* is applied to the Highveld.[5] This uncertainty about the choice of a word is merely academic. It is insignificant when compared with the blatant savage reality of the *Mfecane* – the effects of which would reach as far as Swaziland, Lesotho, Mozambique, Zimbabwe, Zambia, Malawi and Tanzania, and involve the loss of more than a million lives.

The first inter-clan violence to involve the Zulus took place in the 1790s, during a period of prolonged drought, remembered by the Zulus as the *Madlantule,* meaning 'suffer hunger but do not speak'. With clans increasingly suffering the effects of the drought, survival was the people's foremost priority. The advantages in maximizing the territory each group controlled became clear, either through alliance with neighbours in a similar position, or through direct conquest. The survivors faced starvation and cannibalism while, in some areas, villages grouped together to protect their grain stores or moved to abodes elsewhere. Two tribes in particular, the Ndwandwe of Chief Zwide and the Mthethwa of Chief Dingiswayo, were among the first to develop in size and influence, and in 1810 their own pressures to expand and inter-tribal rivalries between them soon spilled over, involving their neighbours such as the Ngwana people living along the White Umfolozi, the Cunu and Tembu to the west and the Qwabe to the south. Rather than submit to overwhelming aggressors, the Ngwana chose to move into Hlubi territory, in turn shattering that society. Likewise, the Qwabe living along the Tugela River consolidated their chiefdom by conquering the weaker neighbouring Thuli and Cele tribes. They, in turn, invaded their neighbours in an explosive pattern that was to wreak havoc and cause misery across southern Africa, with the victors of the day killing vanquished male warriors and absorbing the surviving women and children in the process.

In 1824 the traveller Fynn wrote:

> The region devastated by marauding chiefs exceeds the Cape Colony in extent. It is for the greater part quite void of inhabitants. Many of the inhabitants who escaped from the spear were left to perish by starvation. Their cattle having been taken and their grain destroyed, thousands were for years left to linger on the slender sustenance of roots – some even of a poisonous kind. In my first journey from Natal to the Umtata in 1824 I witnessed awful scenes. Six thousand unhappy beings, having scarcely a human appearance, were scattered over this country, feeding on every description of animal, and driven by their hungry craving in many instances to devour their fellows.[6]

The effects of the ongoing *Mfecane* coincided with the early reign of King Shaka and were most obvious in Natalia. This land had previously been vibrant and sustained a healthy population – only to suffer again from the annual invasions of Shaka's army. Those who did not abandon their ravaged lands took to hiding in the hills and hidden valleys, always on the lookout for any raiders. Larger groups formed themselves into communities that could be defended or were impracticable for marauders to bother with. This gave rise to a number of such communities, which became states in their own right, including the peoples of mountainous Basutoland and Swaziland and the desert lands of Bechuanaland. Had any of the pioneers travelled further south from Port Natal into Pondoland, they would had come across the Natal refugees who had fled the *Mfecane*. Here life was a desperate struggle for survival; chiefs and leaders had been lost with famine and chaos ruled. When the area was eventually explored by missionaries such as Cowie and Green, it was named 'No-Man's-Land'. Nevertheless, regardless of their fears, Fynn and Farewell made regular visits across the area north of Port Natal to trade with Shaka. They found Shaka living well and commanding an army of 10,000 warriors. Fynn wrote:

> The whole country as far as our sight reached was covered with numbers of people and droves of cattle. The king came to us and told us not to be afraid of his people.[7]

Pre-*Mfecane*, no southern Bantu people possessed a permanent standing army with specialized military training or a military hierarchy. It was, however, the implications of the *Mfecane* that provided the base from which the Zulu nation arose and in a relatively short space of time, the *Mfecane* brought a number of famous leaders to the fore, which in turn created strong societies by putting their male populations into designated 'age sets', usually grouping together males of the same age.

The Zulu age set was based primarily upon the Nguni formation of young men, and sometimes women, into *amabutho* (age sets), which had specific civic and military tasks to perform. The *amabutho* originated as circumcision sets, which appears to be a cross-cultural phenomenon among Bantu speakers in southern Africa, as is the transformation of the non-militaristic, civic orientated age sets into militaristic and civic orientated age regiments. Indeed, many groups performed communal initiation rites in association with age from the early Iron Age, although it appears that these lacked the militaristic element for which the Zulus became famous. They were noted for keenly engaging the enemy, bonding together with the national cry '*Usuthu*', which demonstrated allegiance to the king and supported the notion of a system that transcended territory. Apart from shield colours specific to an *amabutho*, individual regiments also had their own dress style, such as headdress colour. The Zulus realized the value of a group identity, seeing it as vital for groups to act in cooperation since it created competition and a feeling of group specialism to benefit the wider institution. It also aided easy and quick identification of friend and foe in the heat of battle, exactly replicating the British army use of regimental colours in battle.

Homogeneity was therefore maintained within the group itself. This can be clearly represented by the Zulus' military barracks, *Amakhanda*, that were designed and built by a principle, common to all *amabutho*, namely to support the king. Consequently, if an age regiment member visited another *ibutho*, the member would instantly recognize the layout and know his place within the hierarchy.

SHAKA AND THE SECOND MFECANE

Interestingly, no soldier in the Zulu army was given formal military training except as a cadet in his youth, nor did they receive pay. This 'obligation' to serve without material reward can be accounted for since they were performing civic duties, which would have benefited their own kin, and therefore, indirectly, themselves. Due to the lack of training in the Zulu army, one might, wrongly, be of the impression that discipline was slack and standards not high. It was through peer pressure and the threat of humiliation and severe punishment that a soldier willingly performed his duties. For example, warriors who were considered by their peers to be below standard or who displayed cowardly behaviour were shamed by their regiments through the practice of rumour, known as *uxoxa impi*, where deeds of bravery or cowardice were passionately discussed by the warriors themselves. The mildest and most common show of displeasure was the symbolic punishment of publicly having one's meat dipped in cold water before eating it. This demonstrates the social constraint that the regimental system imposed upon its members, as well as the wider society, since one would not want to have one's father, brother or son shunned by society.

Until Shaka's maturity, and prior to the *Mfecane,* significant disputes and inter-clan differences were traditionally resolved by each side engaging in *giya*, a relatively formal but harmless process of hurling threats and some throwing of spears for an hour or two until one side felt they were in ascendancy. They were noisy and dusty events, with each side advancing and retreating in turn to the accompaniment of high kicking, stamping and the beating of shields. Such disputes rarely resulted in more than casual bloodshed but this traditional system of challenge was to be short-lived. Otherwise, minor clan disputes were heard before the clan chief, whose decision was final. A tribal chief, deemed to be the sole link between their tribal ancestors and the community, was in charge of matters civil, military, judicial and religious within his immediate clan. He would be aided by a close team of senior men and, in a larger clan, the ever-present prancing witch doctor, whose role was to deal with any misfortune or unexplained community events within the clan. Such events were understood by the people to have been caused by evil spirits, *abathakathi*, and their resolution would devolve on the witch doctor, making both medicine and superstition play an important part in Nguni life.

Meanwhile, at just twenty-three years of age, Shaka's reputation increased, as did, legend records, both his fearlessness when hunting wild animals and great prowess with the spear. On hearing of his success, Shaka

11

was called to the junior ranks of the IziCwa *abutho* of King Dingiswayo. During the next five years he closely studied the king's strategy of controlling other tribes by the use of brutal and aggressive tactics, a policy frequently but incorrectly first attributed to Shaka. By now, Shaka was unique in having lived among the Zulus, the eLangeni, the Qwabe and the Mthethwa tribes before returning to the Zulus. He knew all their strengths but, more importantly, he also knew their weaknesses. Zulu folklore remembers that a shipwrecked sailor, of nationality unknown, was discovered washed up on the shore and brought before Shaka. The sailor recounted the successes of Napoleon, which, according to Zulu folklore, made a great impression on the Zulu chief.

Perhaps with Napoleon in mind, Shaka drilled his Zulu army remorselessly until he had an *impi* numbering no more than 500 warriors, but each warrior was trained only to obey orders, not to think or act independently. By 1817, Shaka's *impi* had grown to more than 2,000 warriors and his sphere of influence was steadily increasing and consolidating. He attacked the Qwabe and, uncharacteristically, let the survivors return to their clan area. The Qwabe chief, Pakatwayo, had been injured in the fighting and, to display his compassion, Shaka ordered his executioners to nurse the chief during his return journey. Unsurprisingly, he died during the night.

Under Dingiswayo, Shaka remained his vassal but was nevertheless accelerated through the ranks until, at nearly thirty years of age, Shaka was appointed to command the iziCwa regiment; it was here that he taught his warriors severe discipline and the deadly close combat for which he became famous.

To the tribal chiefs, discipline and total control of their military and civilian populations were equally foremost. They maintained their control by fear, utilizing their witch doctor's ability to 'smell out' dissenters, dissension being a crime punishable with immediate execution of the offender. Such executions were generally accepted by the people even though they were grisly, frequently involving slow death by impaling. Such executions were performed with horrendous cruelty and the punishment could extend to include members of the victim's family being put to death, along with the confiscation of their family's goods and cattle. Fear of being 'smelled out' was especially a matter of concern for the more wealthy, who, realizing their vulnerability, constantly ingratiated themselves with their chief. Once smelled out, there was no possible appeal.[1] In due course, smelling out became a major tool for Shaka, who would use the process to punish offenders, real or imagined, and instil terror across the Zulu nation by ordering indiscriminate or group executions.

Shaka became a legend for his qualities of leadership. As proof of his stamina and fitness, Shaka always went barefoot, considering sandals to be an impediment. In order to convince his regiment that his close-contact method of fighting was superior, he ordered two of his *impis* to face each other in *giya* fashion. For this demonstration, one side was armed with throwing spears, the other with sharpened reeds. Fynn wrote that the two regiments thus weaponed were ordered to oppose each other with one throwing their spears and the other then rushing in and stabbing with their seemingly harmless but sharpened reeds. Many of the spear throwers were seriously injured and Shaka noted, with satisfaction, that a number had been killed. He ordered the ineffective throwing spears to be melted down and recast as the long and sharp, flat-bladed stabbing *assegai* or *iklwa*, the onomatopoeic term for the sucking sound of the blade being withdrawn from a body. He ordered the *amabuthos'* traditional weighty shields to be cut down and made stronger so that in close combat the new shield could be hooked under that of an opponent and, when twisted sideways, reveal the opponent's body, exposed and vulnerable to the deadly *iklwa* thrust. Warriors who lost their *iklwa*, even in battle, would be classified as cowards, as would returning warriors with wounds to their back, indicating they had fled in battle. Their lives would usually be forfeited to Shaka's executioners.

It was Shaka's ruthlessness that gave him the reputation he enjoyed, yet those before him had been equally brutal – or worse; totally exterminating one's enemies seemed the norm. Shaka was also merciless in battle. To the survivors and their families he was equally pitiless – surviving men were killed but women and children were taken and absorbed into the growing Zulu tribe. Other clans and tribes swiftly sought alliance with the Zulus rather than risk being attacked. Impressed by his success, Dingiswayo realized that Shaka was an organizer and tactician *par excellence* and appointed him to lead the Zulu tribe. On Senzangakhona's death in 1816, Shaka learned that another brother, Sigujana ka Senzangakhona, had been nominated as heir to the Zulu clan. Shaka immediately dealt with the matter by ordering the assassination of Sigujana and a number of his brothers, of which there were about a dozen. Knowing the fearsome reputation of the approaching Zulus tasked with the executions, Sigujana's people didn't await the Zulus' arrival – they knew full well the consequences of defeat so they took it upon themselves to kill

Sigujana by spearing him while he was bathing, and were gratefully brought into the growing Zulu tribe. Shaka meanwhile annexed every group within the Zulu tribe and exiled his half-brothers, Mhlangana and Mpande. The most threatening half-brother, Dingane, was sent back to his own distant clan, an offshoot of the Qwabe tribe.

Shaka now extended his ruthless influence. Opponents and dissenters were mercilessly executed, as were warriors who did not reach the exacting physical standards required for a Zulu *impi*. Executions as a means of control became a powerful feature of Shaka's rule and would be conducted in full view of those present. Shaka expected his warriors to be brave and not hold back. Any warrior deemed by his chief, even by his fellow warriors, as having shown cowardice or a lack of enthusiasm in battle, could expect a grisly death. Adulterers were likewise disposed of. Even if minor transgressions were occasionally overlooked, they could be sufficient to warrant execution; Shaka would regularly and arbitrarily order an execution because someone sneezed in his presence or because he disliked a man's appearance. The raising of Shaka's finger was sufficient for the king's special team of bodyguards, who also acted as executioners, to drag off some otherwise innocent man or woman, firstly to be stunned by a blow from an outsized executioner's knobkerrie, before being skewered through the rectum on a pointed stake. In the event of a number of executions, the favoured method was a simple but practised snap of the victims' necks. Even though executions were accepted by the people, there was still an undercurrent of resentment amongst the Zulus:

> That man used to play around with people. A man would be killed though he had done nothing, though he had neither practised witchcraft, committed adultery nor stolen. Shaka would say, 'Hau! How ugly this fellow is! Take him away.'[8]

The traveller Charles Maclean, who as a youth spent a number of years with his hunter father, witnessed a number of such executions and wondered at victims' seeming indifference to their fate. He wrote:

> It has often excited my pity, admiration and astonishment to witness the fortitude and dignified calmness with which a Zulu will go forth to execution. No fetters or chords are ever employed to bind the victim. He is left at liberty to run for his

life or to stand and meet his doom. Many do run, but few escape for, alas, every man they meet is their enemy. Many stand and meet their fate with a degree of firmness that could hardly be imagined.[9]

Maclean also noticed a distinct absence of the elderly. It is possible that the long established Zulu custom of dispensing with the aged, infirm or disabled commenced with Shaka, who took a dim view of the elderly, or anyone he considered useless to his society. He went as far as to establish a special settlement known as *gibixhegu*, meaning 'death to old men', which was nothing more than a death camp.[10] Tactically, Shaka embraced all the techniques he had learnt during his years with the IziCwa. He perfected the *iklwa* flat-bladed spear and developed the *Impondo Zankhomo*, the feared encircling technique known as the 'horns of the bull', whereby an enemy was surrounded by fast-running flanks of each horn until completely surrounded – from which escape was virtually impossible. This was a technique formerly used for hunting large herds, whereby the fast-running horns, the *umuva*, of the two flanks encircled their prey; it was a tactic equally effective against an enemy. The main Zulu body, the *isiFuba*, would then engage the surrounded enemy at close quarters with their shields and stabbing spears. The Zulus were not inhibited from attacking overwhelming numbers as they had been trained to display incredible heroism and valour and were not afraid to die for Shaka. Wilmot described the tactic as follows:

> They went forth to conquer or to die, 50,000 well-organized, determined savages, giving no quarter, slaying men, women, children and even domestic animals. Their hissing and hollow groans told their progress among the dead. A few moments laid hundreds on the ground. The clash of shields was the signal of triumph. They entered the town with the roar of the lion; they pillaged and fired the houses, speared the mothers, and cast their infants into the flames. They slaughtered cattle; they danced and sang till the dawn of day; they ascended and killed till their hands were weary of the spear.[11]

His re-trained regiment was soon pitched against the nearby Buthelezi tribe and, in due course, both regiments lined up for the traditional *giya*. The unsuspecting Buthelezi, led by Shaka's half-brother, Bakaza, commenced to *giya* in expectation of the usual noisy but relatively bloodless confrontation. Instead, Shaka's foremost warriors rushed upon the Buthelezi and instantly killed Bakaza, whereupon the remainder of the iziCwa fell upon the hapless and unsuspecting Buthelezi warriors, who fled for their lives. Not content with his victory, Shaka led his warriors into the Buthelezi homestead, firing huts and killing everyone they could find, including women and children. The practice of killing enemy wounded, those taken prisoner in battle and occasionally women and children, commenced with Shaka.

Shaka then turned his attention to the eLangeni tribe, who had earlier treated his mother so severely. Shaka's regiments surrounded the unsuspecting eLangeni and, on seeing Shaka's approach, many of the eLangeni people tried to flee in terror. The tribal elders stood their ground in a misguided attempt to placate Shaka. Those elders who had made his or his mother's life a misery, especially those who had taunted Shaka in his youth, were brought before Shaka. Each was asked what he had done to help Shaka or his mother. The few who could offer a plausible account were excused the gathering and rewarded with a cow. Those who failed were savagely put to a slow death by impaling. Once the impaling of the eLangeni chiefs had been completed, Shaka then ordered dry burning grass to be heaped around the victims to accentuate their writhing and increase their death agonies. The surviving eLangeni people were absorbed into Shaka's Zulus, effectively doubling the size of his army. As a further demonstration of his growing power, Shaka attacked and defeated the Gungebeni people, one of the first Nguni clans to have arrived in the area.

Apart from those serving in the army, the majority of the Zulu population lived their lives unaffected by Shaka's rule. Under his protection they enjoyed a relatively easy lifestyle, which inevitably resulted in unsustainable population growth. There was simply not enough land available. This land famine led to increasing disputes, which, in turn, led to widespread violence as tribes sought to expand and then secure their areas of interest. This expansion and conflict spread across Zululand until the state of permanent unrest erupted, extending the *Mfecane*, a term first used by E. Walker in 1928.

Meanwhile, other bordering tribes felt the necessity to engage in destructive inter-clan warfare in order to secure their tribal boundaries. Four neighbouring Nguni chiefs, Zwide of the Mthethwa, Dingiswayo of the

SHAKA AND THE SECOND MFECANE

Ndwandwe, Matiwana of the Ngwane, and Mtimkulu of the Hlubi, were principally responsible for the catastrophic internecine warfare and economic destruction that accompanied such tribal conflict. These chiefs wreaked havoc across the land until Dingiswayo sent his army, including Shaka's Zulus, to defeat his neighbours in order to extend his control. As the Ndwandwe approached, Dingiswayo was captured by one of Zwide's patrols who were monitoring Dingiswayo's advance and promptly beheaded the protesting chief. With Dingiswayo dead, his warriors, including Shaka and his Zulus, departed the battlefield in disarray. It is Zulu folklore that Shaka deliberately held back from the battle knowing Dingiswayo was tactically inadequate. The struggle for power now focused on Zwide and Dingiswayo's heir, Shaka. Zwide's army of Mthethwa warriors attacked first in the knowledge that he heavily outnumbered the Zulus. The battle took place mid-1818 at Gqokoli Hill, but it was Shaka who selected the high ground to suit his tactics. The weather was hot and the location chosen was deliberately far from water, although Shaka ensured his army had adequate supplies from a nearby spring. Shaka decoyed the Mthethwa into approaching the hill through a narrow valley, from which the Mthethwa were encouraged to attack. From their approach the Mthethwa were unable to see the top of the convex hill, where Shaka had massed his army. Thinking the Zulus were few in number and in a weak position, the Mthethwa repeatedly attacked the hill, where they not only failed to make any headway but steadily lost men, including five senior chiefs. The Zulus were able to maintain their line throughout the battle by replacing casualties from their hidden hilltop reserves. Only the Zulus were adept at close combat and in the late afternoon Shaka led the Zulu counter-attack. The exhausted Mthethwa army was very thirsty from the day's fighting and they were quickly savaged and in complete disarray. Nevertheless, because they still heavily outnumbered the Zulus, the battle was inconclusive and both sides withdrew to their own territory. Shaka's army claimed victory and, unlike the Mthethwa, was still intact. Warriors from other clans immediately flocked to swell his ranks of Zulu warriors.

Zwide attacked the Zulus again in the summer of 1819 with a massive army of nearly 20,000 Mthethwa warriors, but this time Shaka was even better prepared. Even though his Zulus were still heavily outnumbered, Shaka ordered the destruction of his own Zulu cattle *kraals* and crops in the immediate area to deny the advancing Mthethwa food or protection. Shaka teased Zwide into following a number of feints across barren terrain, until several days later, on an especially dark night, Shaka's warriors ambushed the Mthethwa patrols and, under cover of darkness, infiltrated Zwide's camp by pretending to be Zwide's returning patrols, seemingly without challenge. The Zulu imposters lay down among the sleeping and exhausted Mthethwa force. Their camp in the Nkandla Forest was not far from where Cetshwayo's grave now is.

At a given signal, each Zulu stabbed the man next to him and then feigned death. The effect was consternation throughout Zwide's slumbering army, which, with no enemy apparent, went back to sleep. With the camp quiet again, the Zulus repeated their attack. In the belief they were being attacked by evil spirits, Zwide's men began fighting amongst themselves, being unable to differentiate foe from evil spirits in the total darkness. During the confusion the Zulus slipped away. Such a guerrilla tactic resulted in the utter demoralization of the Ndwandwe army, who hastily retired towards the Nkomati River and their own territory. Determined to annihilate this army once and for all, Shaka's own army bypassed the retreating Ndwandwe and prepared to attack. The Zulus waited until the defeated, starving and disorientated escapers reached the river, and then Shaka's army attacked, killing every Ndwandwe they found.[12] Although Zwide escaped the battlefield, Shaka gave chase and on reaching the Ndwandwe capital, destroyed it and its remaining population. Zwide managed to slip away and with the surviving remnants of his once proud army gathered around him, fled into modern-day Swaziland. Other tribes were quick to pledge their allegiance to Shaka. Indeed, by the 1820s, many of the groups south of the Tugela had only survived the threat of Zulu attack or of being scattered as refugees by pledging their allegiance. Meanwhile, as A.T. Bryant stated:

> This was now a time of relative peace for the majority of the northern Nguni, a 'Golden Age' where the people lived in peace and stability in numerous small clans and under independent chiefdoms.[13]

Shaka thereafter ruled unchallenged but was rarely inactive, even managing to lead four expeditions into Natal – in 1817, 1818, 1819 and 1820 – only to find that a large proportion of the previously dense population of Natal had been exterminated during the preceding *Mfecane*, leaving Natal a virtual desert. Even so, the few survivors were still prepared to resist Shaka.[14] By the end of the year, Shaka's army had swept all remaining opposition from Natal, forcing many thousands of refugees from numerous tribes, including the Thembu and Cunu, to flee towards the Cape and seek refuge from Faku, chief of the Mpondo.

Shaka's army eventually grew to more than 20,000 trained warriors and was based in a heartland that extended from the Indian Ocean to the Drakensberg, and from the Pongola River in the north to the Tugela River in the south. His principle military settlements were at Bulawayo, Dukuza, Isiklebhe, Gibixhegu and Mbelebele. Collectively they acted as bases for Shaka's standing army. Each settlement was commanded by a military chief, an *inDuna*, specially selected by Shaka, with all the authority previously delegated to local chiefs. With constant guidance from his mother, Nandi, Shaka ruled unchallenged. Shaka forced his ruthless influence still further and by 1822 his clan had grown into an empire that extended into the Kalahari, north to the shores of Lake Malawi and south to the Northern Cape.

At the same time and to the north, Chief Sobhuza consolidated what became the Swazi kingdom. To the south, the Ngwane and Hlubi people encroached upon the Sotho peoples, while Chief Sekonyela settled his people along the Orange River. Instead of finding peace, these tribes suffered raids by the growing bands of Bastaards, themselves refugees from the Cape. By 1824 Shaka had begun limited trade with a handful of white settlers. Two of them, Farewell and Fynn, kept diaries of their experiences. Although permitted access to Shaka's homestead, the two Englishmen had little influence over the Zulu king.

To the south-east, the previously powerful Ngwane (Amanwana) tribe under Matiwane were dealt a severe blow when they inadvertently met with a British force under Lieutenant Colonel Somerset, who had responded to false information from a settler, Thomas Pringle, that a large marauding Zulu force was approaching the fledgling colony of British Kaffraria to steal cattle. No Zulu force was discovered but in 1828 similar rumours re-emerged promulgated by a number of missionaries. Somerset again prepared to intercept the Zulus just north of the Kei River at Mbholompo but he unwittingly crossed paths with the peaceful Ngwane, who were moving back from Lesotho. In the belief he was about to be attacked by the Zulus, Somerset gave the order to attack. The battle raged until 1.00 pm, when the savaged Ngwane withdrew to the Drakensberg Mountains. The slaughter had been terrible, with every man, woman and child killed. An accompanying British officer later rendered his account to Reverend Kay, who wrote of the incident:

> A respectable British officer whose duty required him to be on the spot, candidly declared that it was 'one of the most disgraceful and cold-blooded acts to which the English soldier had ever been rendered accessory.'

He continued:

> It has indeed been said, that a parley was attempted; and for the honour of our countrymen, we cannot but wish that this could have been proved. Unhappily, however, the unanimous testimony of numbers who were personally present during the whole affray is altogether against this assertion, showing too clearly that time was not allowed for anything of the kind.[15]

Within weeks the survivors abandoned Matiwane and fled south, seeking mercy from the frontier tribes who accepted them as refugees and a useful workforce. Matiwane and his few remaining advisers fled back to Zululand to discover Shaka ruling the Zulu people. Shaka knew Matiwane had been a strong dissenter and had once attacked Dingane, causing him non life-threatening injuries. Not prepared to accommodate such a dangerous individual, Shaka ordered his protracted execution. Matiwane's eyes were removed before sharpened stakes were driven up his nostrils. When Shaka became bored with the spectacle the executioners snapped Matiwane's neck to draw the execution to a close.

Most of the immediate area had now been conquered by the Zulus and Shaka had the allegiance of the territory's chiefs. There was only one serious detractor, Chief Mzilikazi, who was in debt to Shaka on account of a number of falsified cattle returns. Rather than face Shaka, Mzilikazi took his clan of several hundred people and fled across the Vaal River, where they established the Ndebele kingdom. As one of Shaka's generals, Mzilikazi was well versed in campaigning and en route north they swept through the Transvaal, the Orange State, and then Botswana before settling in the land known today as Zimbabwe. Like Shaka, Mzilikazi was ruthless, with the difference that his victorious tribe would assimilate subjugated people rather than destroy them, until his horde of belligerent refugees eventually formed their own nation. Meanwhile, Mzilikazi's people migrating northwards could never rest. They were again forced by Shaka's army to move northwards, where Mzilikazi occupied the Tswana chiefdom in the northern Transvaal and there they lived in peace until the arrival of the Boers in 1836. The only tribe ever to make a stand against Mzilikazi and Shaka was the Basotho people under their leader, Moshoeshoe.

Beyond Shaka's immediate sphere of interest, the repercussions from his autocratic reign spread far and wide. With each Zulu purge or victory, a fresh wave of refugees would seek protection from, or fall upon, their neighbouring tribe. Some would blend to form new kingdoms while others fought for ascendancy; this effect also continued the *Mfecane*. It has long been the considered view of some historians that it was Shaka who set in motion the worst effects of the *Mfecane*, causing a strong ripple of mass migrations and bloody conflicts that were responsible for the deaths of so many innocent people. These fresh conflicts were fought with utter brutality over a vast area of thousands of miles. Shaka certainly gained a fearful reputation as a military tyrant bent on regional domination, regardless of the cost in human terms. One result of Shaka's expanding empire was indeed: 'At least a million people, and more likely two, died in a decade.'[16] Charles Maclean was travelling just north of modern Durban and described the area as depopulated. He wrote:

> There was no evidence wanting in our travels by the wayside
> to show what fate of the many had been. The heaps of
> human skulls and bones blanching on the plains were sad
> monuments of the fearful conflicts that had annihilated
> whole tribes.[17]

By 1824 the Zulus had eclipsed all their rivals. Shaka retained the earlier clan system but this was overlaid by subservience to Shaka. The majority of clans and tribes had been forced by conquest into submission, while in others Shaka intervened by replacing existing chiefs with his own nominations. This was done to ensure loyalty to Shaka and to guarantee his monarchy. Nevertheless, there remained a handful of clans, such as the Cube, who avoided conquest by proffering their loyalty, but the balance of power remained totally in favour of Shaka. Although blamed for the

Mfecane, it is a fact that this rolling purge had begun well before Shaka's influence became widespread. It is therefore probable that, rather than cause the *Mfecane*, Shaka might well have brought it to a close. His method was to crush neighbouring tribes and clans, killing the men and adopting the women and children into the Zulu nation. This being the case, post-slaughter, there would have been few men left from a defeated tribe able to conduct their own *Mfecane*.

Shaka perfected the scorched earth retreat before an advancing enemy that would be followed by the pincer movement to envelope their progress. Shaka would follow this tactic up by close combat to kill, rather than wound, the foe, thus preventing his survival to fight another day. It was a unique and ruthless fighting tactic, which changed African warfare. He also developed the most efficient espionage system ever seen in Africa based upon his spies' ability to mingle with his foes; Shaka was well informed before every event. What cannot be overlooked is Shaka's success at forming a single political body from numerous separate and disparate clans and tribes. Conversely, more distant tribes were forced to band together for protection, leading to the establishment of the Ndebele in Rhodesia, the Ngoni in Malawi, Tanganyika and Zambia. Closer to Shaka's sphere of influence, the previously lush and rich land of Natal was left barren, having been utterly destroyed by those fleeing the original effects of the *Mfecane* and then Shaka's rule. Further north, the devastations of the Hubli and Ndebele had produced an identical landscape. The whole area north of Zululand was equally impoverished and only the substantial lion population benefited. Previously, big cats had ignored humans as prey but now, with dying and weak humans abounding, the lions gorged themselves.

It is recognized by historians that Shaka's twelve-year reign resulted in him being recognized as the African Napoleon. Following the death of Shaka in 1828, powerful chiefs such as Dingane of the Zulus, Moshoeshoe of the Sotho, Mzilikazi of the Ndebele, and Sobhuza of the Swazis became the most important leaders throughout the area.

Chapter 3

Zulu Rituals and Customs

Care must be exercised when considering historical and modern Zulu customs and rituals. The European definitions of these terms are clear, but less so in Zululand, where there is much conceptual overlapping. Because of the blending of these terms and to avoid ambiguity, the expression 'custom' to encompass these concepts is used. Likewise, the expression 'Zulu' to denote a person is broad; it encompasses any descendant from the Zulu or Qwabe clans or from any Nguni tribe or clan resident in Zululand or Natal during the lifetime of King Shaka.

Much that happened in this part of southern Africa can be better understood by contemplating the customs and rituals then followed by most of the Nguni tribes. To the Zulus, there has never been any difference between the religious and secular. They saw, and still see, most objects and events being associated with or created by a god, *Umvelingqangi* – in whatever form they see him. Likewise, in Zulu culture and therefore in their folklore, there is little distinction between the living and the dead – whose spirits are omnipresent and influential, even extending to the practice of making sacrifices to spirits in times of need or celebration. The spirits of ancestors, *amadlozi*, or 'shades' as they are more commonly known in Zululand, would be consulted for advice and could make their presence known by appearing as a snake or in dreams to the head of the family or clan chief. It is Zulu belief that dreams show truth because the spirits of the dead never deceive their children.

Senior chiefs or the king would bridge the gap between the living and the dead by employing a *sangoma*, a medicine man/woman, or spirit diviner. Or they could call upon the feared witch doctor, whose powers included communicating with both ancestors and evil spirits, known as *umnyama*, or detecting *umthakathi*, people or animals who secretly used magic to cause harm to the community or king, often by 'smelling out' individuals from the *umuzi* on nothing more than a whim. Any unexplained event or misfortune in the clan could be considered as witchcraft. Even jealousies between families fell to the witch doctor to adjudicate, usually resulting in the death of one or more luckless persons. The king's witch doctors could advocate sacrifices, of cattle or people, and were therefore of vital importance to the chiefs or king to maintain control over the people by instilling fear in them. Witch doctors were greatly feared, being among the king's 'intelligence officers' who looked out for spies, malcontents, cowards and those considered lazy. No one furthered or exploited the power of the witch doctors more than King Shaka, although he quickly let it be known that he considered himself above their deliberations and therefore immune from their decisions, preferring to take his inspiration by sitting on the shore and staring at the great breaking waves rolling in from the Indian Ocean.

Zulu health matters were referred either to the *inyanga*, a specialist herbal doctor, or to a *sangoma*, who was so deeply respected that patients usually recovered after being prescribed a particular lotion or potion. If they didn't recover, the sick person, if seriously ill, could be declared possessed of evil spirits, the *abathakathi*, before being put to death or left to die. Throughout Zulu history and through to present times, illness and black magic have been combined to treat the afflicted either by discounting the disease or by curing it. At the same time a wide range of *muti* (medicines), usually ground to a fine powder, could be used; this included human and animal parts, tree bark, herbs, the dung of ferocious animals and numerous roots. Many of the roots used have stood the test of time and a number feature in conventional European medicine.[1]

Since the time of King Shaka, Zulu children were separated from youths, and youths from men, the youths being put into age set groups. In this way, the king had control over a large proportion of his subjects. It is possible that age sets, perhaps the first organization of Zulu society, developed out of opposition between the youth and the old. Age set research has only fully developed since the 1950s, as it was in these more recent years that anthropology became accepted as an academic profession. Power for the individual in an age set was achieved by one's relative position within that particular age set, and the age set position within the age set hierarchy. Consequently, open resentment or rebellion should not arise, since one's ability and demeanour were constantly mediated by the presence and actions of one's age set colleagues. However, the Zulu system soon developed beyond this age set template into the *amabutho* system.

The Zulu system is interesting not only from this perspective, but also because, during the reign of Shaka, from 1818-28, the standing of age regiments, which arose from the age sets, was drastically reorganized, as were military tactics. The *amabutho* system, however, was in use before Shaka's time; it was used by Zwide of the Ndwandwe tribe, Matiwane of the Ngwane and Pakatwayo of the Qwabe, who all had age regiments, although Shaka was the first to use it militarily as well as to control the nation's economy.

Girls were treated differently from boys; they were tied to their kin, whereas boys, even from a very young age, would learn to herd their parents' goats and protect them – hence the custom, even today, of herd boys carrying sticks and knobkerries. On reaching eighteen all males would be summoned from across the territories to form a new *ibutho*, or troop of a similar age; it was their 'call-up' into the army, itself divided into three divisions. The first was composed of veterans or *amadoda*, the second the *ebuto* or *ibutho* of youths and the third, the *ezibuto*, or carriers of provisions. Under Shaka, this national service was seen as a means of binding the nation together. Members of each *ibutho* would be required to build their own quarters, and were trained how to fulfil and obey orders. Each *ibutho* was given a distinctive name and ceremonial uniform of feathers and furs. Their war shields remained the property of the king, being issued only for special ceremonies or to settle disputes, and to maintain the *ibutho* bond and identify its own warriors, especially in battle. *Ibutho* shields were invariably of a matching colour. An *ibutho* was required to give service to the king only until such time as the men married, when their primary duty reverted to their families and local chiefs. To maximize the time young men were available to serve them, Zulu kings had often refused to allow members of a regiment to marry until the men were in their late thirties. When each regiment assembled to answer the king's call they were fed and quartered at the king's expense. Because it was logistically difficult to sustain such large concentrations of men for long periods, the *amabutho* were seldom mustered for more than a few weeks each year. For the most part, the men lived at home with their families, fulfilling the normal duties of their ordinary civilian lives. Apart from drawing young men into an *ibutho* for military and work purposes, it also served to accustom warriors into identifying the Zulu king as their leader, regardless of their origins. However, where young men came from an outlying area or had recently been absorbed into the Zulu nation, they were initially allocated menial work and were known as *amalala* (menials), *amanhlwenga* (destitutes) or *iziendane* (unusual hairstyles).

Warriors allocated to their regimental *amabutho* remained celibate until the king authorized their 'marriage'. Zulu marriage is another often misunderstood concept. It has invariably been wrongly interpreted through European eyes with overtones of repressed sexuality and transposed with European values of marriage. To a Zulu, marriage denoted the most significant event of his life by giving him the right to take a number of wives, but never from within his own *umuzi*. He was then free to establish his personal homestead and could own land for his cattle and crops. Pigs were not kept, as pork was never eaten.

Historically, prior to marriage, a woman was seen as a marketable commodity and was valued accordingly to the price she was likely to fetch when marriageable. Should she become a widow, her life would become pitiable without a protector. Unmarried Zulus were at liberty to engage in sexual relations, a form of external intercourse, or *ukuhlobonga*, so long as it did not involve penetration. From King Shaka to King Cetshwayo, the royal house controlled marriage as a means of keeping young men under arms and out of the economic structure of Zululand. Had every warrior been permitted to establish his own homestead at will, the effect on various Zulu social processes, including production and reproduction, would have resulted in economic instability. Concomitantly, the king and his council knew that by delaying the time when Zulu women could marry, the birth rate, growth and pressure of an increasing population could be strictly controlled and maintained in line with economic production.

Marriage was a crucial rite of passage for both men and women in Zulu society as it marked the formal transition to adulthood. It was considered so important that a married man and woman would wear their hair in a style that reflected their status in society. An unmarried man remained part of his father's household and any individual rights he may have had were subordinated to his father's will. By extension, this duty also included his father's immediate superior, the *umuzi* chief. When a man married, he assumed all the full rights and responsibilities of adult status. Zulu women were expected to work hard in the *umuzi* and the field, and simply have children. Women were also subject to execution if they did not conform to Zulu custom, especially with regard to infidelity. Two such executions carried out at Rorke's Drift in 1878 were partly responsible for the 1879 Anglo-Zulu War.

Superstition played, and still plays, an important part in Zulu life to the extent that until the early 1900s each clan chief was able to maintain complete control through fear by utilizing his witch doctor's ability to 'smell out' dissenters, dissension being a crime punishable with immediate execution of the offender or, in serious cases, his whole family or homestead. There was no possible appeal. In 1820 Reverend Kay recorded the chilling detail of a typical 'trial by witch doctor'. On visiting a clan, several boxes containing his personal effects had been surreptitiously removed from one of his wagons and a number of items taken. When this was discovered, other contents were found strewn around. The local chief was enraged by the treatment of his visitor and declared that everyone involved would be put to death, together with their wives and children. There were no obvious culprits so the sorceress was called upon, much against Reverend Kay's wishes. He recorded in his diary and later published the following account. One hopes it was more to alarm his readers than to merely record what happened:

> About midday an assemblage of several hundred took place, with the chief at their head. The sorceress, preceded by several other native women, now came forth attired in a dirty black garment, loosely suspended from the shoulders; on her head were three large artificial tufts of hair and in her right hand several sharp-pointed spears. After exhibiting to the assembly a number of ridiculous gestures, and throwing herself into a number of disgusting attitudes, she announced the names of two persons, stating that they were the men who had done the deed, and that she had been made acquainted with the facts by means of a dream. Breathless silence ensued and every eye was instantly turned towards the individuals, one of whom was brought forward in the most savage manner. While two or three held their *assegais* over his head and breast, the others completely stripped him of his garb, and of every ornament possessed. Of one, the lobes of his ears were barbarously torn by the ruffians in their strife about the beads suspended from them. As is usual on such occasions they proceeded to bind the accused hand and foot and to extort from him a confession of the crime by means of torture. For this purpose, recourse is had by severe flogging, lacerations and branding by the application of heated stones to the throat, breast, and inner parts of the

thighs. On this occasion, nothing could be adduced than the bare assertions of the sorceress.

It is likely that before long the people will be again assembled to go through the ceremony called *umhlaho*, when the name of an offender or offences will be announced, and they will as usual be punished and tortured. Their modes of torture are various … and I shudder while witnessing their effects. Beating with the *induku*, or club, until the offenders are almost lifeless is a comparatively mild measure. Those who are doomed to undergo this process are first pinioned to the ground at full length, a poisonous swarm is then let loose upon them and their stinging powers purposefully stimulated. In this way many a poor female is put upon the rack.

Roasting and branding come next in order and constitute a fiery ordeal indeed. The culprit is fixed to pegs with his arms and legs extended to the very uttermost. A fire is then made to each side of him, at his head also, and likewise at his feet. Here he broils, and when he seems likely to expire amidst the encompassing flame, the fires are partly removed but it is only to shift the rack. Hot stones are now applied to the breast, abdomen, thighs or the soles of the feet, which are thus burnt until the sinews shrink, and parts of the muscular system are completely destroyed.

The most common form of execution is 1. stabbing with the spear, 2. stoning or beating with clubs, which, notwithstanding its tragic nature, is not infrequently made a matter of sport until the executioners are tired of their work, 3. burning, he is placed upon the fire and there held until scorched in a dreadful manner. But generally, after protracting his tortures to the utmost of what nature is able to bear, they break his head with a bludgeon, and thus he expires. Many cases of this description have occurred within the range of my own observation.

Horrible as are these penalties, and affecting as are the groans and cries occasioned by them, they are inflicted in ninety-nine cases out of a hundred.

In another hamlet a wife was charged with bewitching

one of the subordinate chiefs. The defenceless woman was bound with thongs and seated upon a fire that had been kindled for the purpose. There she was held by a number of merciless wretches until the flesh on her legs, arms and other parts was literally roasted, insomuch as it fell from the bones. In this melancholy condition she was left to languish under the eye of hovering vultures and within the range of prowling hyenas.

Executions carried out before Shaka were conducted according to the crime. Punishments for minor offences or the execution of a senior man was carried out with one or more blows from an executioner's knobkerrie. Where Shaka's authority had to be made public, death by impaling was used. A sharpened pole would be thrust into the victim's rectum, whereupon the pole would be pushed upright into a previously prepared hole in the ground. The more the impaled victim struggled, the deeper he sank onto the shaft; the victim was usually left until death occurred. Serious crimes were dealt with by the victim having four or more foot-long sharpened sticks hammered into his rectum; this was considered more painful than impaling. He would then be dragged outside the perimeter of the camp and left to slowly die. Warriors accused of cowardice in battle, or just plain laziness, were brought before Shaka. The unfortunate would be permitted to explain his actions and if plausible, would be released with the gift of a cow. If implausible, he raised his left arm and an *assegai* was thrust through the armpit into the heart. Shaka was also known to test his warriors' bravery pre-battle. Selected warriors would be required to raise their left arms and a spear blade would be teased into each man's under-arm flesh. If the unfortunate winced, the spear went the whole way; otherwise the man was returned to his line of warriors.

After Shaka, most power was concentrated in the hands of the tribal and clan chiefs, but they ruled in association with their councillors who, in turn, had an ear to the people, so there was some curb on excessive autocracy. If a chief made too many wrong decisions his power would slip away or, worse, he would be disposed off. There was a range of punishments for different crimes and misdemeanours – most disputes were resolved by the chief discussing with his councillors to decide the guilty party, who was then punished with a fine (goats or cattle). Only extreme cases warranted the death penalty – usually witchcraft. Torture, as such, became rare, although guilty witches could still be impaled; most criminals were killed by a blow from an executioner's knobkerrie. If someone was guilty of something particularly serious – usually passed off as witchcraft, but often political intrigue – not only were they killed but their immediate family might be 'eaten up' too, as they were guilty by association and might be a source of future dissent. Their cattle would then be forfeited to the chief. The normal procedure was to summon the guilty individual on some pretext to the chief's homestead, then accuse and condemn him – and despatch an *impi* against his family before the news could reach them. It is perhaps worth pointing out that Zulu folklore suggests that most people thought this system was perfectly fair – they didn't see it as particularly oppressive, and felt it only right that wrongdoers be punished for their crimes. After all, most of them looked to their chiefs to protect them from criminals and witches.

Each year, an annual four-day gathering of warriors from across the Zulu nation, *Ukuqwanjiswa Kwempi*, occurred, coincidentally about the time of the European Christmas. There the similarity ended; it was an occasion for the chiefs and the king to review the army and herds of the king's cattle. It would also prepare them for any potential conflict with magic *muti*, which involved the killing of a bull by hand by young warriors – a dangerous business. The meat was daubed with magic potions supplied by the *sangomas*. The warriors took a bite of the meat before passing it to the next man. Women were excluded. The warriors were then formed up in a crescent, whereupon the war doctors, special *sangomas*, would sprinkle the assembly with their magic.[2]

At other times, particularly in droughts, the *sangomas* took on the mantle of rain doctors. This was a testing time for the *sangomas* as they needed to succeed or face heavy fines or death. In times of drought they were adept at finding excuses, in the absence of which they could blame someone practising witchcraft and commence the process of 'smelling out'. The practice of calling for rain during droughts continues to this day, whereas 'smelling out' is no longer common.

Modern-day visitors to Zululand, especially in remote rural areas, soon become familiar with beer drinking. The pastime has little to do with becoming drunk; its origins lie in the tradition of drinking beer to communicate with the dead. The custom of beer drinking remains common and is not openly discussed with Europeans. Zulus believe others would disapprove of the activity, which commences with the head of the *umuzi* served first, followed by the guests. Zulus confirm that beer cannot be drunk in isolation as the drinker will always be accompanied by the spirits of the dead. Curiously, the Zulu term for the event is *ukudla*, although the term *iphathi* is more common today – probably derived from the English word 'party'. Women do not participate, even though they make the beer.

Death has always been accepted by the Zulus as a stage in a journey. Their belief was that man originated from reeds; the first person, or God, was known as *Unkulunkulu*, who brought people into the world by snapping off reeds. The belief even includes the white man – who arrived late to scrape the last piece of wisdom. Messengers bringing news of life came in the form of chameleons, whereas death notices came from salamander lizards. Even in modern times, rural Zulus treat both creatures with apprehension and will immediately kill lizards. The reincarnation of the dead is believed to take place by a visitation of a snake, which always causes some concern, not just because of their venomous nature. The Zulu theory of death is adapted from the folklore of the Khoikhoi people, that *Unkulunkulu* decreed that all men must die.

A Zulu custom that was later to be feared, misunderstood, and which tended to give many a Boer trekker and British soldier sleepless nights, was the Zulu post-battle cleansing tradition of disembowelling the enemy, usually with a knife-like weapon – rarely the *assegai*. The custom of disembowelling a fallen enemy, *qaqa*, was standard practice and was directly related to the Zulu view of the afterlife and its relationship with the world of the living. Part of this ritual involved slitting open the stomach of the slain enemy. To the Zulus, it was essential that those slain in battle or clan disputes had to be ritually disembowelled to free any incarcerated spirit and to protect the victor from absorbing any bad spirits previously possessed by their victim. Under the African sun, any corpse will quickly putrefy and the gases given off by the early stages of decay cause the stomach to swell. In Zulu belief, this was the soul of the dead warrior vainly trying to escape to the afterlife. The victor was obliged to open the stomach of his victim to allow the spirit to escape, failing which, the victor would be haunted by the ghost of his victim, who would inflict unmentionable horrors upon him, including causing his own stomach to swell until, eventually, the victor would go mad. As a final cleansing rite, usually after local skirmishes, the victor then had to have intercourse with a woman, not his wife, before returning to his clan. This practice ensured that any remaining trace of evil spirits would be left with the woman, leaving the victor clean and whole to return home. It also ensured that post-battle, the *impi* would rapidly and enthusiastically disperse from the battlefield for the purpose of religious cleansing. Zulu warriors were only accorded any real status when they had 'washed' their spears in the blood of a defeated enemy.

Mehlokazulu kaSihayo, son of Sihayo and an attendant of King Cetshwayo, was present at Isandlwana with the iNgobamakhosi regiment. In his account of the war, which was recorded by the British in September 1879, he made various references to the subject of stripping and disembowelling the dead:

> As a rule we took off the upper garments, but left the trousers, but if we saw blood upon the garments we did not bother. All the dead bodies were cut open, because if that had not been done the Zulus would have become swollen like the dead bodies. I heard that some bodies were otherwise mutilated.[3]

At Isandlwana, some bodies were disembowelled immediately. Trooper Richard Stevens of the Natal Mounted Police survived the battle and recorded his shock of the practice:

> I stopped in the camp as long as possible, and saw one of the most horrid sights I ever wish to see. The Zulus were in the camp, ripping our men up, and also the tents and everything they came across, with their *assegais*. They were not content with killing, but were ripping the men up afterwards.[4]

One aspect of Zulu ritual that did result in mutilation of the dead was the removal of body parts from a fallen enemy that could be added to the ritual medicines used to prepare the Zulu army before a campaign. These medicines were known as *intelezi*, and were sprinkled on the warriors by *izinyanga*, war doctors, before the army set off on campaign.[5] Parts from a dead enemy, especially one who had fought bravely, would be an enormous boost to Zulu morale, thus ensuring supremacy in battle. Since a number of *izinyanga* accompanied the army that triumphed at Isandlwana, they would certainly have taken the opportunity to collect the raw materials for such medicine from dead soldiers. These mutilations included the disarticulation by the Zulus of dead soldiers' jawbones for trophies, complete with beards. Facial hair was relatively unknown to the warriors and the luxurious beards worn by the soldiers fascinated them. Despite the soldiers' deep-seated fears that these mutilations were carried out before death, and therefore amounted to torture, there is no evidence that this was the case. Interestingly, post-Isandlwana, the practice of shaving became widespread throughout the British Army. Soldiers accepted the necessity of dying for their country but were reluctant to be disarticulated after death on the battlefield. The gulf of cultural misunderstanding was so wide that, after Isandlwana, any Zulu who fell into British hands was doomed.

Over the years, little has changed with regard to traditional Zulu family ties and responsibilities. Many modern Zulu values and traditions can be traced back through time and many of these traditions still hold good today. For example, fathers always had an obligation to their children for shelter, clothing, protection, discipline, teaching, being responsible for their wrongdoing while in his care, monitoring their relationships, providing his son's *lobola* and wedding, and ensuring good relationships with his child's in-laws. The granting of honorific names, *isibongo*, is still current across Zululand and remains a paternal responsibility. *Isibongo* stems from the time of King Dingiswayo, who was appropriately known as 'the lion', and Zwide 'the crocodile'. Modern Zulus retain the tradition by having more conventional European honorific names that can be more easily recognized by Europeans.

Mothers had different obligations, including: protecting the unborn and cooperating in her giving birth; caring for and protecting the child; ensuring the child is educated; teaching female children household duties; monitoring her children's relationships; preparing the wedding beer; providing after-wedding care; and offering assistance and advice for the birth and care of her grandchildren for the whole of her life. Since the time of Shaka, when a woman first had powerful influence in all matters, it has been the woman who has been the more stable element in such relationships within families, villages and tribes, a position that has not been relinquished in modern times.

Sons and daughters reciprocate by recognizing their parents' authority. After school in rural areas boys still rear the sheep and cattle and build huts for their fathers. Daughters look after any small children and then assist the mother with her household and pastoral duties. As boys grow up they assume responsibility for the homestead and cattle. When fully grown, sons living at the family homestead must pay their earnings to their parents as a 'down payment' towards their *lobola*. Sons, in particular, must care for their parents – and in the case of the infirm or elderly parent, take them into their own homes until their death. Although marriage is still a different concept from European marriage, there are strong responsibilities on both sides. Traditionally, a husband had to accept all acts and responsibilities of his wife – who until recent times had no legal position. He had to provide the land for his wife to cultivate their food, provide his wife with her living essentials and enable her to have his children. He was required to treat her fairly, support her in disputes and be responsible for her debts. Since the emancipation of Zulu women, women have jointly been able to make decisions about their children's welfare. When a husband was absent at work, the wife would assume all home responsibilities. Today, modern Zulu women have equal rights in law, although many still hold and practise traditional values. In the many rural areas, most Zulu traditions continue to be followed closely.

When pondering or commenting upon Zulu superstitions or beliefs, I am not going to trespass on controversial ground by trying to come to any conclusion. I therefore exercise some caution, not least because I have yet to find a Zulu belief that cannot be equated with its equivalent in recent European culture. There are numerous medical conditions where Zulu medicine is proven to be as efficacious as our belief in the power of certain foods, placebos, acupuncture and counselling. In the case of disasters, major or personal, people of the first world frequently resort to prayer, whereas the Zulu believes such events are caused by the devil manifesting itself, quite illogically, in another person – who must be 'smelled out' and punished. Europeans are blessed with an education that enables scientific solutions to beliefs, usually involving fear, hope or ignorance; the Zulu relies on the *sangoma*, diviner or herbalist to come to terms with medical or spiritual problems – and the club, spear or AK47 is there for retribution.[6]

Chapter 4

White Expansionism in South Africa and the Eight Frontier Wars

Following Diaz's discovery of the Cape in 1486, southern Africa remained of little interest to the Europeans. It appeared to have nothing to offer beyond its geographical location. In the name of King John of Portugal, Diaz and his men erected a marble cross at the site of their landfall, today known as Angra Pequena. That cross lay neglected for hundreds of years but today it stands in the Lisbon Maritime Museum, a treasured memory of Portugal's contribution to Africa's history. It was King John's expectation that the Cape might open a passage from the Atlantic to the Indian Ocean; thence to the Portuguese-controlled East Indies.

Ten years later, Vasco da Gama landed at the Cape, but only to replenish his water supplies. Curious Khoi gathered to stare in awe at their first sighting of white men, only to be shot at by archers armed with crossbows. The Khoi fled and the die was cast for future mistrust between the races. Vasco da Gama then sailed further north along the lush coastline, far beyond the point previously reached by Diaz, and on Christmas Day in 1497 he named the spray-swept coast Terra Natalis before sailing on to cross the Indian Ocean. Due to the dangerous and fast cross currents and treacherous ocean breakers that pounded the African shoreline, the green hills of the interior were to remain unexplored until the mid-seventeenth century. Before then, the only landings made were accidental, usually involving shipwrecks. Few survived the hazardous combination of sharks and turbulent surf. In the years that followed, isolated Portuguese stations were established in modern-day Mozambique and it was to these stations that the handful of surviving shipwrecked sailors rendered the first-known accounts of the fearsome Bantu people. These stations were usually established on the sites of thriving Arab slave and trading posts. As a consequence, the Portuguese adopted the Arab word for these black people: the word used was *kaffir*, which meant 'unbeliever', and at that time lacked the derogatory racist connotations of more modern times.

Although the lucrative East India trade remained the prerogative of the Portuguese, the barren Cape was otherwise of little importance to other maritime nations. After Spain seized Portugal, Dutch vessels were banned from re-victualling at Lisbon; previously, this was their main storage and watering station for their Atlantic-bound vessels. In 1595, the next east-bound Dutch fleet investigated the Cape and discovered new and easily accessible moorings and plentiful water supplies. The only other ships known to have entered the Cape bay in this period of time were commanded by Captain Lancaster, who was later to command the first English East India Company fleet. Using his knowledge, his company ships also used the Cape as a convenient staging post with its excellent facilities and vegetables – grown by the first settlers. Meanwhile, ships of the East India Company regularly used the nearby victualling facilities of Table Bay. Aware of growing foreign interest in the Cape, the dominant seagoing nation of the time, the Dutch actively discouraged other ships from visiting the area, citing the dangers of its allegedly treacherous shore. Nevertheless, Francis Drake had fully charted the Cape coast in 1580, and thereafter the British knew it to be a relatively safe haven. Drake had written:

> We found the report of the Portuguese to be most false. They affirm that it is the most dangerous cape in the world, never without intolerable storms and present dangers to travellers who come near the same. This cape is the most stately thing, and the fairest cape we have seen in the whole circumference of the earth.[1]

As the years went by the number of trading ships rounding the Cape greatly increased. Its natural harbour was ideally suited as a watering point on the long haul around Africa to the Indies, but little more. By 1650 it was common practice for Dutch ships outbound for the Indies to deposit mail at the Cape under a prominent rock, where it remained until collected by a home-bound vessel, but apart from this strange role as a forwarding post office, the Cape saw no immediate further activity.

Then, in 1651, the Generale Vereenigde Nederlantsche Geoctroyeerde Oost-Indische Compagnie, better known as the Dutch East India Company, established the first permanent white settlement in southern Africa. They built a small fortified enclave intended to provide fresh food and water to their ships rounding the Cape en route to their distant destinations. The company was controlled by a powerful council of seventeen members based in Amsterdam, with important commercial interests in Japan, the East Indies and Formosa. As the Company's Far Eastern trade increased, a more permanent victualling station at the Cape became essential and a tenacious former ship's surgeon of the company and a previous visitor to the Cape, Jan van Riebeeck, was chosen as the founder leader to develop the Cape settlement. In 1652, van Riebeeck's growing band of settlers constructed a fortified camp. They duly expanded by trading their European goods with the Hottentots for cattle and sheep and van Riebeeck's settlement quickly prospered, marred only by attacks from the numerous lions and leopards living on the Cape peninsula. In 1662, the Dutch settlers secured vast tracts of additional land from the Khoi in exchange for goods worth only £10, and the whole location became known as the 'Cape of Good Hope' after the vessel *Good Hope*, which sank in the bay. The survivors constructed two flimsy craft from the wreckage and eventually reached Madagascar and the Cape settlement respectively in 1686. The first Dutch East India Company employees and settlers began arriving from Holland shortly afterwards.

In 1688, more than 200 protestant French Huguenots arrived. The Huguenots had been forced to flee France after the Revocation of Nantes made Protestant worship there unlawful. The majority fled to Britain, some 50,000 souls in all; others went as far afield as Germany, Scandinavia and Canada to escape savage persecution and torture in their home country. Many smuggled themselves and their children across the border into Holland by adopting disguises or hiding in wine barrels. Those caught by French officials were severely treated: most were imprisoned and the women detained in convents, where they were punished with hard labour as well as being roundly abused. Although kindly treated by the Dutch population, these religious refugees were not encouraged to remain in Holland but earnestly urged to emigrate to the Cape, and most complied. Within a generation of their arrival at the Cape they had ceased to speak French, yet from those original 200 immigrants, their number multiplied until, by the 1970s, one million white South Africans could trace their descendants back to the original Huguenots.

In 1712, the Europeans inadvertently brought smallpox to the Cape, which reduced the white population by a quarter and virtually wiped out the Cape Khoi. It then spread through the San tribes. Yet the few San survivors of the disease were still feared, partly because of their use of poisoned arrow tips for hunting or when defending themselves, and they continued to suffer persecution by black and white alike. In 1823 a rough count of the total population of the Cape Colony was estimated at more than 110,000, of whom 30,000 were Khoi. By the 1840s, the San were so reduced in numbers due to the 'blind eye' policy of open slaughter that they faced extermination. Sunday afternoon 'Bushman shoots' were still a feature of Boer farming life and, following psalms and hymns on Sundays, the farmers would 'load their guns' and go hunting:

> The unfortunate Bushmen found on the plains were shot down without mercy. Others were dragged out of their hiding places and – bound hand and foot – had their throats cut like sheep, or were roasted alive over slow fires.[2]

Only those who fled towards the desolate Kalahari were to survive. The Khoi fared just as badly. Voight (see note 2, above) tells us that alcohol, crime and punishment, including liberal hangings for petty offences, resulted in their 'improvement', in his words, 'off the face of the earth'. He adds that 'there are only a few individuals of unmixed Hottentot blood to be met here and there throughout all Cape Colony.' It was not until the early twentieth century that Europeans became aware that these supposedly primitive people had an appreciation of music and art. Fine examples of their delicately coloured wall paintings can still be seen today on numerous rocky outcrops across South Africa, including the eastern face of the Oscarsberg at Rorke's Drift. As the famous African explorer Sir Laurens van der Post wrote of the San, 'they were dealt a rotten hand.'[3]

Many of the Freiburgers, the familiar term for those pioneer farmers who had worked out their contracts for the Dutch East India Company, chose to make their homes around the Company settlement of Good Hope rather than return to the uncertainties of life in Holland. Over the years that followed, limited settlement took place and as sovereignty of the Cape changed hands, the vast majority of those displaced by change stayed on as farmers and began to progress further inland. Here there was unlimited land for the taking, blessed not only with better grazing but also with absolute freedom from petty administrators. These people, together with an increasing immigration of French, German and Dutch settlers, created a tough new race. They cooperated with each other and collectively adopted the name 'Boer' to describe their predominately agricultural way of life. Their farms were vast by European standards, as land was free and relatively unpopulated; they had merely to register their property with the supervising chartered company, a process that was nothing more than a simple formality. In due course, this influx grew into a community of more than 10,000 settler and refugee families that stretched for 600 miles inland from Cape Town. Numerous inter-Boer political disputes followed concerning farmers' land rights. By now the largest non-white group at the Cape consisted of Boer-owned slaves and their descendants. The majority of these slave people had been taken from Madagascar, Ceylon, India and the East Indies, the most popular being black men from Madagascar for physical labour while the other nationalities were prized for their domestic skills.

In 1769, and to the Boers' surprise, their own expansion to the north-east unexpectedly came face to face with the migrating amaXhosa, who were moving in even greater numbers from the north. Both sides met on opposing banks of the Great Fish River. Boer accounts report that the Xhosa made a fierce onslaught on the pioneer explorers but were beaten off by musketry fire. As the Xhosa had not previously encountered men on horses or firearms, the fighting did not last long.[4] Previously, neither side had had much experience of the other, although the Boers quickly discovered that this new race was far more defiant than the San and Khoi. The Xhosa fiercely contested attempts by the Boers to cross and settle on their side of the river and ferocious raids and vicious attacks by both sides regularly occurred. The two opposing migrations were competing for the same natural resources and the disputed boundary area created a pattern of conflict between the black and white races that was to shape the future of southern Africa well into modern times. By negotiation, both sides agreed not to cross the river for malevolent purposes but the large number of Boer cattle was too tempting for the Xhosa, who made a number of increasingly violent cattle raids into Boer territory.

In 1780, the first of eight frontier conflicts took place. The Boers retaliated when two Xhosa tribes, the Gaikas and Tslambis, or the amaNdlambe as they are known today, crossed the river, forcing the Boers to retaliate with a once-and-for-all attack designed to drive the local Xhosa tribes from the immediate area. The Boer leader, Van Jaarsveld, adopted a novel approach to the problem: one of his riders would enter the chosen village and throw tobacco onto the ground. In the ensuing melee, Jaarsveld and his men would approach the scrabbling mass and open fire, which resulted in them killing more than 200 on one occasion. The war ended during July, with more than 5,000 cattle seized and an unknown number of Xhosa killed. There followed an uneasy peace that deteriorated into the second Frontier War of 1793, when a sizeable horde of Xhosa crossed the river border, murdering settlers and seizing their cattle. Severe destruction, brutal retribution and reprisals thereafter caused much suffering on both sides.

In 1794, the Dutch formally assumed administrative control of the Cape but in the same year they were defeated by the French in the Napoleonic Wars, which opened the Cape to French warships. This caused considerable concern to the British Admiralty and Britain promptly responded by seizing the Cape in order to protect her own prosperous sea routes to India. In 1795 matters deteriorated to the extent that the two frontier districts of Swellendam and Graaff-Reinet threatened insurrection. It was to avoid such political restrictions and disputes that the isolationist Boers continued to migrate away from the developing administrative complexity of life at the Cape. The year 1799 saw the beginning of the third Frontier War, which was to wage for more than two years. This particular war saw the surviving Khoi join with the Xhosa against white settlers but again their predictable defeat ultimately favoured the Boer trekkers.

Along the Great Fish River border, the most southerly Xhosa people and the Boers lived as uneasy neighbours. The Xhosa prized Boer cattle and the Boers coveted Xhosa lands. During one Xhosa raid, the Boers were forced to abandon more than 100 farms. Limited Boer retaliation was undertaken, but to little effect; each side remaining wary of the other. The struggle for domination of the Great Fish River area finally erupted in the fourth Frontier War, of 1811, which resulted in more than 20,000 Xhosa being forcibly relocated beyond the far bank of the river.

During this period, the inland area of southern Africa was of little interest to Britain and was regarded by most Europeans as *terra incognita*. Apart from the insignificant Dutch settlement at the Cape that had clung to the area for 150 years, it still measured only 200 by 500 miles. It would not be until the 1820s that several thousand British farmers and settlers arrived at the Cape to bring the total population up to 12,000.

By 1814 the border was becoming more of an imperial than a Boer problem. Having temporarily seized the Cape in 1806, the British had acquired the Cape Colony for the sum of £6,000,000 and they now sought to resolve the border disputes through the construction of a series of well-defended military fortifications, known as blockhouses, strategically sited along the border. The plan failed and the fifth Frontier War, now termed 'savage warfare' by the troops, broke out in 1818. In 1819, the settlement of Grahamstown, complete with its British garrison commanded by Lieutenant Colonel Willshire, was surrounded by some 10,000 angry Xhosa warriors. The Xhosa were beaten off during a two-hour battle that left more than 1,000 dead and dying warriors compared with British losses of three killed and a handful wounded. The British solution to the growing border problem was to 'clear' a vast area of land between the Great Fish and Keiskamma rivers and declare the area neutral territory, which they then filled with land-hungry British settlers who had accepted the home government's generous offer of free land. Such an offer resulted in large-scale emigration from Britain, whose working classes were still suffering from widespread agricultural depression following the long war with France.

Meanwhile, and several hundred miles north-east beyond the Great Fish River frontier, one Bantu tribe, the southern Nguni, had settled along several coastal rivers that flowed into the Indian Ocean. The area was populated by a patchwork of independent clans and minor chiefdoms that spoke broadly the same language and followed the same cultural practices. It was little more than a generation after the first conflict occurred near the Cape between black and white that these people, the Zulus, began to emerge as a new tribe among the northern Nguni.

In 1823 the British entered the stage in the form of ex-naval lieutenant Francis Farewell. In 1824 he charted two ships, the *Julia* and *Antelope*, in which he undertook a trading expedition to Natal and was so impressed by the territory that he decided to settle. He persuaded a group of some twenty-five like-minded adventurers who settled the northern shore of the area known then as Port Natal, today as Durban. Most of the men then abandoned Farewell. In the meantime, he and the British Resident in Zululand, Henry Fynn, visited King Shaka of the hitherto unknown tribe, the Zulus, with a view to trading elephant tusks and fine skins against beads and pots. The explorers found Shaka at the height of his power with an army of 10,000 warriors and living a luxurious lifestyle. Fynn wrote:

> The whole country so far as our sight could reach was covered with numbers of people and droves of cattle. The king came to us and told us not to be afraid of his people.[5]

Partly due to trade and partly to Fynn's apparent medical skill, which included disguising Shaka's grey hairs with Macassar, Shaka gifted Farewell with the inlet area of the white settlement together with 40 miles of coastline. Shaka made his mark on a document, which was duly submitted to Lord Charles Somerset, although, in the event, the British authorities at the Cape expressed no interest in Natal. The area around Port Natal continued to thrive and settled into uneasy peace. At the time, Shaka kept his army active with skirmishes against the clans of Celeland and the Kumalo. His final campaign was against Faku in Pondoland, where Shaka's army captured his clan's whole herd of 30,000 Pondo cattle, leaving Faku destitute.

Meanwhile, the local Xhosa increasingly resisted European settlement with cross-border raids against the new settlers, which resulted in the sixth Frontier War of 1834-35. This was another brutal conflict, which resulted in nearly 1,500 Xhosa and 100 colonial fatalities. One noted casualty was Chief Hintsa, who surrendered to the British commander in person, General Sir Harry Smith and his escort. On learning that his tribe would be given an unobtainable ransom demand for his release, he seized a horse and tried to escape from the general's escort:

> He was pulled off his horse, shot through the back and through the leg. Desperately he scrambled down the riverbank and collapsed into the watercourse. A scout named George Southey, coming up fast behind him, blew off the top of his head. Then some soldiers cut off his ears as keepsakes to show around the military camps. Others tried to dig out his teeth with bayonets.[6]

Again, no resolution was found and following the murder of a British escort to a Xhosa prisoner who had stolen an axe, the seventh Frontier War, 'the war of the axe', was undertaken throughout 1846. This war ebbed and flowed until, in 1850, the now desperate Khoi, Xhosa and Thembu joined forces for the eighth Frontier War. The war was fought over land that was again stricken by drought, and in the midst of the starvation and death, a girl gave birth to a two-headed baby. Although the baby died within days, the birth was somehow seen as a sign to continue the war, which the British pursued with indiscriminate shootings and 'scorched earth' raiding. The war lasted two years and only ended with the Battle of Fort Armstrong. The war's end resulted in an even stronger line of defence for the Boers, now fully supported by the British. In 1857, the Xhosa were further decimated when a young girl, Nongqawuse, prophesied that the whites would be driven from their land if the Xhosa slaughtered all their cattle and burned their crops. The Gcaleka chief, Sarhili, ordered his people to fulfil the prophecy; the resultant famine killed thousands of Xhosa while others fled towards the Cape. The famine was used by the British to move waiting German settlers into the region and the whole area was brought under British control.

Meanwhile, Dutch influence had long since failed at the Cape, which, since 1806, had finally and permanently been annexed by Britain. This coincided with a new British colonial policy of self-finance through taxation, a form of revenue that was alien to both the Dutch traders and isolated Boer farmers. Even while the Cape Border Wars were raging new circumstances involving taxation and legislative controls were gradually evolving that would seriously undermine relationships between the British and the Boers, the two dominant European groups at the Cape. Strife and conflict marked the early years of British rule at the Cape, which resulted in a strong British determination to stabilize the colony's borders to the north.

The Cape Boers soon became utterly disillusioned with British rule, taxation and punishments for non-compliance with local laws. These Boers were a hardy new race; they called themselves Afrikaners and they fiercely resented any intrusion with their way of life, especially politically motivated executions. They owed allegiance only to God, themselves and to Africa (hence the name Afrikaners). They were fully aware that the whole of unexplored Africa lay to the east and the north. Surely it was possible, many asked, to move there and live in peace? Being devoutly religious, they fervently prayed for a solution and, inevitably, the solution stared them in the face. Because they had sought help through prayer, the obvious answer took on a religious significance and many Boers came to believe their trek from the Cape was ordered by God. The final indignity to be endured, which precipitated the trek, came in 1834, with yet more British legislation, including the Act of Emancipation, which finally abolished slavery and gave equality to all people, regardless of their race, colour, creed or station in life. As prodigious users of slaves, this was too much for some of the wealthier Boers, who responded by selling their farms and heading for the uncharted African interior. They called themselves Voortrekkers, those who trek to the fore.

Without doubt, the most influential Voortrekker was the aristocratic Piet Retief, who was highly respected by Boers and British alike. Although a failed businessman, he was a wily politician, a wealthy farmer, and a field commandant. His eventual approval of the trek was the spark that ignited the fire of mass disaffection amongst the Boers. His own decision had been made with the passing of the 1834 Act of Emancipation and British offer of compensation for their 'lost' slaves. Compensation was indeed offered but payment had to be made in London. No Boer could afford this undertaking and the loss of their slave workforce would have destroyed many Boer businesses and farms. To gain a few months' grace, the Boers designated their slaves as 'apprentices' while they busily prepared for the trek. Curiously, the undertaking did not have the blessing of the United Dutch Reform Church.

Once under way, the purpose of the Great Trek was to discover new land where they could establish their own Boer law-abiding state and live totally independently of British rule. It was their overwhelming frustration that had led to this extraordinary and carefully considered emigration of nearly 12,000 Boers, probably a fifth of their people, together with a similar number of servants and apprentices. The trek took place over several years and many parties perished at the hands of, firstly, the northern Matabele, and then, as they progressed further east and north, the Bantu. Two other large parties perished when they attempted to cross the vast wastes of the Kalahari Desert. They were never seen again and no trace of their wagons has ever been found. Several influential families initiated the trek and many names are well known to students of South African history; people such as the Tregardts, who were of Swedish origin, and the Van Rensburgs, who were slaughtered by the Matabele as they entered unknown territory to the north. As the treks progressed, three men came to the fore: Maritz, Uys and Retief. Maritz and Uys pressed on, seeking their Promised Land to the north, while Retief pondered the possibility of his Promised Land being somewhere east of the Drakensberg Mountains.

When Retief left his farm and set off with twenty-five families, their wagons, servants and herds, the news spread rapidly and others rushed to join the Retief Column. At the Orange River, more than 300 trekkers and their entourages joined Retief, while others followed the trails left by his wagons. Piet Retief wrote bitterly in his diary of British oppression, which he believed was deliberately biased in favour of non-whites:

> We leave this fruitful land of our birth in which we have suffered enormous losses and continual vexation and are about to enter a strange and dangerous territory. We go

relying on merciful God, whom we shall fear and humbly endeavour to obey.[7]

On 17 April 1837, his group joined a larger column under the leadership of Gert Maritz. At a trekker meeting, Retief was elected overall leader, giving him a command of nearly 5,000 trekkers, with more than 1,000 wagons and huge herds of cattle and sheep. Retief made strict rules and gave orders to control the multitude, which included instructions that the local clans were not to be molested, native servants were to be properly treated and game was only to be shot for the pot. Order was maintained by a system of field commandants and offenders were punished with fines. His policy towards the native chiefs, through whose territory they passed, was one of friendship and, while reports from trekkers to the north indicated hostile Matabele, his advance scouts were reporting most favourably on the land east of the Drakensberg Mountains and towards the Indian Ocean, the unexplored land of the Zulus. This news was warmly received as the trekkers had become disheartened by the unending dry land through which they had been passing. It was too hot in summer, too cold in winter and always short of water. Accordingly, he made plans to cross the Drakensberg Mountains.

Retief had scant knowledge of the inhabitants he was hoping to meet – a little-understood warrior nation, but one with a fearsome reputation. The Boers knew nothing of Zululand and even less of its king, Dingane, other than that he was generally regarded by his people as their king. Retief knew full well that he should meet Dingane and negotiate settlement rights and, accordingly, the Boers travelled to meet the king. Retief was so confident that he could negotiate land rights for his people that towards the end of October, he and his party set off into Zululand. By early October 1837 they had crossed the Drakensberg Mountains but instead of travelling direct to the Zulu king, they first needed fresh supplies and slowly headed towards the small and mainly British settlement on the coast of the Indian Ocean at Port Natal. They arrived to a most cordial welcome from the hundred or so English settlers, who were fully aware that a Boer settlement inland from the British would afford them added security against any marauding Zulus.

Refreshed, they set off. A fluent Zulu speaker from the port community, Thomas Holstead, agreed to accompany the Boers. The land they travelled through was everything the Boers hoped for; the lush and well-watered grasslands were beyond their expectations and clearly ideal for their settlement, especially as they appeared devoid of human population. What was unknown to the unsuspecting Boers was the reason for the depopulation, namely the *Mfecane*, and the subsequent slaughter of surrounding tribes by King Shaka when he had expanded his empire some fifteen years previously. Little was known of King Dingane outside Zululand except that he was believed to be overweight and that he exercised autocratic control over the Zulu people. Retief knew Dingane had killed his famous half-brother Shaka and would execute any opponent out of hand. This included his chief, Matiwana, who was put to the stake, being considered by Dingane as untrustworthy.

To smooth his onward route, Retief sent a warm and friendly letter to Dingane in which he expressed his wish to discuss the possibility of a peaceful and profitable Boer settlement in the vicinity of the Drakensberg Mountains. Retief knew from his conversations with Holstead that an English missionary, Francis Owen, lived at the king's *ikhanda*, the royal homestead, and could translate his letter of request to Dingane.

Dingane's reputation may not have unduly perturbed the well-armed Boers but, with all events considered, perhaps more caution should have been exercised. Dingane was fully aware that Retief's equally well-armed fellow trekkers to the north were being successfully harassed by the Matabele, with whom the Zulus had been in indecisive conflict in 1830. King Dingane's reply to Retief was nevertheless friendly; he even returned some sheep that had previously been stolen from the trekkers. Retief's party set off in anticipation of a successful outcome.

On about 5 November 1837, the party approached the king's *ikhanda* at Mgungundhlovu, near modern-day Ulundi. Retief must have been impressed; the *ikhanda* consisted of a fortification containing more than 2,000 large and well-built huts, each capable of housing twenty people, with another 300 larger huts for the king's personal use, his wives and his senior *izinDuna*. He was even more impressed by the eight days of celebration, feasting, dancing and displays that went on endlessly and, after a week, must have exhausted and frustrated the Boers. Missionary Owen was present throughout and it is due to his meticulous diary – discovered only in 1922 at the Missionary Hall in London – that we now know accurate details of the horrendous events that would shortly unfurl.

At the end of the eighth day, Dingane informed Retief that he would be granted permission to settle where he requested – subject to Retief first recovering cattle that had been stolen from the king by a rival chief, Sikonyela, of the Basotho people. Retief accepted the arrangement and returned to his settlers who, without his permission, had now crossed the Drakensberg mountain range and begun to stake their claims towards the Tugela River. Other trekkers, encouraged by the promising news, were enthusiastically following across the mountains in the anticipation of bountiful grazing. Retief gathered seventy of his best fighting men to undertake the mission against Sikonyela and, immediately following the celebration of Christmas, Retief's expedition set out for Sikonyela's homestead, leaving the main party in the care of the youths and elderly Boers, though without instructions for the remaining families to laager or to prepare defensive positions.

Within the week, Retief's party arrived at Sikonyela's homestead and, on the pretext of presenting the chief with a bracelet, snapped the unsuspecting chief into handcuffs and held him prisoner while the stolen cattle were collected. Sikonyela was then released and Retief headed back towards Dingane's *ikhanda* in optimistic mood with the recovered cattle. Prior to Retief's return to Mgungundhlovu on 3 February 1838, Missionary Owen had observed an unusually large number of young warriors arriving at the *ikhanda*. He also recorded in his diary of hearing rumours that the king was annoyed at reports from his spies that Retief had permitted Sikonyela to live. Retief returned the stolen cattle to an apparently appreciative Dingane but had siphoned off some of the cattle recovered from Sikonyela as his 'reward' before returning the bulk of the herd. This was against Zulu etiquette: he should have returned them all and allowed Dingane to graciously gift him a proportion as his reward. According to Zulu legend, this allegedly made Dingane believe Retief was dishonest.

While Dingane pondered how to deal with Retief, the celebratory feasting recommenced. For several days Retief and his men were obliged to watch the ritual entertainment held in their honour until, on 6 February, following an impressive display of horsemanship and firearm salvoes by the Boers, Retief was finally called before the king. A few days earlier, Dingane had received messages from his spies that, without the king's permission, Boer settlers were crossing the Drakensberg in their hundreds and that they were already staking claims on Zulu territory. Dingane's concern was heightened when he learned that Retief's visiting Boers had ridden their horses, under the cover of darkness, around the king's private compound. The Boers denied all knowledge but were unable to explain the hoofprints around the compound perimeter. By now, Dingane was highly suspicious of Retief and was becoming concerned for his own safety. The Boers were summoned for a final meeting. In the presence of the senior *izinDuna*, Dingane allegedly gave verbal permission for the Boer settlement. Everything promised by the king was written down by the Boer scribe, Jan Bantjes, who then translated it back into Zulu for the benefit of the assembled *izinDuna*. According to Boer legend, Dingane and the three most senior *izinDuna* then signed the document before Retief placed it in his leather pouch for safety.[8]

As Retief was about to depart, he and his men were invited to one final feast. Not wishing to appear discourteous or impatient, Retief reluctantly agreed. The Zulu *izinDuna* respectfully reminded Retief that it was impolite for anyone to enter the king's *ikhanda* with firearms and Retief acquiesced; all their firearms were stacked outside the enclosure next to their horses. The feast commenced and hundreds of young warriors began their series of dances. Suddenly, King Dingane rose to his feet and a chilling silence descended on the multitude. He called out: '*Babulaleni abathakathi*' (Kill the wizards!), and before the unsuspecting Boers realized what fate held for them, they were seized and bound hand and foot with strips of leather. They were then dragged by their feet several hundred yards across rocky ground to the hill of execution, which was deliberately sited by the *ikhanda* main gate to remind residents and visitors of the king's power. The whole event was watched by Missionary Owen through his telescope just as a warrior arrived at his house with a reassuring message from the king to the effect that Owen and his family need have no fear for their lives.

At the hill of execution each Boer in turn had his arms and legs broken with knobkerries before being untied and then either clubbed to death or impaled. Retief was made to watch the orgy of torture and death, including that of his 12-year-old son, before he too was executed. Their bodies were then thrown over the cliff for disposal by wild animals and the resident flock of vultures. Owen wrote in his diary that he fainted from the shock, as did his wife.

Also murdered were the thirty or so native servants who accompanied Retief's party. Only one survived, named Lomana, who was guarding the Boers' horses outside the king's *ikhanda*. He escaped the slaughter by riding off, and lived to tell the tale until he died near Weenen in 1909. Rumours still abound that a number of Boer women were with the party and that they too were murdered. There is no evidence that this was the case, although Owen's diary records that those slain included a number of Boer boy riders, 'some under the age of eleven'. Dingane decreed that no Boer, woman or child, should survive on his land. Owen's next diary entry reveals that, 'within two hours, a large *impi* was gathered and almost immediately departed the king's homestead.' According to Zulu folklore, Dingane's half-brother, Mpande, was present at Dingane's *ikhanda* on the fateful day, accompanied by his 12-year-old son, Cetshwayo.

Disaster of a colossal magnitude was about to befall the unsuspecting Boer families gathering in the area now known as Bloukranze and Weenen; all were totally unsuspecting and eagerly anticipated Retief's return with the promised permission to settle. Under cover of darkness, several thousand Zulu warriors approached the sleeping Boer families and then launched their merciless attack. Immediately south of the Tugela River the most appalling horror and bloodshed was unleashed. Throughout that Friday night and the following day the trekkers further back from the direct line of attack sought desperately to rally whatever men they could and bring the surviving women and children to the relative safety of wagons hastily drawn up into protective laagers. By dawn on the Sunday, the stabbed and mutilated bodies of 531 elderly Boer men, women and children were spread over an area of 20 square miles. An estimated 300 servants had also died violently at the hands of Dingane's warriors.

The surviving trek leaders, Maritz and Cilliers, were helpless to prevent thousands of cattle, sheep and horses from being driven off by the Zulus. While the survivors surveyed the terrible scenes of death and devastation a Boer scouting party arrived with news that the Zulus had withdrawn. But grieving had to wait; much was to be done to prevent the circling vultures from descending. The days ahead were critical in view of the possibility of a renewed assault and the crucial decision had to be made whether to trek back over the mountains and abandon Natal, or take revenge. A clear majority, especially the women, forcefully insisted on punishment and retribution. The decision of a public meeting late in March was that the combination of the highly respected Boer leaders Hendrik Potgieter and Piet Uys would be granted equal status, each to command his own men, in order to punish Dingane.

Early in April the first punitive expedition of 347 well-armed men under the command of Uys and Potgieter departed from the main Boer laager. Across the Buffalo River, at the Italeni Valley, they met the Zulu war party that had been shadowing the Boers. The Zulus had camouflaged themselves as cattle by hiding under their cowhide shields and easily decoyed Uys and his followers into descending into the valley and a carefully planned trap.

Potgieter, deeply suspicious, held back; Uys' strategy of rounding up Zulu cattle did not appeal to him at all. Swiftly encircled by the Zulus, Uys and his men desperately tried to shoot their way clear in order to escape the overwhelming odds but in the process Uys was fatally stabbed, and his young son, Dirkie, not wishing to leave his father, also perished. The Zulus returned to Mgungundlovu to report their continued success.

Potgieter and his men now had to face the waiting trekkers and report their failure. Panic once again set in at the realization of another defeat and, even worse, another leader's death. Renewed thought was seriously given to abandoning Natal. Potgieter was labelled a coward and accused of treason. He left Natal a haunted man and, due to the seriousness of the situation, many others were tempted to follow him back to the Cape.

Once again it was the women who implored their menfolk to remain, this time fiercely demanding that Dingane should be made to pay personally. Conditions for the Boers were extremely difficult and the constant threat of Zulu attacks forced them to remain in their laager. Local grazing was soon exhausted and the Boers' food supplies were minimal. Crisis loomed; Maritz was on his own and within weeks he became desperately ill and died. Like Moses, he saw the Promised Land but was not destined to live in it.

Meanwhile, the English settlers at Port Natal, furious at the loss of their friend Thomas Holstead, prepared a small force to support the Boers and sent out a fifty-strong raiding party. The Zulus watched the party cross into Zululand and prepared an ambush using 10,000 well-concealed warriors. Within minutes, only four of the party managed to escape. Zulu folklore recalls that the Zulu commander was none other than Mpande, accompanied by his son, Cetshwayo, in the role of an *uDibi* boy. Flushed with success, the Zulus advanced upon Port Natal. The residents fled by sea, leaving their settlement to be wrecked and looted by the jubilant Zulus.

A month or so after Maritz's untimely death, another Boer leader, Andries Pretorius, responded positively to a plea to join the trekkers in the vicinity of the Little Tugela near Loskop. The trekkers' situation was extremely grave. Pretorius found a demoralized people suffering an epidemic of measles that was raging through the Boer camps. Pretorius was immediately elected Commandant General and within days he set out with another force of 468 well-armed men, along with 120 servants and sixty-four battlewagons. Each wagon was dawn by only ten oxen, as they would be very lightly loaded. Though cumbersome and considerably slow moving, they would be absolutely essential for forming a laager. Thus, fully aware of the fact that wherever the scene of battle was likely to be, it would be grassland, and it was therefore imperative to prepare *veghekke*, or fighting gates, in order to deny to the Zulus any gaps between the wagons drawn together for protection. Ammunition bags were prepared to make reloading of old muzzle-loading muskets quicker. Biltong, rusks and coffee were to suffice as rations. A strong disciplinarian, Pretorius demanded total obedience and made it clear that he would not tolerate independent dissidence, the factor that had led to the previous undoing of the Boers and was to prove a problem in future.

Ever the tactician, Pretorius had wisely brought with him two of his personal small cannons. These, and a longer-range ship's cannon also belonging to Pretorius, were to prove invaluable. News reached Maritz that a large Zulu force, numbering 10,000 and under the command of Chief Ndlela, was fast approaching his small convoy. On the eve of the anticipated Zulu attack some 700 oxen and 750 horses, along with the wagon leaders and trekkers (among them three Englishmen), were brought into the roughly D-shaped laager. Whip-sticks supporting lanterns were in readiness should the *impi* attack under the cover of darkness. It was 15 December 1838.

During the night a thick wet mist settled over the camp and along the riverbanks, which prevented the Zulu scouts locating the exact position of the Boers. Ironically, the heavy mist seriously alarmed the trekkers as the threat of their gunpowder becoming damp and useless was very real. Fortunately for the Boers, the dawn caught Ndlela's force divided by the river, and at opposing ends of the Boer position. As the mist lifted the trekkers manning their positions waited for the inevitable Zulu attack and the fact that it was Sunday gave the dramatically tense situation a special religious significance, although it was of no consequence to the Zulus. There are two accounts of what ensued. According to Boer history, the Zulus charged the Boer position but found the small but deep Ncome River blocking their advance on the Boer position. Even when the Zulus forded the river they were unable to breach the barrier of wagons. In spite of the din of battle, the animals within the laager did not panic, as Maritz had feared. They could so easily have wreaked havoc by breaking loose and stampeding to escape the confines of a relatively small enclosure. Victory was assured by mid-morning as, according to the Boers, the *impi* fled. Released from the defensive position, the mounted Boers gave chase and hastened the Zulus' speedy withdrawal.

Although the Battle of Blood River has long been considered to have been one of the greatest victories in Boer history, the trekkers had, in fact, laid themselves open to siege. How much longer would those animals have behaved under such stressful circumstances without grazing? How much longer would the ammunition, the food and, above all, the water, have lasted? The lessons learned after the earlier Boer defeat at Vegkop alerted the Boers to the fact that the Zulus, victorious or otherwise, always drove away stock. Chief Ndlela had been determined to attack the Boers during darkness, and in doing so his plan could possibly have met with success had the night not been so dark and misty, resulting in the Zulu army repeatedly losing themselves as they tried to cross the river and surround the Boers.

The official copy of the battle report displayed at the Boers' Blood River Museum boldly describes the short battle and explains how the Ncome River became known as Blood River.[9] Boer history records that hordes of fleeing warriors were shot down by the Boers and that the pursuit lasted until midday, when the commando returned to the laager, where 3,000 Zulus lay dead.

Zulu history tells a very different story.[10] During the previous week, Dingane's spies had relayed reports back to Dingane that the Boers were again approaching, but this time as a compact force. Wanting to deter the Boers, Dingane gave orders for his army to assemble and set in motion a plan to confront the Boers with an overwhelming display of force – which assembled within a mile of the Boers on the night of 15 December. Under the command of Chief Ndlela, Zulu scouts were despatched to within several hundred yards of the Boers but with orders not to cross the river or engage with any Boer scouts. Just before dawn, the Zulu army moved forward and took up its intimidating position. As dawn came, little could be seen by either side due to the heavy mist that hung over the river. The Boers quietly waited, and from the Zulu positions the Boers could be neither seen nor heard. After an hour of inactivity Chief Ndlela sent his scouts a half-mile upriver, where it was shallow enough to ford, and then to advance on the Boers to a point where they could assess the strength of their defence. As the Zulus appeared through the mist, just 30 yards away, the Boers began firing wildly. Being at close range, the Zulus retaliated by throwing their spears and then retreated back across the river. Chief Ndlela ordered his army to wait until the mist cleared to disclose the strength of his army in the naïve expectation that their presence would deter the Boers from advancing further into Zululand. Within the following hour the mist dissipated and both sides were in full view of each other. With his large army intimidatingly arrayed before the Boers, Maritz's force took no further action. An hour later, Chief Ndlela gave the order for his army to move back towards Zululand. He had made his point.

The Zulus certainly acknowledge a Boer presence at Blood River but challenge the account that either a major battle took place or that they suffered such serious casualties.[11] Regardless of the veracity or otherwise of events at Blood River, Boer farmers continued to trickle into the more northern reaches of Zululand while the British concentrated on developing Natal and mistakenly left Zululand and the 'Boer problem' to Dingane's successor, King Mpande. At the same time, the British formally occupied Port Natal and renamed it 'Durban', after Sir Benjamin D'Urban, Governor of the Cape Colony. All the while, the relationship between the Zulu kings and the British authorities in southern Africa remained sympathetic. To prevent further disputes, a peace treaty was drawn up between the British and Zulus using the Tugela River as the acknowledged boundary between them; this was signed on 23 March 1839.

In 1846, four separate Natal Land Commissions under Theophilus Shepstone were set up to consider and decide upon the relocation of the numerous black settlements in Natal. The commission recommended the introduction of magistrate-supervised locations occupying more than 100,000 acres, but the system never properly functioned. It was reintroduced in 1847, with 80,000 people being moved into black reserves that they could self-administer subject to tribal law so long as it did not offend 'natural law and justice'.

In January 1853 and February 1854 respectively, Britain first recognized the Voortrekkers South African Republic (the Transvaal) and then the Orange Free State. It was a desperate gesture to pass off the enormous financial and military burden of protecting these two Boer states. It was also a shrewd political gamble to protect the valuable British coastal colony of Natal from the incessant conflicts of the African interior.

Over the following years, the problem of growing numbers of refugees entering Natal increased; the Secretary for Native Affairs, Theophilus Shepstone, wrote to Lord Carnarvon on 30 November 1874:

> It is impossible to foresee what solution will be found to so serious and dangerous a problem. A safety valve in the shape

of adjoining territory (Zululand) has always been looked at as the only source of relief.

At the same time, Boer settler incursion from the Transvaal into northern Zululand was ruthless and growing out of control. Collectively, the Boers were rugged and hardened, and without pity for those whose land they took. They were described as being:

> a religious people, well versed in the teaching of the Old Testament, which seemed to them to uphold racial inequality and justify summary discipline for the backward and heathen … they concluded that the prestige and authority of the colonist must be upheld and the black man subjected to firm restraint.[12]

The Zulus were losing patience, and the British would be forced to act.

Chapter 5

Passing the Crown:
From Kings Shaka, Dingane and
Mpande to King Cetshwayo

The first significant white movement to affect the Zulus was the establishment of Port Natalia in 1824 under the leadership of Francis Farewell and Henry Fynn. The purpose of their mission was to establish trade with the northern Nguni, especially in ivory and skins, most of which was being traded through Delagoa Bay, the small Portuguese enclave in Mozambique that lay 1,200 miles from the Cape and 200 miles to the north of Zululand. Although the Portuguese trade routes extended throughout Zululand and into Natal, the Portuguese used African intermediaries rather than actively trading themselves. There is evidence to suggest that isolated examples of European trade goods were known throughout Zululand in the 1790s, although Europeans themselves were known only by repute as *abelungu* – sea creatures that were occasionally found washed up on the shores.

In early 1824, while Farewell and Fynn were establishing their trading post, another event occurred that was to bring radical change to the Zulus. Shaka had heard of the handful of white men living at Port Natalia and to satisfy his curiosity, and his desire for their prestigious goods, he sent them an invitation to visit his *ikhanda* at kwaBulawayo (the place of he who kills) under the protection of the king's escort. The party consisted of Lieutenant Farewell, Fynn, Captain Davies of the sloop *Julia*, and adventurers Peterson, Henry Ogle and Joseph Powell, together with a Boer and a large number of gifts. The party arrived in July and were in awe at the size of the royal *ikhanda*. It measured at least 3 miles in its circumference and housed the impressive royal huts and the royal cattle *kraal* containing some 7,000 pure white cattle and 2,000 domestic huts. The party was greeted by Shaka, who was protected by 12,000 of his best warriors. After various displays and feasts, Farewell and Fynn again met with Shaka, using the occasion to request trading rights for the Farewell Trading Company. To Shaka, his visitors were welcomed as a source of exotic trade goods, including firearms. This meeting was a success and Shaka permitted Farewell's expedition to function as a subservient chiefdom at Port Natalia and surrounding area.

With Shaka's permission, the party returned to Port Natalia but without Fynn, who remained at Shaka's request – not as a hostage, but to enable Shaka to learn more of the white men. Fynn was residing at the royal *ikhanda* when an attempt was made on Shaka's life. He was stabbed in the stomach by an unknown assailant and lay at death's door for a week. During this time, Fynn cleaned and bandaged the wound and generally watched over Shaka who, being strong and healthy, quickly recovered. Shaka believed that the attempt had been made by members of the distant iHlambo tribe. Accordingly, two *impis* were dispatched, who captured the iHlambo cattle and destroyed their homesteads and cattle *kraals*. Restored to good health, the settlers' position was assured and a grateful Shaka signed an agreement granting Farewell nearly 4,000 square miles of land around Port Natalia. It was to this ramshackle beginning that all subsequent British claims to the region owed their origin.

In 1826, Farewell and Fynn were requested to accompany Shaka's army of more than 40,000 warriors on an expedition against the Ndwandwe clan. The result was total slaughter of the Ndwandwe at the Battle of iziNdolowane, which distressed even Farewell and Fynn, though Shaka was delighted with the 60,000 captured cattle. Fynn's horror of the post-battle massacre was recorded in his diary:

> The enemy's loss (Ndwandwe) had now become more severe. This urged the Zulus to a final charge. The shrieks now became terrific. The remnants of the (Ndwandwe) army sought shelter in an adjoining wood, out of which they were soon driven. Then began a slaughter of the women and children. They were all put to death. The battle from the commencement to the close did not last more than an hour and a half … Early next morning Shaka arrived and each regiment, previous to its inspection by him, had picked out its cowards and put them to death.[1]

It was during this excursion that the title 'king' was applied to Shaka. Zulu folklore describes a spontaneous gesture by Lieutenant Farewell during an early meeting with Shaka. In deference to Shaka, Farewell took a smear of grease from one of his cannon wheel hubs and ceremonially anointed Shaka on his forehead, after which he was referred to as the king.

King or not, Shaka was a feared leader. When he suspected that some of his younger warriors were visiting the girls of the royal *isiGodlo* he had 200 youngsters paraded before him, only for them to be summarily executed. Their screams could be heard from the surrounding hills. Shaka's message was unambiguous. Shaka's absolute disregard for the sanctity of human life was difficult for the Europeans to comprehend; even in peaceful times a dozen or more daily executions were carried out before Shaka – often for minor indiscretions. It was a gruesome custom that continued through to King Cetshwayo's reign.

The absolute nature of his power was demonstrated when, in 1827, his army subdued the Bheje people, assisted by James King from Port Natal. Then disaster struck; his chief adviser, his mother Nandi, suddenly died. There remains a belief among many Zulus that Shaka murdered his mother out of fear that her powers were becoming too great. He then suffered intense guilt. Fynn was present and later relayed his suspicion to a number of traders that Shaka had stabbed at his mother in a fit of pique. Mortified, he had bound the wound, but Nandi steadily deteriorated and died a few days later. Whether or not her death was by murder or illness, Shaka's shame or grief was so intense that he required every Zulu to experience his loss and ordered a gathering of some 20,000 souls within the royal homestead. On Shaka's order, enforced wailing and summary executions commenced and continued throughout the day until several thousand of the multitude lay dead.

Fynn recorded the day's event in his diary:

> Those who could not force more tears from their eyes, those who were found near the river panting for water, were beaten to death by others who were mad with excitement. Towards the afternoon I calculated that not fewer than 7,000 people had fallen in this frightful indiscriminate massacre. The adjacent stream, to which many had fled exhausted to wet their tongues, became impassable from the corpses which lay on either side of it; while the *kraal* in which the scene took place was flowing with blood.[2]

Shaka then decreed that during the next twelve months no crops could be grown, children were not to be conceived, or milk drunk – all on pain of death.

The decree lasted for three months until Shaka tired of mourning his dead mother, and some normality returned. But the damage was done: Shaka's half-brothers, Dingane and Mhlangana, along with the king's chamberlain, Mbophe, agreed that Shaka must die. They waited until the army was on campaign, but this time the Zulus were routed. When Shaka learned of the setback he sacrificed a number of defenceless women, including wives of some of the vanquished warriors. This was too much for Dingane and Mhlangana, who stabbed Shaka to death during a meeting with his senior *izinDuna*. His body was left out during the night to the mercy of the wild dog packs. Folklore recalls the dogs ignored the body – giving credence to the myth that Shaka had been divine. The body was weighted down with stones and unceremoniously buried in a pit along with his personal possessions.[3] Dingane held equally strong ambitions as the deceased Shaka, and issued a decree across the Zulu nation:

> Let it be known to all. The mighty elephant is dead. The elephant who has killed him is stronger and mightier than he was.[4]

There can be little doubt that Shaka was ruthless beyond comprehension, ruthless to his own people and especially to his enemies. Undoubtedly he was a great soldier and his skill in the use of military tactics bordered on genius, to the point that he used his skills to create a nation from an insignificant clan.

Within days the exhausted and anxious Zulu army, under Dingane's younger brother, Mpande, returned in expectation of Shaka's wrath, only to be relieved when Dingane confirmed Shaka's death and welcomed the army back, fed them and then authorized their leave. Dingane thus ensured their loyalty and sent *impis* to round up the royal herds scattered across southern Natalia before the tribes beyond Dingane's influence sought to recover their stolen cattle. To remove any succession threat from the young brother, Dingane's advisers recommended the execution of Mpande, but Dingane's *inDuna*, Ndlela, dissuaded the king, who instead banished the hapless brother. This rare act of compassion would later cost Dingane his life. Meanwhile, having murdered his remaining brothers, Ngwadi and Mhlangana, along with Shaka's faithful advisers and adherents, Dingane assumed the mantle of king and kept control by retaining Shaka's policy of regular executions. In 1834, Dr Andrew Smith visited Dingane's *ikhanda* at Mgungundhlovu, where according to an earlier visitor, William Wood, 'executions were frequent,' usually two each day. Dr Smith wrote in his diary:

> As characteristic of his system of proceeding, I may only mention that when I was at his *kraal* I saw portions of the bodies of eleven of his own wives, whom he had only a few days previously put to death, merely for having uttered words that happened to annoy him.[5]

With Shaka's death, Farewell's traders realized their predicament. They had previously enjoyed the king's protection and, being uncertain of their future, they commenced fortifying their small fort. They need not have worried because Dingane duly informed them that they were welcome to continue their activities. Farewell set off with presents for the new king and camped en route near the Nqetho homestead without realizing that this particular clan remained loyal to the memory of Shaka. During the night, Farewell and his two fellow travellers were murdered. The principle founder of Port Natalia was dead before he attained the age of forty. At no more than thirty years of age, Dingane settled into a life of luxury and security. Unlike Shaka, Dingane was gluttonous and spent most of his time in the *isiGodlo* or reviewing parades of warriors and cattle. He reduced the size of the Zulu army and Shaka's previous policy of random butchery ceased, although serious miscreants were still summarily executed.

In the spring of 1834, a relatively unknown incident occurred that helps explain Dingane's subsequent suspicion and treatment of the Boer leader Piet Retrief. A Zulu *impi* returning from a minor campaign came across a small party of half-cast hunters from the Cape. Thinking the *impi* was about to attack them, the hunters fired several shots and within minutes were annihilated by the Zulus for their mistake.

News trickled back to the settlement at Port Natalia, where the settlers incorrectly presumed that the *impi* had attacked their own hunting party, who were by sheer coincidence in the same area but had not been involved and were unaware of the incident. The settlers retaliated by mounting a small expedition and ambushed the *impi*, taking the Zulus by surprise and killing scores. The settlers returned to Port Natalia fully expecting a major Zulu attack. Curiously, Dingane did not retaliate, but in January 1837, traders from Port Natalia rendered the king valuable service by helping the Zulus to successfully raid the Swazi kingdom to the north.

Following the 1838 confrontation with the Boers at Blood River, Dingane withdrew his army and regrouped his forces to rebuild Mgungundhlovu. Although defeated in battle, Dingane now possessed large numbers of Boer guns, cattle and horses and spent the following months consolidating his position. The Boers continued to stream across the Drakensberg and began settling on the central plateau. They named the settled area the 'Free Province of New Holland in South East Africa' and its centre of crowded wagons became known as 'Pietermaritzburg', after Retrief and Maritz. Meanwhile, the British occupying Durban negotiated a truce with Dingane, but then abandoned the port area to the Boers following a minor action by them against the British. In consequence of the Tugela Peace Treaty with the British in 1839, Dingane decided to re-establish his control over the non-Zulu tribes by undertaking a punitive expedition against his younger half-brother, Mpande, who promptly fled to the Boers for protection accompanied by nearly 20,000 of his people. Mpande's support had grown to the extent that he was the second dominant chief to Dingane. Even so, he had realized his vulnerability and allied himself with the Boers, and now requested their protection. Fearing for his life, Mpande sought to bring about the downfall of Dingane by forming an alliance with the settlers under their leader, Pretorius. Mpande's Zulus were now settled to the south of the Tugela River at kwaMahambehlala under the protection of the Boers, who realized only too well that the Zulus were in disarray.[6] This allegiance is still known as 'the breaking of the rope that held the nation together', the *ukudabuka bkwegoda,* but the price of Boer support was the abandonment of huge tracts of Zulu territory in their favour. The Boers, now reinforced and supported by Mpande's Zulus, dispatched a massive punitive expedition to recapture lost Boer cattle and horses.

King Dingane was forced to flee across the northern Pongola River, seeking refuge in the Magunda Mountains with the Nyawo, a sub-clan of Swazi origin, where he established his eSankoleni *umutzi.* Angry at Mpande's support of the Boers, Dingane executed Ndlela, his respected and long-standing military commander, for negligence in 'allowing' Mpande to have lived. Dingane was considered by his hosts to be too dangerous so a short while later, a Swazi patrol, supported by Zulus loyal to Prince Mpande, captured and tortured him out of revenge before executing him. Dingane had ruled for eleven years and, like Shaka, was allegedly childless. Although a person in form, Zulu folklore holds that 'Dingane had the heart of a dog and the nature of a witch, truly like a poisonous snake.'[7]

But Mpande had sold his soul; the Boers crowned him 'king' on 10 February 1841, and four days later, the Boer flag of the Republic of Natalia was raised. The Boers had effectively annexed the land between the Black Mfolozi and Tugela rivers, even though they knew they had neither the people to occupy or administer their new territory. Accordingly, they seized such Zulu herds they could find and withdrew to the area south of the Tugela River.

News of King Dingane's death swept across Natalia, and then beyond, to the many tribes who had been displaced by Shaka and Dingane. These homeless people, and indeed Dingane's own *impis*, commenced their own trek back to their established homelands in northern Zululand, only to discover that the Boers were settling on their lands leaving them nowhere to go. As a result, thousands of discontented Zulus flocked south to Natalia, which caused huge animosity on the part of the Natalia Boers, who saw their recently acquired land of 'milk and honey' being resettled. The Boers treated these homeless Zulus with utter contempt, treating them severely – frequently with vicious corporal punishment or mutilation by whipping for even minor irritations.

During April 1839, Mpande attended a meeting with members of the Boer Volksraad (council) at Pietermaritzburg, where it was agreed that Mpande should be acknowledged as the rightful king of Zululand. The cost to Mpande was an agreement that allowed the Boers to annex Natalia and its port, the area to be known as 'The Vassal Zulu State'.[8] The Boer Volksraad then decreed that the natives that had earlier poured into Natal, most of whom were homeless, were to be rounded up and moved into a native homeland well away from the Boer sphere of influence, according to the Volksraad decree of 2 August 1841, 'by force, if necessary'. The British at the Cape learned of the natives' plight when tens thousands of displaced Mpande refugees sought refuge in Natalia and towards the end of 1841, the British forbade the Boer action and re-seized Durban. The British quickly dispatched sufficient administrators to govern Durban while the Volksraad endeavoured to regain control over the increasingly contrary Boers – who had even endeavoured, unsuccessfully, to enlist the support of the King of

Holland who, unbeknown to the Boers, had no intention of provoking Britain. Regardless of events at Blood River, Boer farmers continued to trickle into the more northern reaches of Zululand, regularly taking Zulu women and children as slaves. Children were sold 'for a horse apiece'.[9] The British concentrated on developing Natalia and mistakenly left Zululand and the 'Boer problem' to Dingane's successor, King Mpande, now resident in Zululand and part of Boer-controlled Natalia. There being no further obvious danger from hostile tribes, the Boers felt ready for further development into unexplored Zululand. In 1842, the British formally took control of Natalia by force and renamed it Natal. European immigration into the area thereafter increased, which, in turn, resulted in a shortage of good farmland. Many newly arrived farmers began to look towards the verdant pastures of Zululand.

Mpande was enthusiastic about routing any dissenters, especially his only surviving brother, Gquazi, who was making plans to depose him. In 1843, Mpande acted. He despatched an *impi* and, as usual, an example had to be made. Gquazi was executed, his wives were disembowelled and all his children had their skulls smashed by blows from the executioners' heavy knobkerries.

Meanwhile, Britain was not prepared to allow the Boers total access to Port Natal and in 1843 sent troops to occupy the port. The Boers objected and surrounded the British force, which had to be relieved. On 31 May 1844, Britain seized the opportunity to annex the whole of Natal into the Cape Colony, including Boer-held territory. Reluctantly, the Boer Volksraad acquiesced. The Boers had overreached themselves and by provoking the British, lost sovereignty over much of their lands. Settlers continued arriving from Europe but the biggest change since the Boers crossed the Drakensberg came with the dredging and channelling of the mouth of Durban Harbour. From this single engineering undertaking, Durban rapidly prospered as the influence of Pietermaritzburg declined. During the European upheaval in Natal, the Zulus under Mpande had withdrawn to the north side of the Buffalo and Tugela rivers. By now, the Zulus knew they were hemmed in. To the north they were under political and territorial pressure from Europeans based at Portuguese-controlled Delagoa Bay, and to the south by British-dominated Natal, and by Voortrekkers south of the Tugela and Mzinyathi rivers on the land mass ceded to them by Mpande.

During the relatively peaceful years that followed, Mpande turned his attention to the *isiGodlo* and feasting until he became too obese to walk;

thereafter he was moved about in a small cart. His activities in the *isiGodlo* produced between fifty and sixty sons. The firstborn was named Cetshwayo, who who was born to the daughter of the nearby Zungu chief, and was followed shortly by a brother named Mbuyazi to another wife. Under Zulu custom, the heir to the throne was the firstborn male of the head or Great Wife, but Mpande never nominated such a wife. Mpande was fully aware that the question of succession would be complex; he postponed the matter by sending the two most eligible sons and their mothers to *kraals* separated by some 50 miles. Although only fifteen years old, Cetshwayo took on special significance among the Zulus as they saw him as their future king, especially as the Boers referred to him as the 'Chief son', their obvious preference as Mpande's successor. As Mpande aged, schisms developed within the Zulu nation and gradually the subservient chiefs and clans graduated towards either Cetshwayo or Mbuyazi. The two brother princes were now in their early twenties and led the uThulwana and amaShishi regiments respectively, though neither had any actual combat experience. Cetshwayo was a traditionalist and had undergone long periods of education in Zulu history and culture. It is unsurprising that he hankered after the regal days of Shaka, whereas Mbuyazi was more inclined to intellectual matters, though equally devious and powerful. Both men professed the right to the royal throne.

Chapter 6

The Emergence of
King Cetshwayo

Between King Shaka's death in September 1828 and the 1879 Anglo-Zulu War, the Zulu Kingdom underwent considerable change. There can be little doubt that the territorial integrity of the kingdom was only saved from annexation by the Boers by the timely arrival of the British in 1843. The British Government had watched the progress of the Boers with some concern and, finally, decided to act in support of Lieutenant Farewell's earlier claim to the bay of Port Natal. Troops were marched overland, and a sharp fight took place among the sand dunes, but despite an initial British reverse, the Boers were finally forced to give way. Most of the Afrikaners – who had earlier come to Natal to escape British influence at the Cape – abandoned it in disgust, and in 1843 Natal was officially recognized as a British colony, thus bringing to an end the fledgling Boer republic. During 1845, Britain finally annexed the whole of Natal into the Cape Colony, including Boer-held territory. Settlers continued arriving from Europe, and Durban rapidly prospered as the influence of Pietermaritzburg declined. During the European upheaval in Natal, the Zulus under their new king, Mpande, had decided to avoid further confrontation with the whites and had withdrawn to the north side of the Buffalo and Tugela rivers.

Following negotiations between the British and King Mpande, it was agreed that the border between Natal and independent Zululand should run along the line of the Mzinyathi and Thukela rivers, cancelling all earlier agreements with the Boers. This boundary would not be challenged until the crisis of 1879. However, no formal boundary was agreed between Zululand and its north-western neighbour, the Transvaal, and it was this wild, sparsely populated area that was to become the cause of so much conflict.

The following period was one of relative peace as King Mpande ruled the Zulu nation fairly but firmly according to Zulu custom, although the struggle for power was never far below the surface. Under Mpande's rule Zululand would settle down for the next thirty-two years, but the new king continued the tradition of summary executions. Once, when challenged by horrified officials, he replied, 'I cannot rule Zulus without killing.'[1] Nevertheless, it was also a welcome period of consolidation after the internecine wars of 1838 and 1840. Military expeditions became rare, although Mpande harboured an especially strong resentment against the Swazi people to the north who, he understood, were fostering strong ties and gaining trade advantages with European traders. Meanwhile, to satisfy his warriors' enthusiasm for raiding, he did launch a series of raids closer to home, including attacks against the chiefdoms of Langalibalele, Maganondo and Phutini.[2]

The struggles of the period between 1838 and 1840 had deeply affected the nature of the internal mechanics of the Zulu kingdom. The mystique of the monarchy, which Shaka had striven to build up, had inevitably been damaged by the first civil war of 1840 between Dingane and Mpande, and the Zulu army was weakened and demoralized, both by defeat and by divisions within the ranks. The natural tendency for power to slip away from the centre and into the hands of the regional chiefs, which Shaka had tried so hard to resist, was once more unleashed. By giving the chiefs the chance to choose between two rival kings, Dingane and Mpande, Mpande had acknowledged the chiefs' *de facto* power in a way that would prove impossible to reverse. Mpande, whose carefully cultivated air of indolent stupidity masked the subtle mind of a shrewd political survivor, spent most of his reign trying to rebuild the authority of the state. This relative peace was not to last long. His opportunity to attack the Swazis came in 1846, when Swaziland became enveloped in a dynastic dispute that left its borders unprotected. This Zulu raid was successful and large herds of Swazi cattle were seized. Not content, Mpande commenced a full-scale invasion of Swaziland, which resulted in the southern half of the country falling under Zulu occupation. Perhaps due to his successes, or to remind the British of his power, Mpande broke the Anglo-Zulu Treaty of 1843 by permitting Boer settlers to form an independent republic in the Klip River area of Zululand. The British duly objected to this breach and in 1848 Mpande backed down – probably in the face of threatened British retaliation.

Instead, he turned his aggression back towards the Swazi people and in 1852 his army again invaded Swaziland, capturing a vast number of cattle. The British formally protested and Mpande was once again forced to withdraw back into Zululand. Zulu skirmishes continued around the border of Zululand, with Mpande taking control of the Tsonga people to the northeast, followed by an inconclusive attack against the Pedi people. These attacks and invasions brought Mpande to the pinnacle of his power and thereafter some normality temporarily returned to Zululand. ·

Earlier, the increase in trade following the gradual expansion of white settlement in Natal from 1843 onwards had nevertheless begun to undermine the king's power. With few white men to deal with, both Shaka and Dingane had earlier been able to monopolize European trade goods and use them to accrue further power and prestige. With the proliferation of European traders eager to make a quick profit, it became increasingly difficult for Mpande to control such commerce. Many of the subordinate chiefs began to trade on their own account, expanding their personal power and influence at the expense of the crown. The goods most in demand in Zululand were mainly European tools, particularly hoes, beads, metal wire for decorating the handles of spears and clubs, cloth and blankets. So many beads entered the country that they almost lost their value as a reward from the king, while the indigenous metal industry is generally accepted to have declined after European metal, in the form of metal rods, became freely available. Hitherto the Zulu kings had enjoyed a monopoly on ivory, a commodity that Europeans always desired, and which the *amabutho* could be sent out to hunt. But hunters and traders were now regularly working in Zululand, and this monopoly too was in danger. The hunter William Baldwin, in 1854, describes the king's reaction when one of his parties decided not to await the royal permission to hunt:

> We had not gone more than 2 miles, when one of Panda's [Mpande] captains came up to us in a great fury, swearing awfully by the bones of Dingaan, Chaka, the much-dreaded and cruel, and other renowned warriors of the nation, that if we did not immediately turn back, an *impi* [regiment 500-strong] would be down upon us and kill us instantly. He was in a great state of excitement, and would not hear of our outspanning or delaying our return a moment, said the signal for attack was crossing that watercourse (pointing to a running stream not 20 yards ahead); and as we were entirely in their power, we thought discretion was the better part of valour, and we did as we were ordered, looking very foolish

in both our own and our followers' eyes. Panda had always opposed our wish to go that way, and it was bearding the lion in his den, and most foolish and misjudged on the part of White [Baldwin's companion] to go in direct opposition to his orders. On passing his *kraal* gates we went through two lines, at least 200 yards long, of magnificent men, armed with *assegais*, shields, knobkerries and knives, in close file, waiting only the slightest intimation from his majesty to annihilate us instantly. It was a nervous moment; I did not half admire it, and all our *kaffirs* were in the utmost alarm; a dead silence was maintained by everyone ...

Eventually all was settled amicably; but our long-meditated route was peremptorily forbidden, and we were obliged to rest satisfied with the shooting Panda thought fit to give us in the Slatakul bush, where the old fellow knew well there were rarely any elephants worth shooting ...

Typical though this may have been of Mpande's efforts to control European commercial activity, such sanctions were increasingly ineffective. One commodity, which he did attempt to rigorously control, was the firearm; the king was all too aware that widespread possession of guns had an important bearing on the internal balance of power. However, he faced a further complication in that many traders, nervous about their long-term safety, were unwilling to become involved in the gun trade, which was in any case illegal in Natal. The king attempted to overcome this inhibition by demanding guns as the price of his permission to hunt or trade in Zululand.

Powerful factors were, however, quietly working against Mpande. White authority in Natal was apparently secure, and with the entire might of the British Empire to back it up, the king had little sanction against those who chose to abandon him and 'cross over' into Natal. In the thirty years that Mpande ruled, several entire clans moved out of the Zulu orbit and into Natal, while the number of individual Zulus who slipped across the border numbered thousands. In 1852, one white observer estimated that the outflow numbered about 4,000 people a year. Not all of them were accused criminals or political refugees; many simply sought an easier life, away from the restrictions that service to the Zulu king entailed. Although African custom accounted for the administration of the vast majority of blacks in Natal, there was no highly developed *amabutho* system there, and the price of the *lobola* was generally lower. It was much easier for a young man to marry and set up his own homestead in Natal than it was in Zululand. By the 1850s, two separate estimates suggest that the number of men actively serving in the king's army was not more than 10,000, and perhaps as few as 6,000 – far less than in Shaka's day, despite a general increase in the region's population and more than ten years of peace. Not all the earlier refugees to Natal found life under colonial rule quite as comfortable as they had expected, and the efforts of first Mpande and then Cetshwayo gradually stemmed the haemorrhage. But it was still necessary for the king to relax some of the more vigorous prohibitions that accompanied life in the *amabutho*.

The age at which regiments were allowed to marry was lowered, and Mpande created a number of *amabandla mhlope* (white assemblies); these were regiments that had been allowed to marry but were still required to muster regularly at the *amakhanda*. They were, however, permitted to allow their wives and families to accompany them for the two-week ceremony. Mpande was able to sustain his centralized authority more or less intact for the greater part of his reign, so much so that Mpande strengthened the *amabutho* system until by the end of his reign he had more than 40,000 trained men, more than Shaka could call on.

Having been preoccupied with internal politics and the successful rebuilding of his nation, Mpande was able to turn his attention away from politics and back towards the *isiGodlo* and feasting, until he became too obese to walk; Mpande was able to sustain his centralized authority more or less intact for the greater part of his reign. By the mid-1850s and having held the throne for sixteen years, Mpande's authority began to weaken. The ostensible cause of this decline was a succession crisis that degenerated into a civil war. It was a feature of the Zulu royal household that succession issues were again going to be the bane of its dynastic stability.[3] Although succession within Zulu society was well established and understood, it was also complicated. Unlike his brothers who preceded him, Shaka and Dingane, Mpande had a number of wives and produced many children, including boys. The heir to a king was the firstborn of the Great Wife, who would have been married for this very reason. Sons from other wives succeeded with the first son of the first wife taking precedence. Zulu folklore believes Mbuyazi was the son of Shaka as his mother was already pregnant when she was relocated to Mpande's *isiGodlo*. Although Zulu tradition provided some guideline for the nomination of his heir –

traditionally, the senior son of his appointed Great Wife – in practice, such distinctions disappeared as Mpande's sons grew to manhood and became aware of their potential. The king himself, mindful that by publicly nominating an heir he was undermining his own security, refused to state his preferences, even though he had once presented his 6-year-old son, Cetshwayo, to the Boers as his heir. To avoid confusion over Cetshwayo's identification and status as heir in the future, the Boers had nicked the boy's ear. Mpande originally favoured Cetshwayo to succeed him but later changed his mind and nominated Mbuyazi, deliberately playing one son off against the other.

By 1856, Cetshwayo and Mbuyazi had enthusiastically courted the support of chiefs in their own districts and in that year both openly sought to be the next king. In accordance with tradition, resolution came through the bloody conflict of the second Zulu Civil War, perhaps the worst seen or recorded in South African history. The confrontation took place on the banks of an insignificant stream, the Thambo, which fed into the Tugela River near Ndondakusuka Hill. Cetshwayo mustered 20,000 warriors, the Usuthu, and pitted them against Mbuyazi's 30,000 iziGqoza, with a considerable number of old men, women and children in Mbuyazi's retinue. Many of the Mbuyazi women followed Zulu tradition by supporting their fighting menfolk in action by urging them on from a safe distance; unbeknown to these civilians, Cetshwayo would consider them as combatants.

The battle lasted no more than an hour, with Mbuyazi's army being heavily defeated. In their attempt to escape the survivors fled towards the Tugela River. In customary Zulu fashion, Cetshwayo gave orders for the total slaughter of Mbuyazi's surviving warriors and his followers. Unfortunately, there had earlier been a heavy thunderstorm; the Tugela was now a 100-yard-wide raging torrent, which the remnants of Mbuyazi's force could not cross. Cetshwayo's warriors caught them there and in one of the bloodiest battles in Zulu history, Mbuyazi's army was annihilated with only a handful of survivors escaping across the river. Mbuyazi died when he forlornly charged into a mass of Cetshwayo's warriors, along with five other sons of Mpande. Some estimates put the number of dead as high as 20,000, and their bodies, carried out to sea by the river, were washed up on nearby beaches for days afterwards. Cetshwayo was later song-praised for his victory as being the victor who 'caused people to swim against their will, for he made men swim when they were old.' A white trader, John Dunn, who lived on the edge of Cetshwayo's territory and who had helped and advised Mbuyazi in the action, claimed to have been present during the battle. Dunn managed to escape to tell the tale and confirmed the shocking atrocities that befell the iziGqoza. Dunn was later able to again ingratiate himself with Cetshwayo, who nevertheless remained suspicious of the Englishman. Zulu folklore holds that a young Melmoth Osborn was also present, then a newly appointed resident magistrate at Newcastle.[4]

Following the battle, and to secure his position, Cetshwayo ordered the murder of several of his own brothers and half-brothers who could have challenged him for the kingship. Within weeks he assumed command of the Zulu army, was pronounced heir to Mpande, and immediately took over the running of the Zulu nation, leaving Mpande as a mere figurehead, although he remained king of the Zulus for the next sixteen years. Mpande occasionally reminded Cetshwayo of his vulnerability but such advice usually rebounded, as in the case of two brothers of Cetshwayo, sons of another of Mpande's wives, Umtonga and Umgidhlwana, who had expressed an interest in the accession. Sensing trouble, the brothers fled, but with Cetshwayo's executioners hard on their trail, they sought refuge with Mpande's Boer friends – who promptly surrendered the hapless pair to their pursuers to have their skulls smashed. Cetshwayo nevertheless remained loyal to Mpande, although Mpande never forgave Cetshwayo for Mbuyazi's death. In 1860, Cetshwayo tactfully moved his homestead nearer to the Indian Ocean coast, north of the Tugela River; it was named Gingindlovu.

Cetshwayo had long observed the underlying tension between the British in Natal and the Transvaal Boers and was aware he was in a position of considerable strength. In 1861, knowing the British and Boers were as duplicitous as he was cunning, Cetshwayo 'traded' Boer non-aggression by giving them a tract of land, which enabled the Boers to establish the district of Utrecht.[5] Cetshwayo had known for some time that both powers had taken a fledgling Zulu prince under their respective wings in a secret attempt to undermine him. The British groomed Mkungo: the Boers Mthonga. The deception had come to Cetshwayo's notice when the Boers falsely warned the king that the British were about to invade Zululand and establish their princeling on the Zulu throne. Cetshwayo then confronted Shepstone, Secretary for Native Affairs, who 'backed off' over the issue of the princeling usurper and apologized. Shepstone nevertheless remained cautious of Cetshwayo's contact with the Boers. Interestingly, no Nguni chief was ever empowered to sell tribal land, so in Zulu eyes no contract disposing of land could be valid. In 1867 Cetshwayo was granted full rights to marry, and took his first wife, Msweli, who soon produced their first son, Dinizulu.

Cetshwayo now had full control of Zululand and in order to strengthen his grip further, he courted friendship with the British. Taking the opportunity of the king's offer of friendship, Shepstone went to the senile Mpande and suggested that Cetshwayo be appointed heir apparent, in the name of Queen Victoria, in itself a suggestion of doubtful legality due to the claims of other sons. Mpande accepted on behalf of the Zulus, although Cetshwayo was aware that his future now depended, to a degree, on British support.

King Mpande died in 1872 after a reign of thirty-two years on the Zulu throne, marred only by his two sons' recent battle by the Tugela. He was the only Zulu king to die of natural causes. His death caused panic across the Zulu nation, its people naturally terrified that the new king would unleash another slaughter of Zulu people as had occurred on Shaka's orders when Nandi died. Aware of the people's growing anxiety, Cetshwayo decreed there would be no such mourning, and peace returned to Zululand. The only people to have justified fears from Mpande's death were members of Mpande's royal household. In accordance with Zulu tradition, the king's servants were beaten until their arms and legs were broken, while his personal valet was strangled – his was the honour of having the dead king laid upon him in the grave. The other unfortunate servants were buried nearby so that they could 'support' the dead king in his post-death passage. Cetshwayo succeeded Mpande at the age of forty and became the undisputed ruler of more than a quarter of a million people. Most lived between the Tugela and Mzinyathi (Buffalo) rivers.

In 1873, a year also noted for a traditional wild animal hunt that saw the mass slaughter of a number of rare black rhinoceros, Shepstone decided to hold a coronation for Cetshwayo notwithstanding that he had already been proclaimed king by the Zulu chiefs in a traditional ceremony. The Zulus prevaricated for nearly a month, keeping Shepstone waiting for his meaningless meeting. When Shepstone was finally taken before Cetshwayo, he presented the Zulu king with a tinsel crown and fired a salute from a number of guns that had accompanied the expedition. In the name of Queen Victoria, Shepstone gave a long drawn-out speech, during which he intimated that no Zulu, even where accused by witch doctors, would be executed without a fair trial. Cetshwayo, though, was only interested in the

British stopping the encroachment into Zululand by Boer farmers. The ceremony became lively when a small grass fire swept into the camp. One headman seized the opportunity to steal two dozen bottles of medicine thinking they were gin. Under cover of a firework display laid on by the British, he became the first person to be executed under the new regime.

During post-coronation conversations, Shepstone agreed to control the spread of missionaries and deter any aspirants seeking the Zulu throne. For his part, King Cetshwayo agreed to allow a limited migration of workers, an agreement that had no legal force as Cetshwayo could neither read nor write, and which five years later would be deemed by the British to be a reason for war.

As King of Zululand, Cetshwayo immediately sought British confirmation of his position. He hoped the British promises would be a guarantee of their full support should he again become involved with the Boers. Cetshwayo knew this was a probability. Boer seizure of tracts of Zululand was ongoing and, curiously, this land theft further bound the king's council together and united the Zulu nation. Shepstone readily agreed. With his military position secure, Cetshwayo began to strengthen his economic and political control and one method used was to strengthen the formation of groups of warriors according to their age. Since Shaka, young men had been obliged to serve in the army as a means of binding the nation together; in recent years there had been an increasing number of young men avoiding military service, and the king's policy was now rigidly enforced. Every Zulu knew his or her place and their society was efficient. Those who sought to escape the rigidity, strictness and dangers of the king's rule had only one traditional escape route – to flee to Natal. Cetshwayo built a new base at Ondini, which was constructed in typical fashion but with the king's quarters built of brick in the European style. In keeping with his supposed promise to Shepstone, executions were rare. There was, however, a serious lapse in the peace when one of the female *amabutho* rebelled on being informed that they were to marry much older warriors from the Indhlondhlo, an *ibutho* unknown to the young women. They refused to comply and many absconded, an unheard of event. Cetshwayo could not forgive such a rebellious display and dispatched his bodyguards to follow and execute the women – more than thirty were killed. When news of the incident reached Shepstone he reacted angrily by reminding the king of his 'coronation vows'. It was this note that prompted a remarkable reply from the king:

THE EMERGENCE OF KING CETSHWAYO

> Did I ever tell Mr Shepstone I would not kill? Did he tell the white people I made such an agreement because, if he did, he has deceived them. I do kill – it is the custom of our nation and I shall not depart from it. Why does the governor of Natal speak to me about my laws? Do I go to Natal and dictate to him about his laws?[6]

Cetshwayo, now in his mid-forties, was perhaps the most intelligent of all the Zulu kings. He was supported by his senior advisers, the *izikhulu*, and together they formed the *ibandla*, the highest council of state. He now ruled a united nation, his army was at its strongest, and the Zulus had a most powerful friend, Queen Victoria – and no apparent enemies. The British High Commissioner for South Africa, Sir Bartle Frere,[7] remained suspicious, knowing only too well that Cetshwayo's well-disciplined army was formidable both in number and tactical flexibility. Indeed, whilst Zululand was now at peace with its neighbours, the Zulu army inevitably became restless. Cetshwayo and Frere knew that such a large army needed a purpose, which was previously war, now an inappropriate pastime. It was traditional for a new king to order his army into action in order for his warriors to 'wash their spears', as a prelude to marriage. Shepstone wrote:

> War is the universal cry among the [Zulu] soldiers, who are anxious to live up to their traditions.[8]

The Swazis to the north had always been an easy target for such action but this was discouraged by the British. Even so, the Zulus went north and attacked the Swazi, who, having hidden their cattle on Boer farms, duly submitted. The Boers then demanded a sizeable proportion of the herd but instead took a batch of boys and girls as slaves. The Swazis now called upon Shepstone in his capacity as the Secretary for Native Affairs for assistance but, yet again, he advised the Zulus to desist. The only other solution for the Zulus was to engage the hated Boers, who still retained a foothold in the disputed territory to the north of Rorke's Drift. Cetshwayo withdrew his army back to Zululand and pondered his options. He waited.

Thereafter, Shepstone clamped down on Africans working and living in Natal; compulsory registration, curfews and the prohibition of alcohol sales followed. He also promoted cruel schemes whereby any excess African population could be relocated beyond Natal, eyeing Zululand as a possible location for the refugees. Shepstone knew that Cetshwayo would never accede to Natal interference. He also knew only too well that Cetshwayo controlled a huge workforce that was denied access to work for the British. Shepstone's dilemma was straightforward: growth in southern Africa was thwarted all the time Cetshwayo's Zulus were unavailable for work and, in view of the steady importation of European firearms to Zululand and its neighbours, any dissent could prove serious. And so, leading up to the 1870s, British policy towards the Zulus was to curb their activities while promoting growth along the south-east coast of Africa.

Meanwhile, with the Zulus unlikely to pose any immediate border problem, the British became occupied with minor conflicts elsewhere in southern Africa, mostly brought about because of native disputes over land occupied by white settlers. Land became scarce and, in time, there was little available to offer settlers and migrants still en route to Natal. By the mid 1870s, the British authorities, under Shepstone, were well aware that Natal needed to expand if it was to become a successful colony. It was also seen both as the gateway to Africa and the means to bring lucrative mining and trade beyond Natal under British control. It would also socialize the 'savage to civilisation'[9] and dampen their enthusiasm for conflict.

From the Zulu perspective, throughout the whole existence of the Natal colony, Mpande and then Cetshwayo had both made repeated representations to the government of the colony concerning successive Boer encroachments into Zulu territory. Shepstone invariably dismissed such protests on the grounds that they were 'temporizing and evasive'. Shepstone's despatches paint a different picture – they indicate that the Zulu claims were 'substantially just and those for the republic [Boers] as being simply the result of an unscrupulous lust for land'.[10] Indeed, despatch after despatch indicated that Cetshwayo was implicitly obeying Shepstone's requests to refrain from hostilities and await an amicable solution to the difficulties.

Shepstone's 'do nothing' policy prevailed until the Boers announced on 25 May 1875 – in the name of the Boer Republic – that large areas of Zululand were their territory. Following this announcement, which seriously irritated King Cetshwayo, Boer settlers again began moving into Zululand and these new incursions were opposed by the Zulus with increasing vigour. One such area of heightened tension was an unofficial extension of the Boers' Transvaal into Zululand, which lay between the Buffalo and Blood rivers immediately north of Rorke's Drift and was generally becoming known as the 'disputed territory'. It was evident to all parties that relationships between the Boers and Zulus were seriously deteriorating and action, beyond sabre-rattling, needed to be taken. Cetshwayo decided his armies needed firearms, previously banned by the British. His council reasoned that, without firearms, they would be at a disadvantage in any further conflict with the Boers. The Portuguese traders at Delagoa Bay were keen to supply the Zulus with their redundant firearms and, although the trade in firearms was illegal, there were enough rogue traders happy enough to sell off their old muskets at a premium. Gunpowder was a rare commodity and so a Portuguese entrepreneur, known to the Zulus as Mqhali, obliged by producing a small but steady supply.

Boer intrusion into Zululand was perceptively described by Mr Osborne, Colonial Secretary to the Transvaal Government in 1876, who wrote:

> The Boers, as they have done in other cases, and are still doing
> – encroached by degrees upon native territory.

Cetshwayo now regarded the encroaching Boers as his enemy and treated them with great suspicion, whereas he regarded the British as his true friends – he now expected their help. King Cetshwayo re-alerted the British to the problem created by the Boers when he wrote:

> Now the Transvaal is English ground, I want Somtseu [Sir
> Theophilus Shepstone] to send the Boers away from the lower
> part of the Transvaal, that near my country. The Boers are a
> nation of liars; they are a bad people, they lie, they claim what
> is not theirs, and ill-use my people.[11]

The British made no reply. Then, during April 1877 a serious confrontation between the Zulus and Boers began to develop as a result of trekkers moving onto virgin land within the disputed territory, unanimously recognized as Zulu territory. Secretly supported by Shepstone, Cetshwayo decided to resolve the problem once and for all by massing an impressive force of more than 30,000 warriors at strategic crossing points along the Boers' Transvaal border. Whether or not the king would give the order for a full-scale Zulu attack is a matter of conjecture; Zulu belief is that the king was showing his hand, knowing it was powerful, just as Dingane had done at Ncombe (Blood River). But then two events occurred in quick succession, either by coincidence or by astute British diplomatic design. Firstly, on the very same day, 12 April 1877, Shepstone was actually attending a secret meeting with the Boers, with the sole intention of persuading the Boers to surrender the Boer-controlled Transvaal to British authority. Shepstone's logical claim was that the Transvaal government was bankrupt, which was correct, and the Zulus were about to attack, which was incorrect – but feasible. In a private conversation between Shepstone and his 20-year-old clerk, H. Rider Haggard, it was debated whether both the Boers and Zulus should be allowed to fight each other. The thought process was interesting:

> The Zulus and the Boers will destroy each other and the Transvaal will fall like a ripe apple into the lap of Britain.[12]

Shepstone then and there ordered Cetshwayo to withdraw his army, who were busy assembling along the Boer boundary, knowing only too well that any Zulu advance into the Transvaal would result in the slaughter of the settlers. On 12 April 1877, agreement was reached with the Boers, whereupon Shepstone annexed the Transvaal to the British Crown. The secretary to the annexation team, Melmoth Osborn, then read the declaration to the assembled Boers. He appeared to suffer from a bout of chronic anxiety mid-proclamation; he commenced, trembling, and his voice failed. Rider Haggard stepped forward to continue reading the script.

Even knowing full well that the Boers were in no position to defend themselves, Cetshwayo reluctantly complied with Shepstone's order but sent a strong letter warning him that he had fully intended driving the Boers 'beyond the Vaal River'. The Zulus believe to this day that Shepstone deceitfully encouraged Cetshwayo to amass his *impis* on the Transvaal border in order to coerce the Boers into allowing their submissive annexation to the British. Likewise, the Boers accepted Shepstone's annexation in the belief that at Shepstone's call, a 'cloud of 40,000 Zulu warriors hung upon the Transvaal border' threatening them in the rear.[13] Shepstone's motive behind this annexation may well have been to further Britain's encouragement of its creeping confederation across southern Africa but, in pursuing this noble dream, Shepstone had unwittingly inherited responsibility for the rapidly developing Zulu and Boer land dispute. For sixteen years the British had avoided the issue of the border conflict between Boer and Zulu and prior to annexation, the British had viewed the encroaching Boers as 'foreigners'. Now that these people had involuntarily become British subjects by virtue of the annexation, and because Shepstone was now Administrator of the Transvaal, the problem of the disputed territory converted itself from being an insignificant Boer-Zulu controversy into a potentially serious three-way dispute between Britain, the Boers and the Zulus.

Under the protection of the British, the Transvaal economy recovered dramatically. Rider Haggard wrote that the financial effects of annexation on the Transvaalers were magical and that credit and commerce were at once restored, but only a few months later he was much more cautionary. He wrote:

> When the recollection of their difficulties had grown faint, when their debts had been paid and their enemies [Zulus] quietened, they began to think that they would like to get rid of us again, and start fresh on their own account with a clean sheet.[14]

At the time, Cetshwayo had welcomed Britain's annexation of the Transvaal as he believed it would protect Zululand from further unwelcome Boer attention, and in a note the king informed Shepstone of his relief at the outcome:

> I am pleased that Somtseu [Sir Theophilus Shepstone] has let me know that the land of the Transvaal Boers has now become part of the land of the Queen of England; perhaps now there may be rest.[15]

Later, however, Cetshwayo would describe Shepstone as a 'cheat' and a 'fraud'; until then, the king had perceived Shepstone's actions to have been in the fairest manner and accordingly Shepstone enjoyed the Zulu title 'Somtseu' (father). As for Shepstone, deep down he had never fully trusted the Zulus. In a letter to Lord Carnarvon he wrote:

> The sooner the root of the evil, which I consider to be the Zulu power and military organization, is dealt with, the easier our task will be.[16]

Shepstone arranged a meeting between the Boers and Zulus to discourage any further dispute and warned Cetshwayo that there must be no war. This infuriated the Zulu leaders, who encouraged Cetshwayo to send a strong message to the Europeans. As a potent gesture he dispatched a large *impi* into the disputed territory, which terrified the Boers and forced a large number to flee. This was too much for Shepstone, who intervened and, on behalf of the Natal Governor General, Sir Henry Bulwer, and in what appeared to be a conciliatory gesture, he offered Cetshwayo an independent arbitration to resolve the matter.

Meanwhile, Lord Carnarvon, the Colonial Secretary in London, appointed Sir Bartle Frere as High Commissioner of South Africa and Governor of the Cape in order to accelerate the pace of confederation, a policy that involved, in theory, combining all the territories in South Africa. Confederation would enable Britain to control both resources and policy through a system of central and regional government with locally employed officials. It was to this end that Shepstone had earlier annexed the Transvaal on the pretext of saving the Boers from their own bankrupt economy and to discourage the Zulus from raiding Boer farms in disputed areas of Zululand.

Frere, an experienced senior administrator from his time in India, soon became convinced that the independence of the Zulu kingdom posed a serious threat to the proposed policy of confederation, although initially he was more concerned about the threat posed to the ports and harbours of southern Africa by the rapidly growing Russian Navy.[17] Border problems between black and white apart, the threat of violence was inherent in Frere's thought process since many groups, both African and Boer, were known to oppose British rule.

Frere had long since come to the conclusion that the Zulus were a threat and should be absorbed by confederation, at least as a British protectorate, and by war if necessary. Direction from the British Government was weak and Frere, in his capacity as the British High Commissioner of South Africa, was given a free hand to use his initiative. Frere's communications with the British Colonial Secretary, Sir Michael Hicks Beach (who had succeeded Lord Carnarvon), were vague and led the Colonial Secretary to believe Frere would solve any problems without recourse to military action. This situation is understandable as Britain was on the verge of war in Afghanistan and the long-running series of petty frontier wars against the Xhosa people around the South African Cape was finally coming to an end, due in no small part to the determination and skill of the British military commander, Lord Chelmsford.

THE EMERGENCE OF KING CETSHWAYO

In Frere's mind, the Zulus posed the lesser threat so it was upon them that he focused his short-term attention. He interpreted the Zulu king's protestations concerning the 'disputed territory' as nothing more than belligerence, and came to believe that a demonstration of force against the Zulu nation would not only intimidate broader opposition to the confederation scheme but would also demonstrate Britain's strength. Frere's belief marked a dramatic shift in the relationship between the Zulu kingdom and the British; the first step had unwittingly been taken along the path towards open conflict between the two former friends.

There remained one problem – the Zulus' autocratic king and his army of 40,000 warriors would never agree to an effective surrender and dissolution of an important part of Zululand merely to placate the Boers. To bolster support, Frere's officials orchestrated rumours that a bloodthirsty and defiant Zulu army was plotting to invade Natal. The rumours began to spread, and hysteria among the white settlers was fanned until the general topic of conversation and newspaper reports spoke of nothing else. The Zulus responded with several incursions against isolated Boer farmers and Bantu migrants illicitly settling in Zululand, simply because cattle were the single currency applicable to Boer and Zulu alike, and, as the settlers' wealth increased, so they sought additional grazing land. These retaliatory Zulu raids encouraged European speculation that war against the Zulus was inevitable, though King Cetshwayo appeared to be unaware of this subversive undercurrent. For the Zulus, the writing was clearly on the wall.

Novelist Anthony Trollope travelled through southern Africa and parts of Zululand during 1877, just as European hysteria was mounting, yet he viewed the Zulus as being perceptive and living in sympathy with their time and environment. He wrote:

> I have no fears myself that Natal will be overrun by hostile Zulus – but much fear that Zululand should be overrun by hostile Britons.[18]

Matters again came to a head during early 1878, when a number of Boer and displaced native settlers joined those already illicitly farming the 'disputed territory' directly to the north of Rorke's Drift. The Zulus prized this well-watered area for its winter grazing, especially after the serious droughts of 1877 and 1878, and were not prepared to share. Cetshwayo was now beset with serious problems. He faced an antagonistic Natal and, to the north, Boer farmers were continuing to encroach onto Zulu farmland. It was clear that Cetshwayo would not accept the increasing flow of settlers and time was running out for the British. Urgent action was required.

For the Boers, the matter was simple: they considered they had the right to settle the best grazing land in Zululand. Since the Boers first crossed the Drakensberg Mountains in 1836, their settlements had continued to spread progressively towards the heartland of Zululand, itself protected by a natural boundary, the Tugela River. This temporarily deterred further encroachment by the Boers. In the British tradition of apparent compromise, Frere sought a fresh solution. He believed that war against the Zulus was the sole solution to a number of problems he faced before South Africa was united. Defeating the Zulus, Frere reasoned, would be an easy task for the British. After all, a small British force under Chelmsford had just defeated Chief Sandili's clan to the south of Zululand. A quick victory against the Zulus would have the added benefit of intimidating the black populations of southern Africa into accepting white domination, and remind the Boers that British military rule was not to be challenged. It would also reassure both Boer and settler communities that they would be secure and become prosperous under British rule. But Frere needed time to allow Chelmsford to concentrate his troops around Zululand. Frere's civilian administrator and Governor of Natal, Sir Henry Bulwer, a long-time friend of the Zulu people, was greatly alarmed by Frere's quest for war. He argued that military action would severely damage Britain's reputation, antagonize the neighbouring black nations and damage the colony's economic foundation. Bulwer proposed an independent commission to examine the border issue. Frere concurred in the belief that such a boundary commission would neatly defer the settler problem by adjudicating, once and for all, the settlers' title to the disputed territory.

The proposal was submitted to Cetshwayo, who immediately agreed. His reply shows his grasp of the subtleties of British diplomacy:

> Before sending for people across the sea for the settlement of the boundary, Cetywayo [sic] would be glad if the Governor of Natal would send his representatives to see what the claims of Cetywayo are, and to hear what he says, and to hear what others say, and if these cannot come to an

understanding on the matter, then a letter can be sent across
the sea for other people to see what can be done.[19]

The original proposal for a boundary commission came from Sir Henry
Bulwer. The commission was specifically to adjudicate on title to the disputed
territory and all parties generally agreed the notion of a commission. The
principal members consisted of Michael Gallwey, a barrister who had
become the Attorney General of Natal at the age of thirty-one, and
Lieutenant Colonel Anthony Durnford RE, a distinguished and experienced
army officer who had served in South Africa for many years, who represented
the military. The local Boers were represented by Piet Uys, a farmer, who had
lost several relatives in skirmishes with the Zulus, Adrian Rudolph, the Boer
Landdrost of Utrecht, and J.W. Shepstone, who had taken over from his older
brother, Sir Theophilus Shepstone, as the new Secretary for Native Affairs.
King Cetshwayo was fully consulted. He was invited to send some of his
advisers to attend the commission and local Zulu chiefs would be permitted
to submit evidence. Confident of his people's case and in the appointed
officials – led by Cetshwayo's chief minister, Mnyamana, chief of the
Buthelezi tribe, together with Cetshwayo's personal attendant, Bhejane –
Cetshwayo readily agreed to abide by the commission's decision. The actual
terms of the commission were laid down in a letter of instruction to the
commissioners, who were to report on the matter of the disputed border and
make recommendations, as they deemed advisable, to settle the dispute.

Sub-Inspector Campbell and a troop of the Natal Mounted Police
escorted the members of the commission to the nominated venue at Rorke's
Drift. The location was ideal, being situated on one of the few crossing
points on the Buffalo River, which formed the largely unmapped border of
Natal with Zululand. It was also just within the disputed territory, making
the venue easily accessible to witnesses from both sides. The commission
was provided with eighteen marquees and accommodation tents, together
with the necessary staff of cooks, servants, scribes and guards, over which
the Union flag was flown.

Deliberations commenced on 7 March 1878: Sir Theophilus Shepstone
was, as usual, full of his own importance, to the point that Mnyamana felt
that his king had been maligned. There followed an uncomfortable
exchange, with Shepstone stating:

> I have only come to talk about the boundary of the country;
> but the English nation will come and settle matters for you.

> Go and tell my child [King Cetshwayo] these words, because
> I know he will understand me.[20]

The Zulu delegation was incensed by this discourtesy and their folklore holds that Mnyamana rose to his feet and struck his shield with his *assegai*. Alarmed, Shepstone left the meeting as he knew had been made to look a fool. On 2 January 1878, he attempted to recover his position by writing a vicious report to Sir Bartle Frere to the effect that he had discovered the most incontrovertible, overwhelming and clear evidence supporting Boer claims to Zulu territory. This was followed by a report warning of the danger presented by the Zulus to the peace of southern Africa.[21] Whatever decision the Boundary Commission came to, this report sealed the Zulus' fate, with Frere commenting that Zulu history under Cetshwayo was 'written in blood'.[22]

Notwithstanding official pressure from Frere to reach his favoured solution, the commission sat for nearly five weeks, during which time they considered voluminous verbal and written representations. It was a difficult task. Gallwey utilized all his legal training to evaluate the material impartially, a task made especially difficult because a number of important Boer documents proved to be fraudulent while various Zulu reports were manifestly unreliable. Gallwey concentrated the commission's attention on two main issues: who owned the land prior to the dispute and whether any land under dispute had been properly purchased or ceded. Boundaries claimed by the Boers were frequently hand-drawn onto inaccurate maps, and no two maps concurred. The commission also noted that it had long been Boer policy, if policy it may be called, to gradually force the Zulus from their rich pasturelands.

The Zulu case was strong; no boundary line had ever been agreed between the Zulus and Boers and, for many years, a number of local Zulu chiefs had repeatedly implored the British Governor in Natal for advice and help in dealing with examples of blatant Boer aggression. Hitherto, little notice had been taken of Zulu petitions. On 24 June, Durnford had written home:

> I think our views will be maintained – at least I hope so. You
> see we have gone in for fair play.

The commissioners duly held that the Boers never acquired, and the Zulus never lost, dominion over the disputed territory, and that the disputed

Prince Dabulamanzi and family.

A rare picture from 1840 showing an explorer crossing an African river. *Photo courtesy Dr David Payne*

A trader crossing a river into Zululand in the 1870s. *Photo courtesy Dr David Payne*

Zulu transport in the 1870s.

A collection of native
elephant hunters.
*Photo courtesy Dr David
Payne*

A sketch depicting
Zululand in the 1870s.

A sketch showing a British attack against King Sekhukhuni. *Photo courtesy Ian Knight*

An early photograph of a typical Zulu *umutzi* or homestead.

Zulu girls posing for the camera in the 1870s. *Photo courtesy Dr David Payne*

Wives of Prince Dabulamanzi. *Photo courtesy Dr David Payne*

An 1870s' lantern slide showing the difficulties in supplying the British advance into Zululand.

British troops preparing to travel to Ulundi for the coronation of King Cetshwayo. *Photo courtesy Dr David Payne*

The carriage presented to King Cetshwayo by the Natal government for his coronation. *Photo courtesy Dr David Payne*

A unique photograph taken during the coronation of King Cetshwayo, 1873. *Photo courtesy Dr David Payne*

British hunters post-Zulu War displaying war relics. *Photo courtesy Dr David Payne*

Prince Sikota – brother of King Cetshwayo. *Photo courtesy Dr David Payne*

Prince Dabulamanzi with his council, 1979.

A native workforce
in the 1870s. *Photo
courtesy Dr David
Payne*

A contemporary
sketch of Rorke's
Drift after the bat-
tle. Note the
British graves.

Two Zulu gentlemen posing for the camera in the 1870s. *Photo courtesy Dr David Payne*

A Zulu princess, post-Zulu War of 1879. *Photo courtesy Dr David Payne*

An original Boer oil painting of the scene at the Battle of Blood River.

A modern scene at Blood River, with bronze replicas of Boer wagons.

Prince Dinizulu aged eighteen.

A sketch of British troops smoking out Zulu warriors before shooting them. *Photo courtesy Ian Knight*

King Sekhukhuni, who fought against
the British in 1878.
Photo courtesy Ian Knight

A modern Zulu me-
morial at Rorke's
Drift.

A modern picture of Zulus at Rorke's Drift village.

The co-authors of this book – Dr Adrian Greaves and Xolani Mkhize.

Dr Adrian Greaves with Prince Buthelezi.

Prince Buthelezi.

Dr Adrian Greaves exploring Zululand with David Rattray.

View of Ngwebeni Valley, where the Zulu army gathered before attacking the British at Isandlwana.

Zulu girls collecting wood near Isandlwana. Note their shoes atop the woodpiles.

The authors at the Zulu village at Rorke's Drift.

A King's necklace.

Zulu beadwork.

Modern Zulu beadwork.

A view of Isandlwana battlefield and Zulu memorial.

A modern photograph of Zulu maidens dancing.

A collection of Zulu beadwork.

Author Dr Adrian Greaves with David Rattray at King Cetshwayo's grave.

A museum display of King Cetshwayo's personal possessions.

territory was still properly a portion of Zululand and, furthermore, the developing Boer settlement at Utrecht must also be surrendered. The commissioners concluded:

> No cession of territory was ever made by the Zulu people, and that even had such a cession been made by either Panda [Mpande] or Cetywayo [Cetshwayo] it would have been null and void, unless confirmed by the voice of the nation according to the custom of the Zulus.[24]

The Boundary Commission eventually delivered their unexpected verdict in July 1878 to an astonished Frere, who determinedly sought to coerce the commissioners to amend their findings, without success. In his inimitable way he dealt with the matter by disregarding the document and placing it under lock and key. Although the commission's findings were not legally binding, Frere was nevertheless devastated by the result. Again, he secretly sought to have the commissioners' findings modified, again without success. Realizing his prime reason for the invasion of Zululand had been annulled by the commission, he decided to ignore the findings and keep the decision secret so as to allow Lord Chelmsford time to prepare and mass his troops ready for battle. In the meantime, another reason for the invasion of Zululand had to be found. Frere could only go forward; he could not go back for fear of tarnishing his reputation. Frere requested the British Government send massive military reinforcements but his request was refused. Hicks Beach made matters worse for Frere by sending him a dispatch that stated:

> All the information that has hitherto reached them [Parliament] with respect to Zululand appears to them to justify a confident hope that by the exercise of prudence, and by meeting the Zulus in a spirit of forbearance and reasonable compromise it will be possible to avert the very serious evil of a war with Cetshwayo.[25]

Clearly, Frere had officially been dissuaded from declaring war on the Zulus and he would also have known that he was now acting illegally. As recently as the Ashanti War of 1863, Britain had found itself in a remarkably similar 'ultimatum' situation when its Gold Coast governor unilaterally threatened war. Then, the response of the home government was unambiguous and stated that the principle of military proceedings:

> should be that of defence and not aggression. It is upon this principle alone that the Governors are authorized to make war, and no invasion of neighbouring territories can be sanctioned unless it can be shown that it is really a defensive measure, safer, and less costly in blood and money, and more likely to be decisive in its results, than waiting for an attack that is being prepared, and which no measure can ward off without loss of that position and dignity and position which are essential to our security.[26]

Furthermore, Frere would have been fully aware of Regulation 35 of the Colonial Service, which stated that governors of colonies are ordinarily expected to confine themselves to the internal government of their colony, and distinctly forbids them to proclaim war against foreign states. It reads:

> General Powers of an Officer appointed to conduct a Colonial government.

> He is not to declare or make war against any foreign state, or against the subjects of any foreign state. Aggression he must at all times repel to the best of his ability.[27]

Unable to alter the results of the Boundary Commission, Frere knew that he could not delay the publication of the commission's findings beyond a few months. He was also aware that the eventual publication of the findings would seriously antagonize the Boers. Worse still, there was every likelihood that the Boers would be required to surrender their farms in Zululand. Frere realized that the Boers would probably retaliate by taking military action against British-controlled Natal. From his days in India, Frere also knew only too well that, at a time when Britain faced war in Afghanistan, Russia would be watching events in South Africa. If Russia detected any British weakness, there was the distinct possibility that Russian warships, which outnumbered those of Britain, could arrive off the Cape and sever Britain's supply line to India and beyond. Frere had to act decisively.

After hasty and delicate discussions with his senior political advisers, Frere was obliged to realize that publication of the commission's findings could unleash powerful forces against Britain – both from neighbouring black nations who would believe their campaign against progressive European settlement was vindicated, and from furious Boers who could well retaliate by resorting to military action against British-controlled Natal. Such action could provoke additional antagonism from a number of the Boers' European allies, especially Holland and Germany. Frere had not been idle since activating the Boundary Commission; he and his staff, encouraged by Shepstone in the Transvaal, had wrongly anticipated that the commission would find for the Boers, and Shepstone erroneously believed that the Zulus might retaliate against Britain with a military offensive into Natal.

This opinion had been reinforced by disgruntled missionaries, Norwegian, German and British, whose collective endeavours over many years to convert the Zulus had met with widespread resistance. Bitter at their rejection by the Zulus, they withdrew from Zululand and wrote copious letters to the newspapers and governments in favour of war. With equal fervour, Bishop Colenso argued against the missionaries' campaign for war as a prerequisite of Christianity. Earlier, on 2 April 1878, Durnford wrote to his mother on this subject:

> These missionaries are at the bottom of all evil. They want war so that they might take the Zulu country, and thus give them homes in a good and pleasant land. They have not been turned out. They came of their own accord. The Zulus do not want them and I for one cannot see why we should cram these men down their throats.[28]

In consequence, plans were already well advanced for a British pre-emptive invasion of Zululand. Invasion would also neutralize the dangerous findings of the Boundary Commissioners, now languishing under lock and key in Frere's desk.

On 28 July, a minor incident occurred, which Frere used to generate widespread anti-Zulu sentiment. Two of Chief Sihayo's sons crossed the river into Natal to capture two of their father's adulterous wives. One wife was duly returned across the border at Rorke's Drift and clubbed to death in sight of the Mission Station. The following day, the second wife was recovered and suffered the same fate. Adultery in Zululand was a serious offence against Zulu tradition, especially when committed by the wives of such an important chief, and the punishment for being caught was invariably instant death. This situation was widely accepted by the Zulus and, prior to current times, would have been ignored by the British on the grounds that matters within Zululand were outside their jurisdiction. On this occasion, the incident received officially orchestrated publicity throughout Natal in order to inflame public opinion against Cetshwayo.

After hasty and delicate discussions with his senior political advisers, Frere was obliged to realize that publication of the commission's findings could unleash powerful forces against Britain – both from neighbouring black nations who would believe their campaign against progressive European settlement was vindicated, and from furious Boers who could well retaliate by resorting to military action against British-controlled Natal. Such action could provoke additional antagonism from a number of the Boers' European allies, especially Holland and Germany, and relationships with Russia were deteriorating. Frere had not been idle since activating the Boundary Commission; he and his staff, encouraged by Shepstone in the Transvaal, had wrongly anticipated that the commission would find for the Boers and Shepstone erroneously believed that the Zulus might retaliate against Britain with a military offensive into Natal. Even the pro-Zulu Bulwer was forced to agree that the danger of collision with the Zulus was growing and he wrote that:

> the system of government in the Zulu country is so bad that any improvement was hopeless – we should, if necessary, be justified in deposing Cetshwayo.[29]

There was another serious problem, but it was one that could be dealt with by a successful invasion of Zululand. Frere and Chelmsford were painfully aware that, in early 1878, and to the north of Zululand, British forces had taken military action to control the militant rebel leader Prince Mbilini, whose abaQulusi tribe had a long history of raiding Boer farms around Luneburg and stealing Boer cattle. Worse was Mbilini's enthusiasm for murdering Boer farm workers. Further to the north of Mbilini's sphere of influence was Sekhukhuniland, where the Pedi people under King Sekhukhuni had likewise been in a state of rebellion against anyone white and who regularly interfered with British lines of communication between Natal and Pretoria, the capital town of the Transvaal Republic, which had been annexed by Britain only the year before. By this annexation, the British inherited not only the Boers' long-standing border dispute with the Zulu kingdom but also the legacy of conflict and bitterness with the Pedi nation, which had come to a head back in 1876 following a minor dispute between the Boers and Pedi raiders, and in turn then led to full-scale war when the Boers commenced operations by advancing on Sekhukhuniland. The Boers chose to attack along the course of the Olifants River towards the first rebel stronghold, but after a chaotic two-day operation, their morale had begun to crumble even before they reached the first Pedi stronghold. The Boer commandos had been reinforced by 2,500 neighbouring Swazi allies and it was they who bore the brunt of any skirmishing. The Boers then attempted to advance further towards Sekhukhuni's main stronghold, but when their Swazi allies abandoned the campaign in disgust, Boer morale collapsed and their motley invading force retreated, leaving Sekhukhuni unscathed and free to continue his marauding.

The Boer campaign had been a military and political disaster for their floundering republic and had been one of the factors used by the British to justify their intervention and annexation of the Transvaal in April 1877. Meanwhile, fresh British attempts to establish authority over the Pedi were likewise firmly rejected by Sekhukhuni. In the official history of the Zulu War it is interesting to note that the British blamed Sekhukhuni's recalcitrant attitude largely on the influence of the Pedi's neighbour, the Zulu king, Cetshwayo. Zulu advisers and spies had indeed been dispatched to observe events and to counsel Sekhukhuni. In any event, the beginning of April 1878 saw British troops move towards the Sekhukhuniland border to defeat the Pedi and thereby, in theory, finally resolve matters. There was sound military reason for attacking the Pedi; with the secret invasion of Zululand in advanced preparation, Frere and Chelmsford did not want a rebellious Pedi army actively operating across their northern supply lines into Zululand. Since the recent annexation of the Transvaal, the Boers living in and around Sekhukhuniland had become quasi British subjects. In consequence, Frere had misplaced trust in the Boers that they would not rebel, but many were on the point of abandoning their farms to the Pedi marauders. Frere feared such a move would give the Pedi greater control in the area and send the wrong message to Cetshwayo.

It was clear to Frere that British action had to be taken to pacify and protect the Boers so Colonel Hugh Rowlands VC was instructed to march north to neutralize the Pedi. Rowlands' numbers were absurdly small, in contrast to his arrogance, especially given the recent Pedi successes over the Boers. No more than a few companies of British regulars were available, along with a handful of locally raised irregular units. After several months of sporadic and half-hearted skirmishes around obscure British outposts, a frustrated Chelmsford ordered Rowlands to finally resolve matters and drive on with the attack against Sekhukhuni's capital of Tsate, in the Leolu Mountains. Rowlands assembled his force at a point about 25 miles east of Tsate, known as Fort Burghers, and on 3 October he advanced with a force of just 130 men of the 1/13th Regiment, 338 men of the Frontier Light Horse, and two light 7-pounder Krupp guns. It was autumn but still unbearably hot and the country was dry and parched after several years of below average rainfall. Rowlands advanced just a few miles each day. He was constantly harassed by the Pedi warriors sniping from rocky hillsides or attacking his bivouacs at night, the Pedi tactics being supervised by Zulu advisers. By the evening of 5 October he was still several miles short of his objective and his horses were suffering terribly from the lack of water and grass. That night the camp was again attacked from three sides, stampeding the column's slaughter oxen into the hands of the Pedi. After about half an hour, the attack was somehow driven off by the exhausted soldiers but the cattle were lost. The following morning, Rowlands adopted the earlier Boer tactic, much to the relief of his dejected force; he gave up the advance and ordered the retreat to Fort Burghers, which he reached on 7 October 1878. A full account of Rowlands' misadventure was already with Cetshwayo.

The British expedition to quell the Pedi had proved only marginally less ignominious than the Boers' earlier attempt but Chelmsford's accelerating plans for the conquest of Zululand made it impractical to resume any fresh operations against the Pedi. A series of British-controlled forts were strategically built around Sekhukhuniland with the intention of containing Pedi counter-attacks, and from these sporadic skirmishing would continue up to the end of the year. Emboldened by Sekhukhuni and the Pedi people's stand against Rowlands' force, and as a result of the reports from his observers and spies of the widespread British weakness on campaign, Cetshwayo and his Zulu nation defiantly stood their ground.

A memorandum in July 1878 from Chelmsford to the Duke of Cambridge at the War Office should have alerted the British Government to the threat of war against the Zulus. He wrote:

> It is more than probable that active steps will have to be taken to check the arrogance of Cetywayo [sic], Chief of the Zulus.[30]

In early October there was yet another minor border incident that played into Frere's hands. At one of the Tugela River crossing points a British surveyor named Smith and a trader named Deighton were reviewing the condition of a drift across the river near Fort Buckingham when they were accosted by some Zulus and questioned about their activities. Although they remained on the Natal side of the river, the questioning lasted for about an hour before they were released. The Zulus were on guard at the drift due to the rumours of an impending British invasion of Zululand. The matter was commented on in Smith's routine report as being of a minor nature. The incident came to the attention of Frere, who virtually dismissed it out of hand, although he later included the incident in the list of grievances about Cetshwayo that would form part of his infamous 'ultimatum'. He initially wrote:

> I concur with you in attributing no special importance to the seizure and temporary arrest of the surveyors, which was partly due to their own indiscretion, and was evidently in no way sanctioned by the Zulu authorities.[31]

Meanwhile, Chief Mbilini, a local chief of Swazi origin, who was feared for his ability to conduct savage raids on Boer farms, now turned his attention to their farms' workers, local natives, most of Swazi origin. During the first week of October, a specific raid was undertaken. Mbilini led his warriors through the Pongola Valley in the very area under dispute and attacked their *kraals*. Their herds of cattle were driven off, many of their women were abducted and then their *kraals* were destroyed. When the news reached Cetshwayo, he realized the incident could be used against him and authorized the Boers to kill Mbilini. Indeed, this action played straight into Frere's hands. He was already preparing the terms of an ultimatum and secretly made Mbilini's raid the third item in the ultimatum.[32] Frere wrote:

> the indiscriminate massacre of every human being, armed or unarmed, including women and children, is by no means a new feature in Zulu warfare.[33]

To make matters worse for the Zulus, Frere and Shepstone encouraged the press to promulgate the belief that Cetshwayo now possessed a standing army of 50,000 warriors, which was poised to invade the developing British colony of Natal and its principal towns of Pietermaritzburg and Durban. On 5 November, Frere telegraphed London:

> Troops asked for urgently needed to prevent war of races …
> On other side of fordable river Zulu army 40,000 to 60,000
> strong, well armed, unconquered, insolent and burning to
> clear out white men.[34]

By the end of December 1878, Britain stood at a high point in its history and enjoyed a second-to-none position in world affairs. Few outside Frere's immediate circle of officials knew of the ignominious results of the recent Pedi campaign. This was fortuitous as Britain was, or so she thought, the greatest power in the world, both economically and militarily, and competently commanded a fine empire. Its cities were modern and efficient, its utilities and network of modern communications were the best in Europe, and London's Underground system was already in operation, as was St Pancras Railway Station, and Londoners were already enjoying tennis at Wimbledon. Nevertheless, Britain as a mighty industrial nation was preparing to commit its army to invade a previously friendly black nation that still lived in mud huts, a nation that had been at peace with the British for thirty-seven years. As for the British Army, it was not in the practise of shirking a battle, and not since Waterloo had any power contested Britain's right to rule as and where she chose.

Chapter 7

Defending their Nation

But all was not well in Zululand. Various frictions between the British and Zulu authorities during and towards the end of 1878 were developing beyond King Cetshwayo's control, the consequences of which would accompany both sides along a difficult path. The results of the Boundary Commission were already known to Frere but would be withheld from the Zulus until 11 December that year. There can be little doubt that, had King Cetshwayo been informed of the results, and had the commission's recommendations been adopted, the Zulus would have accepted the findings in their entirety and both sides could have maintained a peaceful relationship – but that would have negated Chelmsford and Frere's wish for war and all the glory with another military victory, even from a quick and easy campaign.

With a mighty army assembling itself at five points along his border, Cetshwayo was still perplexed by the British demands for the surrender of Sihayo's sons. Ordinarily, whatever action Cetshwayo would wish to undertake, he would not act without the authority of his inner council, whose judgement he respected. In the event, most of his council reluctantly agreed that giving up the two sons was a small price to pay, and one that might just prevent war. But Cetshwayo was not prepared to give up the sons of his most trusted councillor and discreetly sent them into the care of his northern ally, Prince Mbilini, an action that would antagonize the British and consequently disappoint the Zulu council. Cetshwayo increased the stakes, hoping the British might realize he would resist them; at the end of September he mobilized his army. The orders went out to take up arms, *maihlome*, and to 'doctor', or spiritually prepare the army, *ukuqwanjiswa kwempi*. Three of his regiments, the uMbonambi, uMcijo and iNgobamakhosi, were ordered to report to Ondini to prepare for interim manoeuvres along the border, and these began at the end of the month. It was intended as a serious show of force; warriors began moving along the Tugela and the Mzinyathi rivers, carrying their war shields and spears. Some had guns. Unusually, UDibi boys and women carried the warriors' equipment, a phenomenon hitherto restricted to the days immediately before the Zulu army advanced to war. In spite of his own army's posturing, Cetshwayo was still desperate to avoid war.

The British merely watched but did not respond – other than to steadily build up their own troop numbers north of the disputed territory near Utrecht. The campaigning *amabutho* soon tired of pointless patrolling and an undercurrent of disobedience began to grow among the warriors, a previously unheard of event. When rumours of the dissent reached Cetshwayo, it was sufficient to force him to agree to their requests and the *amabutho* were allowed to go home, with the proviso that the whole army would assemble at Ondini the following month. During October the *amabutho* again assembled at both Ondini and Gingindlovu – which brought a strong repost from Frere, claiming British troop movements, as reported back to Cetshwayo by Zulu spies, were merely in response to Zulu movements. The repost was sufficient to alarm Cetshwayo, who, again and reluctantly, permitted his warriors to depart. Having given the permission, he was disturbed to learn that several of the *amabutho* had already departed for home – and he could do nothing but risk losing credibility by recalling them.

Cetshwayo's very position as king was now under unprecedented attack on all sides. The British were clearly preparing to invade Zululand; he faced serious dissention among his advisers and some of his senior regiments, and only the younger *amabutho* chiefs wanted to stop the British, by war, if necessary. Other leaders, including Chief Hamu, the firstborn biological son of King Mpande, still counselled inaction as late as November. Little did Cetshwayo know that this trusted chief had already committed treason and negotiated his own peace treaty with the British in advance of hostilities. As the month progressed, British reinforcements along the Zulu border reached their high point. It was now that Cetshwayo realized that the surrender of Sihayo's sons was a mere ploy – the British were going to invade Zululand regardless. At the end of November, Frere informed Cetshwayo that the result of the Boundary Commission would be announced by the Secretary for Native Affairs, John Shepstone, at a formal gathering at the lower reach of the Tugela River that took place between 9 and 11 December. At the end of the two days, the findings were relayed to the Zulu officials but in heavily worded terms deliberately designed to cause confusion.

DEFENDING THEIR NATION

The hitherto secret ultimatum was then read to the Zulus, who, astonished by the about-turn, committed everything to memory and anxiously set off to report the ultimatum's terms to Cetshwayo. The main requirements of the ultimatum included some conditions to be fully met within twenty days. All were impossible within the timescale. For example, the Swazi Chief, Mbilini, was required to surrender and pay a fine of 500 cattle for his previous cattle raiding activities, as were Chief Sihayo's sons for crossing the river border into Natal and then murdering two of Sihayo's adulterous wives. A fine of 100 cattle was also to be paid for having molested two British officials, Deighton and Smith, at the border crossing. The conditions of the ultimatum were such that both Frere and Cetshwayo knew the demands could not be complied with; an awful milestone in the history of both cultures had been reached. (See Appendix D for further details.)

There were further conditions to be fully met within thirty days. King Cetshwayo was to observe his alleged coronation 'promises' – of which he was certainly unaware. A number of prominent Zulus were to be surrendered for trial (no names were specified), summary executions were forbidden and the Zulu army was to be disbanded along with the abolition of the Zulu military system. Every Zulu was to be free to marry – a reflection of the European misunderstanding of marriage within the Zulu society; missionaries were to be readmitted to Zululand without let or hindrance; Zulus were to be permitted to attend religious classes without obstruction; a British resident official was to oversee Zulu affairs; no sentence of expulsion from Zululand could be enforced without the permission of the resident; and any dispute involving a European was to be dealt with under British jurisdiction.

Even by this late stage, and notwithstanding the impossible nature of the ultimatum, King Cetshwayo sent a conciliatory message to the Lieutenant Governor of Natal stating:

> Cetshwayo hereby swears, in presence of Oham, Mnyamana,
> Ntshingwayo and all his other chiefs, that he has no intention
> or wish to quarrel with the English.[1]

Again, this faithful endeavour for peace was ignored.

In the final weeks leading up to the British invasion, Cetshwayo had been fully aware that events were rapidly moving beyond his control. All along the border with Natal, Zulu women and children, often leading their cattle, could be seen moving away from the probable British invasion routes and going into hiding. Cetshwayo ordered wild animal hunts to be held along the borders of the territories neighbouring Natal. These hunters were instructed to ensure that Shepstone's spies observed the Zulus' advanced state of preparedness as well as the strength of the Zulus opposing them. Notwithstanding soothing reassurances from Shepstone, Cetshwayo was not to be caught off-guard; shrewdly, he decided to wait, prepare and watch. Aware of the growing consternation of his people at the menacing gathering of British troops along the Natal border, the king sent a number of *inDuna* emissaries to implore British restraint but on presentation of their credentials they were arrested and imprisoned. In the meantime, the British invasion force was already gathering along the border of Zululand in total confidence that King Cetshwayo could not comply with the ultimatum.

At last the tide of Zulu opinion was beginning to turn in favour of Cetshwayo; his chiefs and advisers were now focused on resisting the inevitable British invasion. Knowing he had achieved unity across Zululand against the threat of invasion, Cetshwayo made one final attempt to prevent the British invasion; he ordered a herd of royal cattle to be taken across the river as a peace offering, along with a request that the ultimatum date be deferred to allow further negotiation – both of which the British refused. Unbeknown to Chelmsford, the timing of the ultimatum was unwittingly in favour of Cetshwayo, whose army was, by coincidence, already in the process of assembling at Ulundi for the annual *umKhosi*, the first fruits ceremony. This was traditionally held before the king each year to allow him to review his army and herds. The next gathering was due to take place on 8 January at his Nodwengu *ikhanda* – just three days before the expiry of the British ultimatum. As a precaution, the warriors were instructed to come prepared for war. It remains a belief among the Zulus that the king had already decided to resist the British, even if it meant outright war. Cetshwayo left a token force in place to watch the border river crossings and report on British movements.

At each year's *umKhosi*, the normal procedure was for young men who had attained the age of about sixteen, known as *inkwebane*, to be formed into companies, or *amaviyo*, which after a year's probation were placed in an *ibutho*, or regiment. This first year also symbolized the transition from boyhood to manhood as a warrior. The new *inkwebane* might either belong to another regiment with which the young one was incorporated, or it might be newly formed. As a rule, several regiments of different ages were combined at the same *ikhanda,* or barracks, so that the young soldiers might have the benefit of the experience of their seniors, and on the latter dying out, might take their place and maintain the name and prestige of the *ikhanda.* In this manner loyal corps were formed, occasionally some thousands strong.

The Zulu army now gathering was soundly structured and consisted of twelve such corps, each with one or more regiments with its own *ikhanda.* These corps necessarily contained men of all ages, some being married, others unmarried, some being old men scarcely able to walk, and others boys. Five of these corps consisted of a single regiment while the remaining corps comprised several regiments. Each corps or regiment possessed its own military *ikhanda* and was controlled by one commander, one second-in-command and several junior commanders who controlled the flanks in action. The uniform of the Zulu army was clearly laid down and was different in each corps. The great distinction was between the married and unmarried regiments. The former were obliged to shave the crown of the head and to wear a ring made of hemp, coated with a hardened paste of gum and grease. They also carried shields with predominately white colouring. The unmarried regiments wore their hair naturally and had coloured shields. For this *umKhosi* the total number of regiments in the Zulu army amounted to thirty-four, of whom eighteen were married and sixteen unmarried. Seven of the former comprised men over sixty years of age, so that for practical purposes there were only twenty-seven Zulu regiments fit to take the field, amounting to some 44,000 warriors. British intelligence figures of the day break these down as 17,000 between twenty and thirty years of age, 14,500 between thirty and forty, 5,900 between forty and fifty, and 4,500 between fifty and sixty.

At Ulundi the *ibutho* in residence was the *uThulwana.* These were the men who looked after the king and their work was rarely of a military nature; they maintained the nearby military *amakhanda* and engaged in planting, reaping and fulfilling the king's wishes. Each *ikhanda* was cared for by a skeleton staff and was only occupied when the king called up his *ibutho.* There were twenty-seven *amakhanda,* or royal homesteads, scattered about the kingdom, thirteen of them being located in the region of Mahlabatini Plain, near Cetshwayo's residence at Ulundi. Ulundi itself was a huge complex of some 1,200 huts whose garrison was more or less permanently in residence.

Unlike the lumbering British invasion force being assembled, the massing Zulu army required but little commissariat and no clumsy transport. Three or four days' provisions consisting of maize or millet and a herd of cattle were prepared to accompany each regiment. The older boys were briefed to follow their allocated regiment and assist in driving the cattle. They also carried the provisions and camp equipage, which consisted of sleeping mats and blankets.

Before marching, a circle, or *umkumbi*, was formed by each regiment, each company together and their officers in an inner ring with the first and second in command at the centre. The regiment then proceeded to break into companies, beginning from the left-hand side. Each company formed a circle and then marched off, followed by *uDibi* boys carrying provisions, mats and food supplies. The company officers marched immediately at the rear of their men, the second-in-command at the rear of the left wing, and the commanding officer at the rear of the right. This tried and tested plan was now set into operation to defend Zululand from the massing British invasion force.[2]

Nothing would now stop Frere and Chelmsford's deceitful masquerade or deter them from precipitating the invasion. Even though Britain threatened Cetshwayo with an impossible ultimatum, and had moved their massed troops along the Zululand border, Cetshwayo still withheld the order for his army to attack in the hope that his final request to delay the implementation of the ultimatum would be accepted. Cetshwayo had given up wondering why the British, his former friends, were now his enemy. Anticipating rejection, he secretly gave his *izinDuna* their orders for a specific attack on Chelmsford's main Centre Column, though with certain restrictions. In view of his reports from the Pedi defeat of the British, they must attack the British while on the move. He insisted his army must not attack any fortified or static position and not threaten the British Natal border. Presuming his orders would be complied with, he was confident that his army's presence would, by itself, force a British withdrawal back to Natal and gain him additional time to state his case, but he nevertheless sent one final plea. It said:

> What have I done to the great house of England, which placed my father, Mpande, over the Zulu nation, and after his death, put me in power? What have I done to the great white chief? I hear from all parts that the soldiers are around me, and the Zulu nation asks me, what have I said to the white people?

I hear that war is intended, and the reason for it is that I said I was as great as the Queen of England.

I feel the English have stopped the rain and the land is being destroyed. They have told me that a *kraal* of blood cannot stand, and I wish to sit quietly according to their orders, and cultivate the land. I do not know anything about war, and want the great chiefs to send me the rain.[3]

Meanwhile, in conversation with his adviser John Dunn, Chelmsford expressed his concern that he might not be able to get Cetshwayo to fight and made the chilling observation:

I must (then) drive him into a corner and make him fight.[4]

For the senior British officers invading Zululand, the main focus for their military intelligence gathering was to learn the Zulus' intentions and predict their tactics. Henry Curling wrote that the advance into Zululand was handicapped by a lack of accurate maps.[5] Chelmsford was, technically, invading Zululand blindly and so had to rely on local information for his intelligence. Much of this intelligence came from local officials, men such as John Robson and Henry Fynn, both local magistrates who were familiar with the countryside and Zulu ways. As late as 6 January, Robson's string of agents were reporting regular patrols of well-armed Zulus along the Buffalo River who appeared to be eager for a fight. Right up to the point of the British invasion, daily reports were reaching Chelmsford that indicated massive concentrations of Zulu warriors between Ulundi and Isandlwana. The reports were correct. Cetshwayo had assembled the Ulundi Corps (8,000 warriors), the Nokenke (2,000), the Ngobamakosi (5,000), the Umcityu (4,000), the Nodwengo (2,000), the Mbonambi (3,000), and the uDloko (1,000), making a total of more than 20,000 warriors. The supremely confident Chelmsford did not want to be bothered or confused with the facts – he treated the reports, most of them accurate, with indifference and ignored them. It was a simple case of having made up his mind.

Britain invaded Zululand on 11 January 1879, forcing Cetshwayo to finally confront the problems being thrust upon him by the formidable British. Even on the date of the invasion, the British received the sixth appeal from Cetshwayo to negotiate. Bulwer simply replied that he should communicate with the British commander, General Lord Chelmsford. The Zulu nation had been at peace for twenty-three years and no British settler or traveller had ever been harmed. The scene was now set for a dramatic confrontation between the British and Zulus. A hush of anxious suspense descended across Natal and Zululand, both sides fearing invasion by the other.

Even though Cetshwayo had purposefully withdrawn his army and *impis* away from the border, the British commenced actual hostilities in the early hours of 12 January 1879. The Centre Column, led by Lord Chelmsford, crossed the Buffalo River at Rorke's Drift and commenced its slow advance towards Ulundi with the intention of making an interim supply depot next to a rocky hill, then known to the British as Isandula. Isandlwana lay about 10 miles from the river crossing and was an ideal site with fresh water and firewood readily available. In between Rorke's Drift and Isandlwana, some 5 miles into Zululand and en route to Ulundi, was a high row of steep red cliffs that formed the backdrop to the homestead of the Zulu chief, Sihayo ka Xongo, an anglophile who wore European clothes and owned two fine English shotguns, and who had been a good friend of James 'Jem' Rorke, a local trader. It was Sihayo's sons who had murdered two of their father's adulterous wives within sight of the Mission Station a month earlier, an act that was used by the British as one of the grounds for the invasion. More to the point, Sihayo's homestead lay directly in the path of the invading column's main supply route. Chelmsford had already ordered that the stronghold be neutralized, and during the day, Major Dartnell, one of Chelmsford's senior colonial officers, escorted by a few mounted police, was sent on a reconnaissance. On their way up the Bashee Valley, which led towards Sihayo's stronghold, they heard a war song being sung, evidently by a large body of natives. But in reality the singing was by the remaining old men and boys looking after Sihayo's cattle. Where they were, or what became of them, the reconnaissance party were unable to discover. However, as this was the ground over which they were going to attack the next day, it looked as if they would meet with some opposition. Other parties had also been out in various directions, and although no Zulus were to be seen, they captured a considerable number of Zulu cattle.

On 12 January, Chelmsford and most of his Centre Column formed up to watch as the untrained Natal Native Contingent, the Natal-recruited black auxiliaries of Commandant Rupert La Trobe Lonsdale – formally of the 74th Regiment (Black Watch) – spearheaded the first attack of the invasion against Sihayo's homestead. Chelmsford commented:

> I am inclined to think that the first experience of the power of the Martini-Henrys will be such a surprise to the Zulus that they will not be formidable after the first effort.[6]

Colonel Glyn was in overall command of the attack. Responsibility for leading the attack was passed to a young staff officer, Lieutenant Charles Harford. This was to be the first engagement of the Centre Column, which sensed some fun to be had from watching the inexperienced Harford and his 'untrained untrainables' going into action under their equally untrained hotchpotch of non-English speaking colonial non-commissioned officers (NCOs). Led by Harford in his first action, the attacking Natal Native Contingent (NNC) warily advanced towards the steep cliffs and soon came under desultory fire from the handful of Zulus who had been left to protect the homestead in the absence of the men who were now at Ulundi. The target for the British attack consisted of old men and boys armed with ancient muskets and spears. Under wild and inaccurate fire from these defending Zulus, who had quickly taken shelter in caves set deeply into the rock face, the NNC adopted the attack formation rehearsed only the day before and then stormed the stronghold over seriously rocky terrain. Bearing the brunt of the mostly inaccurate Zulu fire, the NNC slowly advanced but such was the close range of Zulu firing that the NNC soon lost half a dozen men killed to point-blank shots, with a similar number badly wounded. The Zulus, on the other hand, lost most of their defenders; more than thirty old men and boys were killed in the exchange of shots and final violent hand-to-hand fighting, including another of Sihayo's sons.

Following the skirmish, several captured Zulus, including a number badly wounded, had been taken prisoner and forcefully interrogated – an unpleasant process but normal British Army procedure of that time. It was a procedure that was to seriously rebound on the British a few days later. The tortured Zulus nevertheless kept the secret that a great force of 25,000 warriors, accompanied by another 10,000 reserves and camp followers, was steadily moving towards the invading British column from Ulundi and was already approaching Isipezi Hill just 20 miles distant. Released the following day, the captured Zulus took refuge at the neighbouring village, which spanned both sides of the river border at Sotondose's Drift, soon to be known as Fugitives' Drift. Angered by the destruction of their village and the death of one of Chief Sihayo's sons, and with their own brutal treatment, not to mention the theft of their 400 head of cattle, they would not be well disposed to the British fugitives who were to flee from Isandlwana through Sotondose's Drift a few days later. News of the British attack on Sihayo's defenceless *umuzi* soon reached Ulundi, and this further angered the gathered Zulus.

On 17 January, the Zulu army, totally inexperienced in warfare apart from a handful of older chiefs, formed up to undergo the final ritual purification against evil influences during the coming conflict. This purification was performed by two war doctors, one with special powers to reduce the effect of British bullets. Later that same day the Zulu army began leaving its base on the Mahlabatini Plain to face the invaders, and the trail they left in the grass was to remain visible for many months. Their orders were to march slowly so as to conserve their energy. Their destination was a gorge, 50 miles distant, near the border with Natal, and just 3 miles from Isandlwana. Faced with the inevitable British invasion of Zululand, Cetshwayo's overall strategy was to either trap or inflict a decisive preliminary defeat on the British invaders. Knowing the British possessed overwhelming firepower, Cetshwayo decided against the traditional Zulu mass frontal attack, preferring the use of siege tactics. He remembered the reports from his spies during the recent Pedi expedition that the British were weak and relatively defenceless when in the open or on the move. He reasoned that, once trapped or starved into submission, the invaders would be forced to withdraw to Natal rather than face a humiliating defeat on the battlefield. He accordingly instructed his generals to harass the invading columns and isolate them from their supply lines.

The Zulu king was also a shrewd diplomat. Cetshwayo knew that once the British invasion force was trapped he could seriously embarrass Britain internationally and even force her invading army commanders to sue for peace. Unfortunately for Cetshwayo, his field commanders would instead take autonomous action, being either unable or unwilling to follow the king's orders.

By 21 January, most of the British Centre Column invading force had arrived at Isandlwana. The location was ideal as there was an ample supply of both water and wood for cooking; and the position was elevated, with a sheer rock face to its rear and, therefore, appeared easy to defend. It dominated the vast open plain towards the Zulu capital at Ulundi so that any approaching Zulu force, advancing from Ulundi, would be observed for several miles before it could form up for an attack. The camp under construction would hold some 750 tents, neatly erected according to strict military regulations, company by company, street by street, over an area nearly 1 square mile, and all under the gaze of Cetshwayo's spies.

Having settled the British invasion column into the camp site at Isandlwana, considerable misgivings on the part of certain experienced officers soon arose, including Major Dartnell. All were alarmed with regard to the selection of the site, owing principally to the broken and wooded country to its immediate rear, which would offer ample cover for a large force of Zulus to concentrate unseen and to attack suddenly. To an officer of the Natal Mounted Police who had suggested to one of Chelmsford's staff officers that the British camp might be attacked from the rear, Chelmsford retorted, 'Tell the police officer my troops will do all the attacking.' Another protested, 'Do the staff think we are going to meet an army of schoolgirls?'[7]

That morning, several natives from the Natal side of the nearby river came into the camp with a warning for Chelmsford that Cetshwayo intended to decoy the British and, when lured into the bush, the Zulu army would make for Natal. The same report arrived from Chelmsford's own local adviser, Mr Fannin; Chelmsford dismissed their multiple warnings. He believed the river crossing points were adequately covered and resolved to push on deeper into Zululand without delay. The *Natal Witness* reporter with the Carbineers submitted the following despatch to his newspaper on 18 January (it was published on 23 January):

> We have already had three different patrols into the enemy's quarters. Rumour had it that there were thousands near to us: but, though we hunted up hill and down dale, 'saw we never none.' It is impossible to know what to believe. The Zulus must assuredly be somewhere, but wherever we go, we only come across deserted huts. It is evident that a large number of the people have taken to flight, but whether they have done so through fear of us, or of their own 'noble savage' defenders, I cannot undertake to say. As a change, however, on the last occasion, we came across a Zulu, whom we took prisoner. On questioning him as to why there were so few men about, he said that they were quite scared away at the manner in which ·

we had taken their mountain fortress (Sihayo's) from them –
as they had not ever dreamt that we should venture up it. This
amount of fear does not look very much like the wonderful
prowess of the Zulus, of which we heard so much in Natal. I
imagine they are much like other natives – very great at
bragging, but easily depressed and panic-stricken by any
sudden reverse.

As the day progressed, Chelmsford experienced frustration heaped upon
frustration. The initial stage of the Zulu decoy was effective and resulted in
a perplexing tangle of information and disinformation reaching the British
headquarters. Chelmsford's situation was made worse by a local Zulu chief,
Gamdana, arriving at the camp. Gamdana had considered defecting to the
British but was still wavering. As a sop to Chelmsford, Gamdana correctly
reported that the Zulu army was approaching Isipezi Hill but he and his
information were dismissed. Rebuffed by Chelmsford, Gamdana was able
to assess the strength and layout of the British camp, a point of accusation
that would later be levelled against Chelmsford by some of his own staff
officers. That afternoon, Chelmsford received incorrect reports from
Dartnell's reconnaissance party that they had found the approaching Zulu
army. Dartnell was sent orders to attack the Zulus the following day and
supplies of food were sent out from the camp to sustain Dartnell's force of
mainly NNC, some 12 miles from Isandlwana.

Later that afternoon, Chelmsford decided to accompany a
reconnaissance patrol to the top of the Nqutu Plateau. One of the officers
leading the patrol, Lieutenant Milne RN, later wrote:

> On reaching the summit of the highest hill I counted fourteen
> Zulu horsemen watching us at a distance of about 4 miles; they
> ultimately disappeared over a slight rise. There were two
> vedettes at the spot from where I saw these horsemen; they
> said they had seen these men several times during the day, and
> had reported the fact. From this point the ground was nearly
> level; there were slight rises, however, every now and again,
> which would prevent our seeing any men who did not wish it.[8]

From their vantage point high on the Nqutu Plateau, these Zulu chiefs were
reconnoitring the British position around Isandlwana. Neither Chelmsford

nor his accompanying officers realized the significance of so many mounted Zulus; only senior Zulu chiefs rode horses and no one expressed any curiosity why the riders were there. Throughout that night the Zulu army silently consolidated its position on the Nqutu Plateau and their scouts were sent forward to the lip of the plateau to observe the unsuspecting British sleeping on the plain below. On one occasion, less than 2 miles from the main camp, some Zulu scouts came so close to an NNC picquet on Magaga hill that they conversed with them.[9]

Chapter 8

Isandlwana

Faced with the inevitable British invasion of Zululand, King Cetshwayo had singled out the British Centre Column for his main attack, not least because it was commanded by General Lord Chelmsford and posed the nearest threat to his capital at Ulundi. He meanwhile dispatched token forces to deal with the subsidiary columns of British troops facing Zululand. These were at the coast, to the north and facing the Middle Drift crossing point at the Tugela River, leaving a small reserve to protect Ulundi consisting of the iNdabakawombe *amabutho*, most nearing sixty years of age. His spies had reassuringly reported that the other three columns – those of Colonels Wood, Durnford and Pearson – were unlikely to pose an immediate threat to Ulundi due to their smaller size and the difficult terrain facing them. The Zulu leaders were confident of victory knowing that, just a few months earlier, the British had not succeeded in suppressing the less sophisticated Pedi, a much smaller tribe living to the north of Zululand.

With the doctoring rituals of the assembled Zulu army completed, Cetshwayo's regiments departed Ulundi on 17 January full of confidence that they would easily crush the invaders. The mighty Zulu column of 25,000 warriors together with 10,000 uDibi boys and camp followers was led by the veteran chief, the 70-year-old Ntshingwayo, and his deputy, the younger Ntuli chief, Mavumengwana ka Ndlela. Accompanying the Zulu commanders was Mehlokazulu, one of Sihayo's sons who had returned from his enforced exile after having riled the British authorities for murdering his mother. By the second day the army reached the Isipezi *ikhanda*, just 15 miles from Isandlwana before dividing into two, more manageable, columns. The following day the huge army continued its advance, with the two columns marching side by side. Some of Sihayo's men had horses and, knowing the area, they rode ahead of the columns to deal with any British scouts. In accordance with the king's orders, the army marched slowly so as to conserve its energy, taking three days instead of the usual two to cover the 50 miles to their destination. On 20 January, the army passed the lower reaches of the Isiphezi Mountain and under cover of darkness moved to the nearby Ngwebeni River depression, where they could camp out of sight from the British at Isandlwana, now only 6 miles distant. Ntshingwayo learned from his scouts' reports that the British had erected their tents over a wide area and that their camp, located on the south side of Isandlwana, was undefended. Of greater interest to Ntshingwayo was his scouts' collective opinion that the British camp appeared oblivious of the Zulus' nearby presence.

The main Zulu army's actual position was so well concealed from Chelmsford's scouts that Chelmsford continued to ignore a number of intelligence reports warning of the possible presence of the Zulu army, choosing instead to believe incorrect reports that suited his plan. Only the day before, Chelmsford and his escort had seen Zulu scouts in the distance – but he ignored the evidence growing before his own eyes. By pure coincidence, other scouts reported seeing a Zulu force in the hills towards Ulundi. They had not; they had seen some of Chief Matyana's warriors on their way back to their own tribal lands following a leadership dispute between Matyana and Chief Ntshingwayo as to who would be in overall command of the advancing Zulu army. Matyana had stormed off, taking his warriors with him, and it was part of this force that Chelmsford's scouts had seen, albeit some 10 miles distant from Isandlwana. Chelmsford accepted their reports, delighted that his decision was correct, and wrongly presumed this was the Zulu army approaching his position. The following day, he accordingly sent a large detachment of four companies, under Major Dartnell, to investigate and confront this imaginary force. Later that evening, Chelmsford received a message indicating that Dartnell, commanding the reconnaissance force now bivouacked on and around the Isipezi hills some 12 miles towards Ulundi, was still awaiting orders for the following day. This presented Dartnell with difficulties, especially as darkness fell, he could see many hundreds of Zulu cooking fires on the hills towards Ulundi. He sent his final warning to Chelmsford that a massive Zulu army was to his front. The fires were part of Ntshingwayo's decoy. Events were about to get messy and uncomfortable for the British; the final stage of the Zulu decoy had begun.

During the latter part of 21 January, Ntshingwayo had given orders for an elaborate decoy to begin. He instructed that, after dark, camp fires should be lit on the first range of hills some 12 miles from Isandlwana in the direction of Ulundi. The decoy would suggest the Zulus were closing on

Isandlwana from the east, whereas Ntshingwayo's army was already to the north of the British camp.

At about 1.00 am on 22 January, Chelmsford received confirmation from Dartnell, who was completely taken in by the decoy fires, believing that he had found the Zulu army. Within the hour Chelmsford committed the cardinal sin for a general in occupied territory: unaware of the true location of his enemy, he divided his force. He ordered one infantry battalion, the 2/24th Battalion Warwickshire Regiment, and a battalion of the NNC to march out to support Dartnell. Chelmsford and his deputy, Colonel Glyn, rode in command. Those left in camp under the command of Colonel Pulleine included the 1/24th Battalion of the Warwickshire Regiment. All those left behind bitterly resented that they would not have the chance to defeat the Zulus.[1]

Well before dawn the remaining Zulu forces had arrived from Isipezi Hill to join the main advance on Isandlwana camp. News from the Zulu scouts began reaching Ntshingwayo that Dartnell's column had remained 10 miles out from Isandlwana and, even better, they were now actively spreading out among the empty hills between Isipezi and Mangeni looking for the Zulu army. The decoy of cooking fires had worked but of even greater importance was fresh information coming to Ntshingwayo from his scouts that during the early hours of that morning, another large column, accompanied by both Chelmsford and Colonel Glyn, had departed the British camp and was at that very moment marching to support Dartnell's scattered force. The Zulu decoy had succeeded beyond Ntshingwayo's expectations.

One can only imagine the old Zulu chief's pride when his scouts confirmed that the five companies of soldiers with four guns and most of the remaining mounted men were no longer at Isandlwana camp. It was this force that had departed the camp during the night to rendezvous with Dartnell at the base of the bare shoulder of Hlazakazi, some 10 miles beyond Isandlwana. Ntshingwayo realized that the main British camp was now deprived of its most formidable weapon, the mounted troops, and half of the infantry and artillery. Isandlwana was now in the care of the inexperienced Pulleine. No wonder that a group of Zulu chiefs was moved to say, after the battle:

> You gave us the battle that day ... for you dispersed your army
> in small parties all over the country.[2]

ISANDLWANA

It was at about 3.00 am when Pulleine and the men left behind to guard the Isandlwana camp, some 1,600 men in all, had heard Chelmsford's column march out of camp. In compliance with Chelmsford's orders to defend the camp, Pulleine dispatched the remaining infantry to form an extended 1-mile line facing Ulundi, approximately 1,000 yards to the left front of the camp. Further positions were taken up at dawn by several companies of the Natal Native Contingent. These covered the base and shoulder of the Nqutu Plateau to the north of the camp while a mounted patrol was sent to observe the top of the plateau itself. Pulleine and his officers were totally unaware of their looming predicament. Their camp was now highly vulnerable to the unseen massed Zulu army hidden on their flank, only 5 miles distant. The British were now unwittingly spread over a vast area, from Rorke's Drift to Isipezi Hill, and from the Ngwebeni Valley to Mangeni; they were all in the wrong place covering an unmanageable 200 square miles.

As dawn broke, the situation for the British began to deteriorate further. Ten miles to the east of the Isandlwana camp, the small decoy force of evasive and fleet-of-foot Zulus began teasing Dartnell and Chelmsford's force by making a sufficient show of themselves to further attract the attention of Dartnell away from Isandlwana towards Ulundi, thus giving the main Zulu army the potential to advance on the British camp and take them by surprise, mostly from behind. At the same time, the Zulus began to move out from their protective Ngwebeni Valley position onto the Nqutu Plateau some 5 miles from the British camp. Ntshingwayo ordered his force to prepare for action and sent his chiefs forward to make their final reconnaissance of the camp from the edge of the Nqutu heights that overlooked the unsuspecting British camp a half-mile below them.

The few British scouts on the top edge of the plateau would shortly see the approaching chiefs and, in the far distance, the Zulu army spreading out over a 4-mile front and, in places, a half-mile deep. Ntshingwayo knew his army could approach Isandlwana camp unseen by the main British force until they reached a point less than a mile from their front line (see map *British positions and direction of Zulu attack at Isandlwana*, page xi). Under orders, the Zulus approached at a fast walking pace.[3] At 7.00 am and completely unexpected by Pulleine and his officers, a group of Zulus was observed on the rim of the plateau overlooking the camp about a mile to the north. These Zulus consisted of a number of senior Zulu chiefs completing their pre-battle reconnaissance. The Zulu commander, Ntshingwayo, now fully appreciated that the British were in unwitting disarray.

At 7.30 am, the first British scouts' reports that reached Pulleine revealed that a sizable force of Zulus was approaching the camp from the direction of the Nqutu Plateau. This caused Pulleine and his officers some confusion; the reports so far received indicated that the Zulus would be to their front, not behind them. Nevertheless, Pulleine strengthened his front line of infantry with the two guns of the Royal Artillery. For the next three hours, the soldiers were alternately stood to, or stood down, during which time the still unsuspecting Pulleine busied himself by allocating about half his force to commence dismantling the camp in anticipation of their next move, which they would still be doing when the Zulus shortly crashed into the camp.[4] One Royal Engineer officer, Lieutenant Chard, who had earlier witnessed the first group of Zulus watching the camp, was so concerned that he returned to Rorke's Drift, 10 miles distant and on the Natal side of the border, rightly anticipating that the tiny garrison there could be in danger.

At about 11.00 am, the central body of the main Zulu force, consisting of some 15,000 warriors, advanced off the plateau and suddenly came into full view of the thin red line of unsuspecting British infantry and guns of the Royal Artillery, who opened fire. The Zulus observed the gun crews' firing procedure, directed by Major Stuart Smith and Lieutenant Curling, and as each gun was fired the Zulus threw themselves to the ground. Thereafter, the shells passed over the Zulus and exploded with minimum effect. The British gunners thought that several rounds of their case shot (shrapnel) landed amidst the Zulus, still advancing with no untoward hurry.[5] This may have been wishful thinking; Zulu accounts state that the artillery did little damage, which was in direct contradiction to Lieutenant Higginson's later report that the artillery 'swept them away'. These Zulu accounts are probably correct because the British front line was unable to see the Zulus massing in the shallow valley immediately in front of them. The Zulus prepared to charge the British infantry line either side of the guns from the relative safety of the dead ground. Using this depression was an important aspect of the Zulu attack and they used it to their advantage to form up for the final attack. Because the British facing this dead ground, including the artillery team, could not see the massing Zulus, they sought to rectify their disadvantage by advancing their line another 100 yards in the hope of getting a better view, and in so doing advanced far enough that Pulleine could not see his front line from his headquarters. The most senior British officer in the camp was now fighting 'battle blind'.

ISANDLWANA

To the right of the guns, the three *amabutho* making up the main body, the iNgobamakhosi, the uKhandempemvu and the uMbonambi, all began to suffer heavily from British rifle fire as they advanced across the last few hundred yards of open terrain. The officers and NCOs in the British front line calmly controlled their men's volley fire and the main Zulu attack faltered and then stopped. The soldiers reportedly laughed and joked about the drubbing they were giving the Zulus even though they could see the advancing Zulu warriors were more than a half-mile deep. The long line of redcoats anticipated victory. After all, they knew only victory; their last major failure had been against the American colonists in the 1775-83 war. To make matters worse for Pulleine, he and his camp officers could now see another massive force of Zulus pouring off the Nqutu Plateau and heading for the small conical hill a mile in front of the camp. They would shortly drive a wedge between Chelmsford and the camp. Pulleine would have been further dispirited had he known a third force of Zulus was about to enter his camp from behind. The full Zulu attack on Isandlwana had begun. Without giving any further orders, Pulleine went into his tent to write a report. Various Zulu accounts claim Pulleine was killed at the height of the battle while still writing at his desk. Wherever he was, he had lost control.

When the main Zulu attack seemingly stalled to the front of the main camp, the Zulu commanders on the overlooking heights of the iNyoni cliffs dispatched Chief Mkhosana kaMvundlana, a sub-commander of the Biyela, to exhort the warriors to the attack. The Zulu chief, untouched by the British bullets, strode among the prostrate warriors urging them to fight. Chief Muziwento recounted that his men were exhorted to fight with the words:

> Never did the king give you the command 'Lie down upon the ground'. His words were: 'Go and toss them to Maritzburg.'[6]

The uKhandempemvu rose to the attack. Chief Mkhosana was then shot dead but he deserves to be remembered as the Zulu hero of the day. Had it not been for Mkhosana, the Zulus might have lost the will to fight, and the battle. In the final analysis, the Zulu attack was perfectly and courageously executed across several miles of rugged and difficult terrain; the British would be powerless to meet the challenge.

British volley fire reduced the visibility of the attacking Zulus to the defenders by creating a thick smokescreen at the front of their line, a vital

109

component of the battle usually overlooked by most authors and historians. Lieutenant Wilkinson, a veteran of several Zulu War battles, subsequently made two relevant and revealing observations: 'We followed suit, firing volleys by sections in order to prevent the smoke obscuring the enemy.' He added, 'Independent firing means in firing in [sic] twenty seconds, firing at nothing [due to the thick gun smoke not clearing], and only helped our daring opponents to get close up under cover of our smoke.'[7] As the charging Zulu masses appeared from the protection of the dead ground only 100 yards in front of the British firing line, it was evident to the Zulus that even sustained British volley fire was no longer going to stop them, the volleys having given way to single shots. The Zulu army rapidly closed in like ghosts through the thick smoke caused by British volley and artillery fire; the temperature was already more than 30°C and there was not even a breath of wind to clear the smoke. Although the soldiers were fast becoming fully aware of their vulnerability, the Zulus still had to deal with men who obeyed their orders to remain in extended line right up to the final bugle call to retreat. Just as the desperately awaited call sounded, the Zulus broke through the British line stabbing and slashing the retreating soldiers. The fighting and slaughter raged for little more than half an hour before the sheer force of numbers overwhelmed the last surviving soldiers. Whilst no front-line soldier lived to tell the tale, several accounts survive from Zulu warriors interviewed after the battle:

> Ah, those red soldiers at Isandlwana, how few they were, and how they fought! They fell like stones – each man in his place.[8]

> They threw down their guns, when the ammunition was done, and then commenced with their pistols, which they fired as long as their ammunition lasted; and then they formed a line, shoulder to shoulder, and back to back, and fought with their knives.[9]

> Some covered their faces with their hands, not wishing to see death. Some ran around. Some entered into their tents. Others were indignant; although badly wounded they died where they stood, at their post.[10]

The Zulus pressed home their attack. The Zulu left horn and main body moved in for the kill. Having completed their encirclement of the camp, their right horn had slipped unnoticed behind Isandlwana and began advancing to attack the retreating soldiers from their undefended rear. According to Commandant George Hamilton-Browne, who watched the battle from a low hill crest 2 miles from Isandlwana, the Zulus emerged in force from behind the mountain, driving the column's bellowing and terrified cattle through the wagon park and into the undefended rear of the British position. The Zulus then broke through the British front line just after the call to retire on the main camp finally rang out across the battlefield. The Native Contingent supporting the British front line broke ranks; this was understandable as they were ill-equipped with only one rifle per ten men. They knew they faced certain death if they stayed, so they ran. Many of them cast off their red NNC headbands in the hope of saving their own lives, and pretended to be Zulus, joining in the attack on fleeing soldiers. Their attire, demeanour and lack of Zulu weapons soon gave them away – the Zulus killed them on the spot. The British withdrawal back to camp was more rout than retreat and those fleeing from the firing line, hopeful of the camp's protection, found it already overrun from the rear by the Zulu right horn.

As the survivors of the Centre companies of the 24th fought their way back towards the main camp area they began to lose men at a steadily increasing rate. They eventually reached the wagon park, where they tried to form a defensive square. Some of those on the edge of the fighting turned and fled in the direction of Rorke's Drift only to be pursued and cut down. One of those fleeing was Lieutenant Curling of the Royal Artillery, a short-sighted mounted officer. He survived to tell a remarkable tale, the only officer to have continuously engaged the Zulus until the impromptu last ditch defences were breached and the camp fell.[11]

With dying and wounded British soldiers everywhere, no wounded man could be cared for; obeying the law of survival, anyone still alive had to flee or be killed. The road to Rorke's Drift taken by those who had earlier fled was now a mass of stabbing Zulu warriors so, no way being open, the remaining fugitives followed a crowd of natives and camp followers who were already attempting to escape across rocky terrain towards a nearby ravine. The fleet-of-foot Zulus were quickly among them, stabbing men as they ran. The artillery's guns were swiftly overtaken and their crews killed.

As soon as his guns were lost, Curling galloped off, his horse picking its way across the rocky ground. He was hotly pursued for about 5 miles until he came to a cliff overhanging the river. As he began to climb down the face of the cliff he saw a number of the survivors fall, injuring themselves seriously, including Major Smith. Curling got down safely and jumped his horse into the turbulent flowing river, which was 100 yards wide, very deep and swift. Once in the water he collected up three floundering soldiers, who desperately clung to his swimming horse. The bedraggled group eventually reached the safety of the Natal bank. Many of the exhausted survivors who attempted to cross the river were swept away and drowned and a number of swimmers caught in a whirlpool were shot by the chasing Zulus.

Back at Isandlwana, the scene in camp had long been one of nightmare proportions with gunfire, the noise of shouting and screaming and terrified panic and confusion at the sight of the slaughter being unleashed. Once they were in the ascendancy, the Zulus busied themselves with massacring the remaining soldiers, and then their horses, cattle and those camp dogs they could catch, such was their fury. By about 1.00 pm, only one British soldier remained alive. He had climbed up the side of Isandlwana and took refuge in a small cave beneath a sheer cliff. For another two hours, according to Zulu reports, this soldier husbanded his ammunition and killed any Zulu who approached the cave. Eventually, the Zulus lost patience with this lone sniper and gathered a force armed with captured Martini-Henry rifles. They poured volley after volley into the cave until the soldier was killed. His body was discovered some ten months later by Captain Mainwaring's burial party, with a rope around his neck. Zulu folklore records their sorrow at having had to kill such a brave man. His name and regiment remain unknown.

Following the battle, the victorious Zulus gathered up their walking wounded and in accordance with Zulu custom, dispatched those too injured to walk. They then plundered the camp, and there was much to be plundered. The most prized items were Martini-Henry rifles followed by ammunition, cattle and red jackets from the soldiers. Blood-stained jackets were ignored but there were plenty of unbloodied jackets to be had. In the heat of the day, several hundred soldiers had been detailed to dismantle the camp and had placed their jackets in neat piles throughout. The victorious Zulus were in no hurry to depart Isandlwana as there was no sign of Chelmsford's column, which was still more than 10 miles off and oblivious of the camp's fate. There were still wounded soldiers to kill and there was much that was new to the victorious Zulus, and even more to plunder. The concept of tinned food was still unknown to the Zulus so this was stabbed and medicine bottles smashed or drunk, making a number of Zulus seriously ill or incapable. As dusk began to fall, Chelmsford's column could be seen approaching. Now alert to the fate of the camp and their colleagues, it was still several miles distant, giving the Zulus a good two hours to depart. The Zulus calmly gathered themselves and set off carrying what they could. They all headed back to their previous night's campsite, where they remained for several days tending their wounded and burying those who died of their wounds. The bodies were placed in nearby disused grain pits.[12] Over the next two days, many hours were spent by the warriors who had taken ammunition from the battlefield, because they were unfamiliar with the rifles and ammunition, they pulled off the bullets from their cases and poured the powder into their powder horns – for use with their antiquated but trusted muskets.[13]

The Zulus had lost a significant number of men. The first few British volleys, especially those at close range, would certainly have accounted for between 1,000 and 2,000 warriors, and perhaps another 1,000 or even 2,000 were seriously wounded. The Zulus had not previously witnessed the effects of Martin-Henry or artillery fire and many had appalling wounds; they died in agony as a result.[14]

The post-battle tradition of a victorious Zulu army was to return to Ulundi, where the chiefs could report their success to the king. Although it is acknowledged that Isandlwana was a great Zulu victory, the Zulus had lost so many men killed and wounded that any euphoria was short-lived. Uncharacteristically, instead of making for Ulundi, the majority of the warriors returned to their homesteads. Undoubtedly, many would have been wounded, in shock or just too exhausted to walk the 50 miles to Ulundi. Depression would have been another issue; modern times describe the condition as post-traumatic shock. Instead, with warriors dispersing across Zululand, it was left to senior *izinDuna* to report back to the king, indicating a general feeling throughout the Zulu army that the whole event had been less than successful. It was another week before the army could muster sufficient men to present themselves before the king. In accordance with Zulu tradition, the brave were applauded and the cowards humiliated. Cetshwayo realized that victory at Isandlwana, although initially hailed across the land, would eventually end in his downfall. His army was dismissed to their homes to complete their traditional post-battle rituals – but with the order to reassemble in a month's time. Cetshwayo knew the British would re-invade Zululand.[15]

THE ZULUS AT WAR

After the Zulu success at Isandlwana, Natal was utterly helpless to defend itself. The British invasion force was in part defeated and part surrounded, yet Cetshwayo was unwilling to capitalize on his victory. As a gesture, he offered the surrounded column at Eshowe safe passage back to Natal. Had he ordered his army into Natal, the consequences for the Natal population and the subsequent history of southern Africa would have been difficult to imagine. Meanwhile, the Zulu reserve at Isandlwana, which had not taken part in the battle or been fed for two days, headed off towards Natal in search of food – against the king's orders. Rorke's Drift was in their way.

Chapter 9

To Rorke's Drift

Any British soldier on foot at Isandlwana was doomed. Only those scouts who had managed to keep hold of their horses had any chance of reaching the Tugela River and with little doubt, many of the survivors, with the exception of Lieutenants Coghill, Melvill and Curling, left Isandlwana before the main battle got under way. Based upon information from his spies, Cetshwayo had ordered the Zulu army to concentrate on red-jacketed soldiers in the mistaken belief that only they were the imperial troops. The majority of the survivors were wearing blue jackets, including Coghill and Curling. The 24th's officers had a choice of regimental jackets to wear in the field so there is no special significance in Coghill and Curling's jackets being blue, other than the fact that Zulu warriors may have paid them less attention. It may have saved their lives on their desperate ride along the fugitives' trail from Isandlwana to the safety of Natal.

The surviving disciplined troops still in camp, those under Durnford and some of the 24th Regiment, probably no more than 200 men in all, made a hopeless but gallant stand in the area of Isandlwana wagon park. Durnford and his men were forced into a back-to-back struggle next to Black's Koppie, the small hillock next to the camp's wagon park; all died making their final stand. The 24th's survivors similarly fought against overwhelming odds that increased with every moment. The last few soldiers then tried to effect a fighting retreat following the earlier fugitives. A few individuals managed to get as far as a mile to the rocky ledges overlooking the Manzimyama stream but all were cut down and died in the attempt. An unknown number of other fugitives were killed in the Buffalo River under the hail of Zulu gunfire or spears. Curling later wrote to his mother:

> I saw several wounded men during the retreat, all crying out for help, as they knew a terrible fate was in store for them. Smith-Dorrien, a young fellow in the 95th Regiment, I saw dismount and try to help one. His horse was killed in a

minute by a shot and he had to run for his life, only escaping by a miracle.[1]

The NNC and auxiliaries who had managed to flee Isandlwana fared no better. Those that reached the riverbank found themselves trapped against the raging torrent of the Buffalo River, now 100 yards across, fast-flowing and dangerously swollen from the torrential rain of the previous week. Several hundred tried to make a stand against the overwhelming Zulus but to no avail as they were no match for them as they caught and systematically killed them. In the midst of this slaughter the last of the escapers, including Coghill, Melvill and Curling, independently reached and swam cross the raging river, though of these three, only Curling would survive to write an illuminating but terrible account of what he had witnessed that day.[2]

At the small Rorke's Drift garrison, just 5 miles further upstream, and out of sight from the dramas witnessed by Curling, most of the soldiers were lazing in the sun, unaware that a 4,500-strong Zulu force was heading in their direction. To a number of observers on the top of the Oscarsberg behind the camp, a long Zulu column could be seen in the distance, slowly approaching from Isandlwana. They were led by Prince Dabulamanzi, a half-brother of the king, and included the uThulwana, iNdlondlo and uDloko *ibutho*. They had crossed the river about 3 miles below Rorke's Drift and, once across, divided into several raiding parties. One group advanced along the Natal bank and moved onto the plateau behind Rorke's Drift, where they rested and took snuff before closing in on the mission station. At the river crossing point the king's younger brother, Prince Ndabuko kaMpande, had urged his uMbonambi warriors to join Dabulamanzi's force crossing into Natal. Because of their casualties, or because they were reluctant to cross into Natal, they declined and returned to plunder Isandlwana.

Whether or not Cetshwayo had ordered his generals to stay out of Natal is open to conjecture. Addressing his assembled army only days earlier, the king had ordered his army to drive the British back, if necessary, to the Drakensberg mountain range well into Natal. It must also be remembered that only three hours earlier, the whole Zulu army had attacked Isandlwana, a defended camp and in direct contravention of the king's orders. The Zulus' decision to enter Natal is perfectly understandable as the Zulu reserve had not been called upon to participate in the battle and faced national derision for missing the action. Their potential ignominy would have been offset by them swiftly crossing into Natal, where they could murder a few farmers and their workers and by seizing food, burning farms and plundering cattle. With this in mind, it becomes apparent that the small mission station at Rorke's Drift was not necessarily an objective; few Zulus even knew of its existence. They would certainly not have been aware that it was defended by a company of British infantry and, had they known, it is unlikely they would have considered it an obstacle after the earlier Zulu victory at Isandlwana. Indeed, once across the river, the Zulus divided into four raiding parties, which suggests that they were free-ranging and unaware of the mission station. It was one of these groups moving several miles into Natal that intercepted Major Spalding's Relief Column marching from Helpmakaar to strengthen the garrison at Rorke's Drift. The Zulus' very presence forced the column to retire back to Helpmakaar, even though they were close enough to hear gunfire and see smoke rising from the mission station. Another group of Zulus went south and then inland, while others followed the river northwards towards Rorke's Drift, where they came across an abandoned farm belonging to an absent local farmer, Edward Woodroffe, which they burnt to the ground. Still following the course of the river, this column continued towards Rorke's Drift.

The two buildings at Rorke's Drift were originally built by a border agent named Rorke, but had recently been purchased on behalf of the Swedish Church for occupation by a Swedish missionary, the Reverend Otto Witt. Witt's stone-walled and thatched house, now converted by the soldiers into a temporary hospital, included three rooms. Adjacent was another similar-sized building, once used as a church and meeting house, now being used as a commissariat store. These two buildings were 20 yards apart and not connected. With Lord Chelmsford's instructions to fortify camps during the British invasion in mind, Commissary Dalton had already fortified and entrenched the site together with its two buildings, the bulk of the work having been completed by 11 January.[3]

The tiny Mission Station was overlooked on its south side, at about 200 yards distance, by a hill, the Oscarsberg, so called in honour of the King of Sweden. The terrain around the buildings was broken with clumps of bush, gulleys, caverns and boulders, giving excellent cover to the advancing Zulus. To the south-west of the hospital stretched thick bush, through which a wagon track and garden had been cleared. This scrub and a taller clump of trees, along with the garden wall, gave shelter to the first Zulus to approach the Mission Station, just as the Oscarsberg and a group of outbuildings did to the south side of the two buildings. With less than an hour's warning of the pending Zulu attack, Dalton used additional stores to reinforce the previously built protective wall around the two buildings. These stores were ready for moving to Isandlwana and therefore luckily at hand and in some abundance – sacks of mealies (Indian corn), bags of flour and potatoes, biscuit boxes, and such other materials as were readily available.

Enclosing the right-angle of the hospital and running in front of the bush and garden, along the top of a broken ridge that fell steeply for about 6 feet, was a barricade of mealie bags about 3 feet high. This, the first line of defence, was continued from the left of the hospital to the commissariat store, which was fortunately divided by a shallow ravine from the broken ground of the Oscarsberg. Besides these defensive lines, both buildings were loopholed and barricaded. In the hospital a guard of four men was stationed along with all the sick fit enough to stand and use a rifle. Some of the rifles had recently been patched up for service with tacks and strips of hide, rifles that were probably as damaged as their users.

The first Zulu scouts were from the iNdluyengwe, whose main force was working its way along the riverbank towards the drift looking for plundering opportunities. Having detected the Mission Station, the warriors gathered about 500 yards from the two buildings to assess the situation. They then advanced at a slow run, darting behind their shields to confuse the soldiers' aim. In the midst of the initial attack, one of the two mounted Zulu chiefs, Prince Dabulamanzi's deputy, was shot from his horse.[4]

The Zulus were skilled at hunting but had received no training for warfare against an enemy armed with accurate rifles. Instead they were indoctrinated with a lifetime of parade-ground rituals, which included imitating *giya* tactics, and they therefore approached the British position using the only tactic known to them. They made a number of prancing attacks at the slow run, showing they cared nothing for the slaughter awaiting them, and each time they would advance, then halt for a moment, and then advance again quietly, but running quickly, taking advantage of every bit of cover. Local Zulu folklore suggests they attacked in a very deliberate manner, more akin to their traditional dancing, by prancing and high kicking as they attacked. It is Zulu belief that the Zulu chiefs had expected to surprise the camp and that their melodramatic approach would scare the British into fleeing back to Natal. Instead the soldiers opened fire at about 200 yards.[5] Numbers of Zulus fell at once; the battle for Rorke's Drift had started.

By using this tactic, many Zulus got to within 50 yards of the first barrier until organized volley fire forced the surviving attackers to retreat and take refuge among the many boulders littering the lower slope of the Oscarsberg. The remainder hesitated, broke ranks, and the greater number scattered to their left and occupied the garden and orchard, where there was plenty of cover. As more Zulus arrived, many took refuge behind a long 5-foot high garden wall directly in front of Witt's house, now being used as a makeshift hospital, and crept to within 20 yards of the British wall of mealie bags. With darkness falling, the Zulus made several attempts to charge the British perimeter but failed to make any headway due to the steep incline capped with a 4-foot high wall of boxes. From British accounts, supported by Zulu folklore, it appears that the first Zulu assaults were initially conducted by single groups of twenty or so warriors who repeatedly attacked the end room of the hospital.

A few got up close to the two buildings by hiding behind the nearby field oven and kitchens, which had previously supplied the small garrison. Others came on in a continuous stream, gradually encircling the two houses. Only a handful of the Zulus had Martini-Henry rifles, weapons that had earlier been taken as loot from Isandlwana. These warriors were stationed on the hillside and kept up a continuous but highly inaccurate fire on the garrison just 200 yards distant and below them. This sporadic fire occasionally caught the soldiers in their backs as they were guarding the garden side, and five men were thus shot dead. Had the Zulus been good marksmen the whole garrison's position would have been untenable. But they were untrained in the use of the weapons and were further hindered by darkness, and so they fired wildly and badly for the most part, as if the noise had as much effect as the bullets.

Under cover of the dark, the bushes and the long grass, the Zulus were now able to get within 25 yards of the hospital without being seen. From this point, in parties of fifteen to twenty, they again attacked the end room of the hospital. Many times, seven or eight at least, they began to be a dangerous nuisance to the defenders. Lieutenant Bromhead, collecting a few men together, had to drive one persistent group off with a bayonet charge. Then the Zulus would retire, and in chorus would shout and strike their shields. The soldiers cheered in answer and kept up a steady rate of fire. Initially, there was plenty of ammunition but it was quickly realized by the officers that too much was being wasted.

The Zulus at last smashed their way into the far end of the hospital but only after some thirty of the patients were rescued by their able-bodied colleagues. Most of the escaping patients were pushed and pulled through a window at the far end, which opened onto the yard next to the main British defensive wall. The Zulus now set fire to the hospital, probably from one of the houses' many oil lamps used to illuminate the hospital after dark. The roof thatch was still damp from the earlier rain, though it would burn steadily for several hours. By its light the soldiers were enabled to see the Zulus better, and many were shot down before they retreated to better cover. After a pause, encouraged or commanded by a chief who shouted his orders from the hillside, the Zulus repeated their attack. The fighting in places became hand-to-hand over the mealie sacks, with the Zulus using their *assegais* as stabbing weapons against the soldiers' bayonets. Directly a soldier showed his head over the parapet to get a shot, he was thrust at. On several occasions the leading Zulus actually seized the bayonets and tried to wrench them off the rifles.

The defenders then fell back on an inner defence consisting of another 4-foot high wall of biscuit boxes stacked upon each other that extended across the yard from the commissariat store, and formed part of a second line of defence, including the store and an open space round it, and extending as far as an adjacent cattle *kraal*, all of which formed part of the final defence position. This second line of defence was not resorted to until the fire from the Oscarsberg, which took the defenders of the mealie-bag barricade in flank and rear, together with the burning of the hospital, had rendered the first line of defence untenable. This second line of defence was never assaulted by the Zulus at close quarters, unlike the outer barricade of mealie bags. From this small fortified position, about the size of a tennis court, the soldiers would hold their positions until morning.

As the night wore on both sides were aided by the light of the burning hospital. This guided the Zulus' fire from the Oscarsberg until Chard gave the order to fall back upon the second line of defence. To avoid hand-to-hand fighting, they established themselves behind the outer wall of the cattle *kraal* within 10 yards of the inner wall still being held by the soldiers. The rifle fire from the mealie-bag redoubt and the biscuit-box rampart was fatal to any Zulu standing still, even for a moment; thanks to the light from the burning hospital they presented the soldiers with an easy target.

After midnight the sporadic but forceful Zulu attacks slackened, but continued intermittently through the small hours until 4.00 am. The last British shot was aimed at a Zulu who was trying to fire the thatch of the store. The Zulus were clearly more exhausted than the British; not only had they run from Isandlwana, they had been without food for two days and had last drunk water when they crossed the river some nine hours earlier. Their attacks had stopped but their marksmen continued to fire into the British position from the safety of the Oscarsberg. The final flickering from the remains of the burning hospital died out at about 5.00 am and thereafter there was nothing to indicate a Zulu presence. Not knowing what the Zulus were doing under the cover of darkness and fearing an attack at any moment, Chard ordered his weary men to remain at their posts. Shortly after 5.15 am, the early dawn lightened the sky and the British realized that the only Zulus in sight were the dead and wounded. The main Zulu force had vanished.

The defeated Zulus had steadily made their way back to the drift and after quenching their thirst had assembled on the far bank of the Buffalo River. It was at this stage that they first noticed, some 2 miles off, the approaching column led by Lord Chelmsford. The column was retracing the route it had taken a few days earlier and was approaching the drift from the direction of Sihayo's stronghold. Not wishing to engage the British, either as soldiers or ghosts, the Zulus turned right and followed the riverbank, presumably to avoid further conflict. It is uncertain whether the Zulus knew that Chelmsford and a portion of his force had survived. Zulu folklore explains that the distant column 'looked like ghosts' coming through the early morning mist thrown up by the river. The departing Zulus genuinely believed the whole of Chelmsford's column had died at Isandlwana and many would have thought they were seeing the ghosts of vanquished British soldiers returning to Rorke's Drift. The theory is credible. In any event, Chelmsford's direct approach surprised the retreating Zulus; indeed, both groups passed each other at a distance of 400 yards. Chelmsford's men had but twenty rounds of ammunition each and the Zulus were exhausted, so neither side had any enthusiasm for a fresh fight.

It was not until dawn that the lookouts at Rorke's Drift could confirm the disappearance of the Zulus from the hill, and it was not for another two hours that Chelmsford's column could be seen approaching from the drift. The sight was greeted by a ringing round of cheers. Within the outpost, the scene was disturbing. The whole area was awash with pools of congealed and smeared blood, which bore witness to the death throes of both British and Zulu warriors. The area was littered with dead and dying Zulus; empty ammunition boxes were strewn around along with torn cartridge packets and piles of spent ammunition cases. The remnants of discarded red army jackets lay in the dust. They had been torn apart by the soldiers as improvised binding for their red-hot rifle barrels in the desperate attempt to save their hands from burning as they fired. The whole inner area was covered in trampled maize that had poured from the damaged sacks along the walls, walls that had successfully borne the brunt of the Zulu attacks. The heat from the burnt-out hospital gradually abated and, not deterred by the smell of cooked human flesh, the defenders found the charred bodies of the patients who had died within its walls. As there were many more charred bodies than the defenders had expected, they naturally presumed that these were Zulus, killed either by the defenders or by the hospital fire. During that same day, Lieutenant Curling RA returned to Rorke's Drift, and that night he wrote:

> The farmhouse at Rorke's Drift was a sad sight. There were dead bodies of Zulus all round it, in some places so thick that you could hardly walk without treading on them. The roof had been taken off the house as it was liable to be burnt and the wounded were lying out in the open. A spy was hanging on one of the trees in the garden and the whole place was one mass of men. Nothing will now be done until strong reinforcements arrive and we shall have much bloodshed before it is all over.[6]

The killing of seriously injured Zulus around the mission station then commenced. It was an act reciprocated by the Zulus, who killed any British soldiers left wounded at Isandlwana. Indeed, it was a fate well understood by both sides. Regrettably, the subsequent British action of killing exhausted Zulus or those who had gone into hiding well away from the mission station was to be more disturbing, even in the climate of such total warfare. Comment on the Zulus' fate was deliberately omitted from official reports to prevent the gruesome details being published in the British press. Such merciless mopping-up operations were, nevertheless, deemed necessary by those present and would be repeated as a matter of military policy by the British after each of the remaining battles of the Zulu War, especially after their victories at Gingindlovu, Kambula and Ulundi. The total number of Zulu dead from Rorke's Drift will never be known. The most likely figure of immediate Zulu casualties would tally at about 500, with probably another

300 or more being accounted for during the subsequent securing of the surrounding area. By comparison, British casualties were comparatively light, with fifteen men killed and one officer and nine men wounded (two mortally). The subsequent publication of details of indiscriminate and wholesale killing of Zulu survivors in hiding or fleeing from the battlefield was later to cause the military authorities much embarrassment.[7]

The engagement at Rorke's Drift was initially viewed by the British military in South Africa as nothing more than a skirmish, and, in military terms, they were correct; it was obvious to those present that a single concerted attack by the Zulus would easily have overwhelmed the small garrison. The praise and fame immediately heaped on the defenders increasingly rankled with many who saw the unexpected status of those present elevated to that of popular heroes. Even General Wolseley wrote on the matter:

> It is monstrous making heroes of those who saved or attempted to save their lives by bolting or of those who, shut up in buildings at Rorke's Drift, could not bolt, and fought like rats for their lives which they could not otherwise save.[8]

Major Clery was one of Chelmsford's staff officers who commented on the action:

> Reputations are being made and lost here in almost comical fashion.[9]

The homecoming for the Zulus was no better. It was as a result of their failed action at Rorke's Drift that Dabulamanzi's returning warriors were chided and mocked. Zulu folklore holds that it was said that 'you marched off, you went to dig little bits with your *assegais* out of the house of Jim, that had never done you any harm.'[10] Zulu folklore also relates that the surviving warriors who had attacked Rorke's Drift were seriously dejected by their failure and worse was to come. The retreating warriors were jeered and mocked by the villagers through whose homesteads they passed. The gist of the baiting calls included 'shocking cowards' and 'you're just women – running away for no reason at all, just like the wind'.[11]

Of greater significance to the Zulus was the result of their victory at Isandlwana. They were left with a hurt and vengeful opponent soon to be bent on total victory, and the loss of many thousands of young warriors at Isandlwana seriously weakened the Zulu army. Ever the astute politician, Cetshwayo had realized that, given time, he could achieve peace and independence by calling on the international community for help – but the British invasion forced his hand and, in the final analysis, his commanders let him down by failing to obey his tactical orders. He was now left with nothing but to await the reinvasion of his country. In an attempt to hold off the inevitable, his southern army investing the Coastal Column was reinforced with some of the warriors from Isandlwana – this brought the size of the force, under Somopho ka Zikhale, to 10,000 men. Cetshwayo's intention was to starve the British force and try to force the politicians to negotiate. Although decimated by their losses at Isandlwana the remaining Isandlwana *impis* underwent their post-battle rituals and slowly recovered. Cetshwayo still faced the growing problem of the British column to the north; he feared this Northern Column could move south to relieve the besieged Coastal Column. He therefore ordered the refreshed Isandlwana *impis*, under his experienced general, Ntshingwayo, and prime minister, Mnyamana, to attack the British in the north, where the rocky terrain would better suit Zulu tactics. Based on his spies' intelligence from the earlier unsuccessful British action against the Pedi, Cetshwayo's order was simple, and would be effective if obeyed: 'Bring the whites into the open field and make them die of hunger.' In other words, drive off their cattle and engage in guerrilla warfare.[12] Refreshed and encouraged, Cetshwayo's army of 20,000 warriors set off northwards.

Although Cetshwayo now had Natal at his mercy, he never attacked the colony. He realized that by defending Zululand while remaining within his border, he had secured the moral high ground. The British would not forgive the Zulu king for his successes.

Chapter 10

Nyezane and Gingindlovu

On 22 January, at the very moment when the main Zulu army was attacking the British at Isandlwana, another but smaller Zulu force engaged the second advancing British column that had entered Zululand across the Tugela River, just a few miles from the Indian Ocean. Although known today as the Battle of Nyezane, the name of a small river, the fighting took place on a nearby hill known to the Zulus as Wombane.

Under the command of Colonel Pearson, the British Coastal Column had crossed the 200-yard-wide Tugela River at Fort Pearson, a purpose-built fort on the Natal bank of the river that separated Natal and Zululand. It had access to the sea for supplies and had been built to give the British a clear all-round view for several miles into Zululand. British orders were to move the column the 35 miles from Fort Pearson to Eshowe to occupy and convert its small Norwegian mission station into a fortified advanced supply depot. Mission stations were conveniently situated at strategic points across Zululand so it was no coincidence that both the Centre and Coastal columns planned to use the missions at Rorke's Drift and Eshowe respectively as their forward bases. Once established, the columns' supply wagons were to return to Fort Pearson to collect additional stores before Pearson could advance at the same rate as the Centre and Northern columns to assemble for the final mass attack on the Zulu capital at Ulundi.

Soon to confront the Zulus was a powerful military force. The Coastal Column's infantry was composed of the Buffs and the less experienced 99th Regiment, with the column's heavy firepower coming from the Royal Artillery and the Naval Landing Brigade, who each supplied two 7-pounder guns and a rocket battery. The 136-strong bluejackets from HMS *Active* and HMS *Tenedos* provided a further two rocket tubes and were supported by the American-built Gatling gun, about to be used in action by the British for the first time on land.[2] With the column was a force of about 2,000 black retainers of the NNC. These locally recruited Natal auxiliaries were poorly trained, ill-equipped and not expected to fight; their role was to scout and disperse the beaten foe and they eagerly awaited the opportunity. The Royal Engineers supplied eighty-five sappers, and the 312-strong squadron of horsemen was made up of mounted infantry as well as from local units such as the Natal Hussars, Victoria Mounted Rifles, Alexander Mounted Rifles and the Durban Mounted Rifles, making the total number of fighting men in excess of 4,000. In addition, 620 civilians were employed to drive the 384 ox wagons. All in all, it was a formidable force, but it constituted a logistical nightmare.

Strategically, the concept of a coastal column in support of the main Centre Column was a logical strategy but it overlooked some important factors. British military planning had not taken into account that their invasion would take place in the middle of the rainy season and the task of moving several thousand men and heavily-laden wagons over 37 miles of rugged terrain following nothing more than a rough twisting track across numerous watercourses soon proved extremely difficult. Furthermore, debilitating sickness had begun to spread among the men and there was the constant threat of an enemy whose tactical aptitude and enthusiasm for battle were unknown quantities. So far, the few Zulus watching and reporting the column's progress had kept their distance, content to observe the struggling column and report back to King Cetshwayo. Under the command of Colonel Pearson, the Coastal Column set off on 19 January into enemy country towards the abandoned Norwegian Mission Station at Eshowe. Because of the heavy rains, the track quickly became treacherously boggy and the many dongas and rivers crossing the route were swollen with deep rushing water. Steady but slow progress was made. The route had to be cut through the dense virgin shrubland, although the most difficult part was manoeuvring the heavily-laden wagons through stretches of deep mud and across the many flooded watercourses. These hazards necessitated the Native Pioneers digging away the steep banks to create crossing points. Soaked to the skin from the constant heavy rain, and exhausted from each day's toil, the men endured miserable nights in their leaky tents. When on night guard, the inexperienced and nervous recruits of the 99th further tried their comrades' patience with regular false alarms. During the day, and notwithstanding Chelmsford's orders, no attempt was ever made by Pearson to laager the wagons and, with his advance divided into two columns, they stretched out for several miles along the track. They were highly vulnerable to Zulu attack but the Zulus were biding their time.

Unbeknown to Pearson, a Zulu *impi,* numbering some 3,500 warriors from the uDlambedlu, izinGulube and umXhapho regiments, had already been detached from Cetshwayo's main army at Ulundi and was steadily marching to intercept his straggling column. On 21 January, Pearson received information that between 4,000 and 5,000 warriors were assembling at the royal Gingindlovu *ikhanda* close to his proposed route to Eshowe. In order to verify this information Pearson detached a fast-moving fighting column consisting of two companies of the Buffs with most of the Naval Brigade, together with his artillery, some mounted men and two companies of NNC. It was certainly good luck for this strung-out British reconnaissance force that the report was inaccurate otherwise they might have been decimated, if not annihilated. The British found the *ikhanda* deserted. Pausing only for some target practice on the deserted huts, the detachment safely returned to the main column.

Unseen by Pearson's men, the destructive activities of the column had been observed from a distance by the advancing Zulus' scouts, which forced their leader, Chief Godide, to hasten his plan to attack the column. After dark on 21 January, the Zulu force of 5,000 warriors assembled at their smouldering homestead and then followed the detachment's trail until they approached the sleeping British camp. Fortune again favoured the British; the gathering Zulus surrounded Pearson's camp but did not attack, being uncertain of Pearson's exact position in the dark and deterred by the regular calling out between the sentries. The dawn discovery of heavily trampled grass around the camp alerted Pearson and his column to their narrow escape and the proximity, somewhere, of a large force of Zulus.

During the night the Zulus were joined by increasing numbers of local warriors until their force totalled more than 6,000. Under the cover of darkness they retraced their route and silently moved away from the unsuspecting column. They crossed the Nyezane Valley and ascended the nearby Wombane Hill, a hilltop location that dominated the area and bode well for the Zulus, having been the setting of an earlier Zulu success against a Boer commando. Godide knew that on the left of the track and nearing the summit was an abandoned *umuzi*. The whole Zulu force began to assemble in their attack formations on the far side of the hill, making them completely unseen to the unsuspecting and strung-out British column, now highly vulnerable as they approached the river crossing. Less than 2 miles away, Pearson had no idea the Zulus were so close and preparing for battle.

The Wombane hillcrest overlooks and leads directly down to the Nyezane River. At first light the watching Zulu scouts hidden in the *umuzi* were able to assess the main advancing British column as it slowly approached the river in the valley far below them. Their reports were quickly passed back to Chief Godide. Knowing the position of the column, Godide gave orders for his army to move forward the last half-mile and to assemble for the attack behind the crest of Wombane but remain out of sight of the British. He also ordered the chiefs who were to lead the attack forwards to the hill crest to observe the layout of the British column. Godide's Zulus had followed their king's orders by advancing slowly from Ulundi. They were fit, well fed and watered; all they wanted now was the signal to attack the invaders. The scouting chiefs moved forward until they reached the hilltop. Far in the valley below they could see the column straddling the Nyezane River. Due to their lack of experience, and a high level of excitement, the chiefs unwittingly edged forward onto the skyline to get a clearer look at the slow-moving troops below, not realizing they were now highly visible from the British column. But with just the chiefs being visible, they presented themselves to the British as an insignificant and easy force to deal with.[1]

Opposing Godide was Pearson's column. They had ponderously set off from their interim camp at 7.00 am using its advance scouts to secure the existing traders' track that led towards a plateau between two low hills, one of which was Wombane Hill.

To Pearson, now only 3 miles from his column's destination at Eshowe, Wombane Hill posed no hint of any problem and it had been ignored by his scouts, who had failed to see the Zulus observing them and the column crossing the river less than a mile distant. The infrequently used traders' track now being followed by Pearson's column was leading the British into a trap. The shallow Nyezane River was to be the column's first obstacle of the day. As the column approached the river, Pearson sent Captain Barrow ahead to find a convenient stopping point. He reported back that he had found a flat plateau just beyond the far bank that was ideal to halt the wagons for breakfast before ascending the plateau. The track from the river followed a low ridge that ran the whole length of the valley leading to the plateau. Either side were gullies that were filled with dense riverine growth and long grass. Despite having reservations about halting in an area surrounded by such thick undergrowth, Pearson decided to accept Barrow's suggestion and ordered the first wagons across the river.

The laborious task of bringing the whole column across the Nyezane River got under way. The day was already stifling hot and some of the troops took the opportunity to bathe in the river as the first wagons passed them by before halting at the open area below the centre spur. Shortly after 8.00 am, one of the British scouts reported to Major Barrow that a small party of Zulus had been seen gathering on Wombane. It was clear to Barrow that the column was being observed so he passed this information on to Pearson, who immediately ordered the native auxiliaries forward in order to engage the small party of Zulus now clearly visible from the column. Led by Captain Hart, the Natal Native Contingent advanced up the track and along the centre spur, which suddenly revealed the leading edge of the gathering Zulus. The Zulu trap was prematurely sprung. Seen from below, a small party of Zulus was observed moving off the skyline above, melting into the bush and then reappearing on the lower slopes of Wombane to the right of the British.

Realizing they were facing a much larger Zulu force already commencing their encirclement tactic, the British immediately attacked by sending a large party of NNC up the slope of Wombane with the intention of clearing the hill of Zulus. They left the track and crossed through the thick undergrowth in the ravine before emerging onto the lower reaches of the hill. The NNC officers in question, all of German extraction, had been locally recruited and few had any military training. They had no knowledge of their troops' language and during their advance a growing confusion inevitably ensued, especially when their leading scouts became aware that Zulus were hiding in the long grass to their immediate front. The NNC scouts desperately tried to warn their officers. In turn, the officers could not understand their men's warnings or their reluctance to advance, and tried to urge them on. At the sight of a party of emboldened Zulus advancing towards them the NNC panicked, probably because they possessed only a dozen rifles between them, and ran back down the slope towards the protection of the ravine. At the same time, with surprise lost, hundreds of Zulus emerged from behind the crest of the hill and fired a number of ragged volleys towards the column before charging down in pursuit of the retreating NNC. Several white NNC officers and NCOs were either over-confident, or rooted to the spot with fear. They appeared to try to hold their ground for a moment but were quickly overrun and killed.

Meanwhile, the sudden sounds of gunfire and shouting alerted the remainder of the column still crossing the river and those just arrived at the wagon park. The bathers hastily dressed and rushed forward towards the centre spur. Sapper Cullern later wrote:

I am thankful to say I escaped. We expect another battle in a few days. We were taken by surprise in the bush.[2]

The Zulu charge was the premature attack by their left horn. They were supposed to be part of a carefully planned ambush, but due to the unexpected British action, the Zulu centre and right horn were not yet in position to pose an effective threat. The Mounted Volunteers quickly formed a firing line to the right of the track and fired into the approaching left flank of the Zulu horn as they tried to work their way towards the wagons.

The Zulu chiefs could see that the British were in a highly vulnerable position. Their wagons were strung out for more than a mile and the river was dividing them. Initially, Pearson was in no position to form an effective defence and his only course of action was to rush as many reinforcements forward as possible. One Zulu later stated:

The whites shot us down in numbers, in some places our dead and wounded covered the ground, we lost heavily, especially from the small guns, many of our men were drowned in the Nyezane River.[3]

Another recalled:

We went forward packed close together like a lot of bees. We were still far away from them when the white men began to throw their bullets at us, but we could not shoot at them because our rifles would not shoot so far … the battle was so fierce that we had to wipe the blood and brains of the killed and wounded from our heads, faces, arms, legs and shields after the fighting.[4]

Pearson was now able to order a defensive deployment by his column – and ordered his men to fire steadily into the mass of Zulus who were now streaming down Wombane Hill clearly with the intention of surrounding the wagons that had already managed to cross the river.

The Zulus to the right of Pearson's position were difficult to see as they advanced through the long grass. To make things worse, other groups of Zulus began to appear from behind the hill and also put down heavy long-range fire into the gathering British defenders. One casualty was Colonel

Pearson's favourite horse, which was badly wounded, necessitating its destruction. Pearson's casualties were mounting and, in response, several officers directed a series of carefully aimed volleys into the Zulu sharpshooters who were causing the most damage.

The Zulu centre and right horn then advanced into the attack but Pearson had pre-judged their intention and already manoeuvred his force to counter them. Earlier that morning, Midshipman Coker and his Gatling gun team had been with the assembled wagons servicing the weapon. On hearing the firing they had hurriedly completed their work and ran forward with the Gatling to a prominent knoll. From here they put down a devastating rate of fire among the Zulus. Machine-gun fire was a new experience for the Zulus and the warriors began to panic and retreat once more, picking up further heavy casualties as they withdrew. On seeing the Zulus' alarm, Pearson audaciously gave the order to advance. There was a race between the Buffs and sailors to close with the Zulus but their combined advance slowed towards the top of the rise as the assembling Zulus made a determined stand. Led by Commander Campbell, the sailors made a wild cutlass charge and the Zulus finally broke and fled in disarray. Groups of Zulus were seen to take refuge in the undergrowth but well-placed artillery shells rapidly forced them into the open and onto the spears of the pursuing NNC.[5]

The battle lasted less than ninety minutes and a potential disaster for the British became a remarkable victory. Pearson's men had behaved admirably under fire but he was undoubtedly lucky. If the Zulu attack had been properly co-ordinated against the strung-out column, especially while it was crossing the river, the outcome for Pearson's whole column could have been catastrophic. By the end of the battle the British had lost twelve men killed and some twenty wounded, two of whom later died of their wounds. The Zulus suffered in excess of 500 killed, with many hundreds wounded. Indeed, the condition of the wounded shocked many soldiers, one of whom wrote:

> It was pitiful to see the fellows lying with fearful wounds. They were very quiet, and seemed to bear pain well, no groaning or crying out … one of them had crawled at least a quarter of a mile with a broken leg. One poor fellow was in an ant bear hole about 70 yards from the vedettes in front of them, and they did not see him for a long time until he called out – asking them to find him.[6]

The battle was, in the words of Colour Sergeant Burnett of the 99th, 'terribly earnest work, and not at all child's play'.[7] During the aftermath of the battle the British assisted the Zulu wounded but such humanitarianism ceased when the slaughter and mutilations of Isandlwana became known to the troops. During questioning of wounded Zulus, Pearson learned that the Zulu plan to attack the column had been pre-empted due to the early attack by the NNC. He was also left in little doubt that an even greater Zulu force was gathering to oppose him. In later actions of the Zulu War wounded were never spared – by either side.

The Zulu dead were left to the circling vultures and scavenging wild animals. The day had been unbearably hot and after a further arduous march onto the high ground of the Eshowe plateau, Pearson called an early halt for the night. At 3.00 am on the following morning, the column resumed the march. Only 2 miles remained and the column reached Eshowe without further incident at 10.00 am on 24 January.

The siege, defence and relief of Eshowe

The abandoned Mission Station occupied conveniently high ground and the first troops to arrive discovered that it was in good condition. Like Isandlwana, Eshowe was intended to be little more than a temporary staging post on the line of advance and Pearson did not expect to remain there long. Nevertheless, the following day his Zulu-speaking Colonial mounted pickets heard Zulus in the surrounding countryside calling to one another across the hilltops. They were relaying the message that they had won a great victory at Isandlwana. The next day a runner from Fort Pearson brought the first of a series of confusing messages, which confirmed that the Centre Column had been defeated. Pearson and his column were shocked by the incoming news. It seemed inconceivable that the Zulus, primarily armed with spears, could overcome an army equipped with sophisticated modern weapons. Furthermore, Pearson's force all knew that they were now a long way from the safety of the Natal border. They were surrounded, vulnerable, and possessed limited supplies.

Pearson was reluctant to withdraw. He was aware that the Zulu army was heading for Eshowe and that any slow-moving column retreating to Fort Pearson would seriously risk being overwhelmed. The officers were divided; some felt that they should try and reach Natal, where they could assist in its defence against the anticipated Zulu counter-invasion, while others sought to stay in order to force the local Zulus to maintain a siege rather than allowing them to intimidate Natal. Captain Wynne of the Royal Engineers put forward a robust case for remaining at Eshowe. It would require a large force of Zulus to contain it. His recommendation was adopted by Pearson. Boosted by the arrival of an incoming convoy bringing fresh supplies, all hands worked with a will to strengthen the defences. As the fort was cramped for space, some 1,000 oxen were sent back to Natal, along with their drivers. Many oxen strayed along the way and were immediately lost to the shadowing Zulus. The remaining cattle were laagered alongside the entrenchment until it dawned upon the defenders that it was a noisome health hazard.

Cetshwayo was understandably indignant that Pearson's column had settled at Eshowe. He responded to his advisers' growing anger by ordering the local Zulu regiments to encircle the British position, cut their supply lines and prevent their withdrawal. Within days the Zulus had completely surrounded the British position, and settled down to watch the proceedings and listen to the bands playing. Their siege was to last seventy-two days.

Pickets and vedettes were regularly detailed to keep the Zulus away from the immediate area around the fort. These were dangerous assignments as the Zulus would regularly fire on such patrols. The Zulus now had nearly 1,800 men effectively under siege with no immediate prospect of them receiving supplies or reinforcements. In response, Pearson ordered the commissariat to put the garrison on three-quarter rations. The garrison was completely isolated and totally unaware of events in the outside world. Not knowing whether the war was being won or lost the men were prey to every type of rumour and imagination. A system of sending messages using black volunteer runners was tried but most were caught and killed by the Zulus.

It was generally acknowledged by all at Eshowe that until Chelmsford received additional troops from Britain, he was powerless to offer any hope to the beleaguered garrison, so the garrison had to fend for itself. To maintain morale, Pearson detailed several mounted forays against nearby homesteads. One such homestead belonged to Prince Dabulamanzi but this action merely provoked the Zulus into harassing Pearson's patrols with greater determination.

The Relief Column, led by Chelmsford, eventually crossed into Zululand on 29 March and was ferried by ponts across the Tugela River. It began its advance further to the east than the obviously difficult route originally taken by Pearson. Although unopposed by the Zulus, Chelmsford's advance was now more cautious. After his recent calamities at Isandlwana and Hlobane, he selected open country where he could laager his wagons and entrench his column each night. The Relief Column travelled light; no tents or baggage were allowed even though it was known that the column would suffer from the heavy rain and intolerable heat that marked late summer in Zululand. Chelmsford's scouts reported to him that the Zulus were gathering in considerable numbers near Gingindlovu to oppose his Relief Column. The Zulu force consisted of the *impis* who had so successfully besieged Eshowe, reinforced by regiments from Ulundi under the command of Chiefs Somopho kaZikhala and Phalane kaMdinwa.

On the evening of 1 April, Chelmsford's rain-soaked Relief Column formed a square laager on the top of a low rise leading from the southern bank of the Nyezane River. It was close to the ruins of kwaGingindlovu, the Zulu homestead that Pearson had attacked on the way to Eshowe, and within sight of Pearson's earlier Battle of Nyezane on 22 January. Knowing that a force of Zulus had detached itself from those surrounding Eshowe and was fast approaching, and having learned his lesson at Isandlwana, Chelmsford ordered the column's wagons to be parked in a tight square, with a trench dug around the outside of the camp. The earth from the trench was then stacked to form a solid rampart, which the men lined with the wagons behind them. All the column's animals were brought into the square at dusk in anticipation of a Zulu attack. Chelmsford and his column were ready.

The Zulus gathered between the British position and Wombane, and then formed themselves into their attacking formation. Having successfully held the British at Eshowe, Zulu spirits were high. As dawn broke over the Nyezane Valley, the scene was partially obscured by a hanging mist that evidenced the heavy rain during the night. Then, through the gaps in the mist, several large columns of Zulus could be seen advancing towards the camp from the direction of the river. In preparation for their attack the advancing Zulus had already formed into their horns battle formation. Chief Somopho was in command of the Zulus, with Prince Dabulamanzi, Chiefs Masegwane and Mbilwane, and *inDuna* Sigcwelegcwele leading approximately 12,000 warriors from the uThulwana, uMbonambi, umCijo, inGobamakhosi and the uVe regiments, plus an unknown number of local irregular Zulu units.

As the Zulus advanced, Chelmsford's men rushed to man the barricades. They patiently held their fire until the first Zulus reached the 400-yard marker posts. The battle was opened at 6.10 am by a siting burst from a

Gatling gun followed by a number of well-aimed volleys that cut through the advancing Zulus' front ranks. In the still of the early morning, the British were quickly enveloped in their own dense volley smoke and were forced to cease firing until the light breeze cleared their view. Meanwhile, in the beleaguered fort at Eshowe, those with telescopes and binoculars keenly followed the opening moves of the battle.

Undeterred, the Zulus sought to surround the British and steadily advanced through the tall grass. The first Zulu attack, on the leading front of the square, came so close to the British position that one young Zulu warrior broke through the British line and was promptly seized by a marine. The warrior was kept as a mascot and later enlisted in the Royal Navy.

Due to the determined efforts of their officers and NCOs, the soldiers were steady enough to repel the attack. Meanwhile, the Zulu centre commenced its attack against the west face of the square, but well-aimed volleys again stalled the warriors' charge. The Zulu right horn then attacked the south wall but was similarly beaten back. The remnants of this attack moved round to launch a final assault on the east side of the laager, which was defended by older and more experienced soldiers whose steady firing prevented any warrior getting close. Due to the main Zulu force advancing through very long grass, those defenders with rifles had a better field of fire from atop the wagons, from where they inflicted many casualties. As the Zulu attack appeared to falter, Chelmsford prematurely ordered Barrow's mounted troops out of the laager to drive off the warriors, only to hastily recall them when he saw they were in danger of being surrounded.

As the shrapnel from the 7-pounders continued to take its toll, the Zulus' assault on the square suddenly ceased. Unable to break through the British defences, the Zulus lost their momentum and began to retreat to the comparative safety of the long grass and some nearby clumps of palm bushes. The officers then directed their men's fire into the groups of sheltering Zulus; this had the effect of killing a large number and forcing the survivors to flee back towards the river crossing and then onto Wombane Hill, where the Zulu reserves were observing the final stages of the battle. The final shots were fired at 7.15 am, just as the Zulu reserves on Wombane, seeing their force unexpectedly beaten, also withdrew.

Finally, after an hour's fighting, Chelmsford reordered Major Barrow to take his mounted men and drive the remaining Zulus further away from the laager. They were followed into the fray by the riders of the Natal Carbineers, who rode out with alacrity, cutting down exhausted and wounded warriors without mercy. The NNC were ordered to follow suit to seek out and deal with any Zulus attempting to hide. They killed every Zulu they could find, a task they relished with brutal enthusiasm. More than 500 Zulu bodies lay around the laager, including one Zulu wearing an officer's sword belt taken from Isandlwana, and many more bodies could be seen along their line of retreat. The Zulus lost more than 1,100 killed or seriously wounded; as many died in the post-battle mopping-up as were killed during the actual assault against the British position. The ruthless pursuit and killing of fleeing and wounded Zulus had first been witnessed at Rorke's Drift. The post-battle operation at Gingindlovu was identical and towards the end of the war would give rise to many uncomfortable questions about Chelmsford's conduct during the campaign.

Although the Zulus were in retreat, they were still capable of putting up a spirited and deadly resistance. The following day, Pearson's men began their retreat towards Fort Pearson while Chelmsford took Major Barrow and a mounted detachment to destroy Prince Dabulamanzi's empty homestead before joining Pearson's retreating column. There was little left to destroy as it had already been ravaged by Pearson's patrols. They failed to surprise the Zulu chief, who retreated to some nearby heights, from where he watched the remains of his homestead put to the torch. Collecting the rest of his men, Chelmsford abandoned Eshowe and marched after Pearson's column. As soon as it was deemed safe, the ever-watchful Zulus entered the deserted mission and burnt it to the ground.

Cetshwayo nevertheless contacted Chelmsford to negotiate peace terms to end the war. He was the wrong person to ask as Chelmsford was in disgrace for his losses at Isandlwana and he sought revenge. Cetshwayo was left one course: to re-arm and re-build his army. Chelmsford was smarting from the reality that he had achieved nothing since the original invasion of Zululand on 11 January. Worse still, the border between Natal and Zululand was effectively undefended. Superior Zulu forces and tactics had destroyed his Centre Column, and the Northern Column under Wood was locked-in at Khambula. He now faced restarting the campaign. Fresh troops, new columns and different tactics would all be necessary before the reinvasion of Zululand could begin. The task of facing the now triumphant Zulus was daunting, yet, unbeknown to Chelmsford, the tip-over point to British success was rapidly approaching.

Chapter 11

Ntombe, Hlobane and Khambula

Ntombe

Hitherto, the area along the Transvaal border to the north of the Zulu stronghold at Hlobane had not caused Chelmsford any real concern. Following Colonel Hugh Rowlands' timid advance against the hostile Sekhukhuni in 1878, and in consequence of having lost Chelmsford's confidence, Rowlands was moved away from active service to Pretoria in order to monitor the growing militancy of the openly disgruntled Boers. His No. 5 Column had been relegated from an independent invasion force to one in reserve. It was now a reduced 'care and maintenance' force of the 80th Regiment holding the northern border between Zululand and the Transvaal settlement at Derby, under the command of Major Charles Tucker. By March, the 80th had moved to their new post at Luneburg so all that remained to be transported from Derby were stores and ammunition. The route between Derby and Luneburg crossed the Ntombe River only 4½ miles from Tucker's base at Luneburg, but the British had to be vigilant as it was within sight of the mountainous stronghold of Prince Mbilini, who was of some concern to Wood. Chief Mbilini waMswati was a prince of the Swazi royal house who had fled Swaziland following a succession dispute in the 1860s. He had offered his allegiance to King Cetshwayo, who had granted him permission to settle on the remote Zulu/Swazi/Transvaal border north of Hlobane. Mbilini had built himself a homestead in the Tafelberg hills in the Ntombe River Valley and, having cultivated a good relationship with the abaQulusi leaders, had built another homestead further south, beneath the southern cliffs of Hlobane. A young man, still in his thirties, over recent years he had tried to rebuild his following and princely influence by conducting occasional raids against Swazi settlements on the Swazi or Transvaal side of the borders. Local white settlers regarded him as a dangerous and vicious marauder and he would emerge as the most dynamic guerrilla leader fighting for the Zulu cause during the war.

Due to the proximity of the Zulus, who were well known for their raiding abilities, these British convoys required strong escorts and so Tucker's companies were rotated to march out to rendezvous with the wagons and bring them safely to the hamlet.

On 1 March, Captain Anderson's D Company marched from Luneburg and linked up with a floundering twenty-strong wagon train bringing the garrison urgently needed supplies, including a rocket battery and 90,000 rounds of Martini-Henry ammunition. Progress was painfully slow as the torrential rain had not abated for five days, making the track virtually impassable. The wagons had to be manhandled most of the way and continually sank up to their axles in thick mud, and after days of toil the men were exhausted to the point that the convoy was in dire straits and all but unprotected. Anderson and his weary men returned to Luneburg and in so doing temporarily abandoned the wagons to the care of their civilian drivers. Unbeknown to Anderson, a small force of Mbilini's scouts had been shadowing the convoy and when they saw the escort withdraw they seized their chance and raided the bogged-down wagon train. They ignored the defenceless and exhausted wagoners and made off with a small amount of stores and some oxen. More importantly, they reported back to Mbilini that the wagons were undefended and contained a large shipment of rifles and ammunition.

When Anderson arrived back at Luneburg without the wagons, Tucker was horrified and immediately ordered out a fresh company of 106 men under Captain David Moriarty and his deputy, Lieutenant Hayward, to pull the stranded wagons from the mud and escort them to safety. The heavy rain had also caused the normally fordable Ntombe River to flood beyond its usual sedate 30-yard width and was now a fast-flowing 50-yard wide torrent, more than 5 feet deep. This forced Moriarty to leave thirty-four men under the command of Lieutenant Hayward and Sergeant Booth on the south bank. Two wagons had been brought across earlier before the flood waters had risen. The remaining seventeen wagons on the north bank were drawn up by Moriarty and his seventy-one soldiers in a defensive V formation, with its base to the river. During the confusion, some of Moriarty's cattle had wandered off. A small search party traced the cattle to the nearby foothills and, having recovered them, killed a number of Zulus responsible for the loss. This incident was witnessed by Mbilini's scouts, who reported back to their chief.

Although deep in mud, the soldiers settled down for the evening and began to have dinner. Sergeant Booth had managed to cross the river and was in the laager when one of the European drivers drew his attention to an unknown black man eating corn and talking with some of the wagon auxiliaries. The driver expressed the opinion that this stranger was none other than Prince Mbilini, whose stronghold was only 3 miles way. Booth reported this suspicion to Moriarty, who assured him that the locals were friendly. Moriarty added, 'You're as bad as your pals said of you; you would shoot your own brother.'[1] Booth was later to write that he was not reassured and believed that, Mbilini or otherwise, the stranger was there to spy out the camp's defences.

The interior of the wagon laager covered little more than half an acre and was filled with the soldiers' tents and oxen. Moriarty gave instructions for just two sentries and even felt safe enough to pitch his tent outside the noisome confines of the laager. Moriarty's exhausted men were grateful to have the shelter of their tents for the first time in days and retired early. Mbilini's visit had disturbed Booth and he later wrote that he began to feel increasingly uneasy. Booth had every reason for, unbeknown to the sleeping soldiers, Mbilini had mustered 1,000 warriors with the intention of attacking the camp to seize the guns and ammunition therein. Having silently advanced under cover of the early morning mist, the barefoot Zulus saw no sentries and were expecting little resistance from the sleeping camp. They carried only their stabbing spears and knobkerries, having left their shields behind, though a few were armed with pillaged Martini-Henry rifles seized from the convoy just two days earlier.

At about 4.45 am, and now less than 50 yards from the British position, the Zulus fired a ragged volley into Moriarty's tents and then charged. Within seconds they were overwhelming the sleeping camp and began killing the sleepy and confused soldiers. A small group of survivors on the south bank formed into a tight square under Sergeant Booth and prepared to retreat toward Luneburg. The Zulus crossed the river and made a number of concerted efforts to overwhelm the small retreating square of soldiers, but thankfully for the few survivors the Zulus turned their attention away from pursuing the soldiers to plundering the two wagons. On receiving news of the attack from the convoy's fleeing officer who deserted his men, Lieutenant Harward, the garrison at Luneburg rode to the scene as fast as they could only to find hundreds of Zulus moving away from the camp towards their nearby stronghold; most were laden with plunder. On riding into the wrecked camp they discovered that all their colleagues were dead, naked and mostly disembowelled. The Zulus had killed the camp's dogs, scattered mealies and flour and shredded the tents, and all 300 cattle and draught oxen had been driven off. Later, Hayward was arrested for abandoning his men and court-martialled. The column had lost 100 men compared with the Zulu loss of twenty-five out of a force numbering 1,000. Realizing that the British would react to this disaster, Mbilini took the precaution of moving his clan, with all the captured rifles and ammunition, to strengthen the abaQulusi Zulus at their Hlobane stronghold.

Colonel Wood's scouts reported that Mbilini's force was approaching Hlobane and it was these sightings that concerned Wood and his deputy, Colonel Buller. Hlobane, and the surrounding area, was home to several sizeable clans of Zulus who were particularly loyal to the Zulu royal family. Originally, 100 years earlier, and in order to secure his hold over this hilly region, King Shaka had established a royal homestead in the area, known as Hlobane, which served as a centre of royal authority. Originally Swazi-speakers, by 1879 they considered themselves true Zulus, calling themselves the abaQulusi after the area in which they lived. Their settlements extended along the northern side of Hlobane Mountain towards the Swazi border. They felt privileged to be a section of the royal house and were ruled by a chief appointed by the king himself rather than by hereditary chiefs. In times of war they mustered as an independent Zulu force and operated under the direction of their own chiefs; they were about to be reinforced by Mbilini's warriors.

Hlobane

By the middle of March 1879, Lord Chelmsford had put the early disasters of the Zulu war firmly behind him and was now contemplating a second invasion. Seeking to maintain Britain's reputation as an invincible world power, the home government now threw its weight behind Frere and Chelmsford by sending massive reinforcements. Chelmsford's plan for the reinvasion of Zululand was well advanced but he was deeply concerned that the belligerent abaQulusi Zulus, who were fiercely supportive of King Cetshwayo, now occupied the Hlobane hills and territory immediately to the north of the proposed second invasion route. This could cause him two serious difficulties. Firstly, the Zulus could move south in support of Cetshwayo's main army and hinder Chelmsford's relief of the besieged column at Eshowe. Alternatively, they could menace and sit across his second invasion route and plunder his main supply line. Either possibility constituted an unacceptable risk for Chelmsford. His commander in the north, Colonel Wood, appreciated the serious danger posed by the abaQulusi Zulus, having already skirmished with them around the lower slopes of Hlobane when his men clashed with them on 20 and 21 January. This engagement had occurred at the very same time that the Zulu army was manoeuvring to attack the British at Isandlwana and then Rorke's Drift some 40 miles to the south.

The mountain stronghold of Hlobane had long been a critical element in abaQulusi strategic thinking. It lay at the centre of an uninhabited chain of rugged, largely flat-topped features that extended eastwards from Zungwini in the west, past Hlobane in the centre, and ended in a long ridge that the British knew as Ityenka. Of these, Hlobane was an almost perfect natural fortress, with a 4-mile level but rocky summit plateau, more than a mile wide and surrounded by sheer 300-foot cliffs at its upper level, which was accessed by a few steep paths known only to the local Zulus. At the western end, Hlobane was abutted by a lower plateau called Ntendeka but known to the British as 'little Hlobane', and the two were connected at one end of Ntendeka by a seriously steep and narrow staircase of rock just 15 feet wide that dropped 250 feet from the Hlobane plateau to the lower Ntendeka plateau. Both Ntendeka and Hlobane were entirely devoid of cover and were desperately exposed to the full fury of violent rain and electrical storms that had hitherto discouraged the Zulus from inhabiting the heights. Historically, when war threatened, the Zulus would gather and hide their cattle on the Hlobane plateau, being well watered by a stream flowing across the plateau's width and draining by a spectacular waterfall off the southern edge. Being protected by cliffs, Hlobane was an enormous and effective cattle *kraal*, which the abaQulusi could further fortify with stone walls to block the paths behind them after their ascent. Unbeknown to the British, the south-facing ridge of Hlobane was pitted with a series of interlinked natural caves that ran from the summit ridge of Hlobane to the lower slopes, which the Zulus would soon use to their advantage. Likewise, the whole length of the north side was a 3-mile long, 300-foot high vertical cliff face.

Energized by Chelmsford's request to commence action, Wood organized mounted forays towards Zungwini and Hlobane. Between 15 and 17 January, patrols led by Wood's equally energetic cavalry commander,

Colonel Redvers Buller, pushed along the course of the White Mfolozi River from Bemba's Kop, probing towards Zungwini. Although they returned with large quantities of captured Zulu cattle – probably intercepted en route to the safety of Hlobane – they also reported an obvious increase in Zulu activity. The abaQulusi were apparently preparing to defend themselves and Buller had noted a fresh determination in the way his patrols had been shadowed and threatened, though not attacked.

Wood did not trouble himself with the exact identity of these warriors but they probably represented the coming together of various local groups – the Mdlalose, Khubeka and, of course, abaQulusi – and the formations he describes correspond to those adopted during the performance of rituals necessary to prepare men for war. Unbeknown to Wood, the assembled warriors may well have included another element as reports from the Luneburg settlement in the Ntombe Valley suggested that Prince Mbilini had recently abandoned his Tafelberg homestead to join the abaQulusi. Not only were the local Zulu clans gathering but another 20,000 warriors were on their way from Ulundi.

In mid-January, Wood wrote in his diary that he was already:

> uneasy concerning the Zulus to the north of our left flank, and obtained the general's approval to my going in a north-easterly direction to clear the Ityenka Range, including the Inhlobane [Hlobane] mountain, of Zulus under Umsebe and Umbiline, hoping to be back before the general was ready to advance with No. 3 Column.[2]

While Wood was pondering how to tackle the abaQulusi, he received an order from Chelmsford to seize the Hlobane stronghold to both neutralize the abaQulusi and draw Zulu forces away from central Zululand, where Chelmsford's Relief Column was attempting to lift the Zulu siege on Eshowe.

Chelmsford wrote to Wood on 19 March proposing a diversion in the north of Zululand and accordingly requested Wood to consider a distraction on or about the 27th. Chelmsford wrote that the main Zulu army was some 50 miles from Wood's location:

> Reports say that all the Zulu Army that Cetshwayo can collect is now, or will be in a few days, out or about Eshowe.[3]

Accordingly, Wood decided to attack Hlobane on the evening of 27 March with two columns of mounted troops led by Buller and Russell. By the time Wood received the request he was laagered at Khambula, some 25 miles from the flat-topped mountain of Hlobane. Wood's scouts reported several large herds of Zulu cattle, which were currently grazing the top of Hlobane, and a serious attempt to seize these cattle would certainly concentrate the minds of the local Zulus and deter them from moving south. His overall plan was to rout the Hlobane Zulus and seize their cattle. Wood's logic was militarily sound; a successful action would wrong-foot other local Zulus as well as deprive any Zulu reinforcements of essential food supplies. He proposed to mount a night attack against the Hlobane range of hills with two independent columns of mounted Colonial troops supported by black auxiliaries, half of which would assail the mountain from the east and the other from the west. The total strength of the force was 1,300 men and it was led by Lieutenant Colonels Buller and Russell, with Buller in overall command. Apart from Buller's skirmishing along the lower level of the mountain in January, the location had never been visited by a European and its precipitous ascent, and later the descent, would severely test Buller and kill many of his men.

The operation was, like so many of the Zulu War, based on the over-confidence of its leaders, who ignored the necessity to reconnoitre their objective and arrogantly ignored their scouts' intelligence reports. Even though the defeat at Isandlwana was still fresh in his mind, Wood had not considered it appropriate to subject Hlobane to any form of reconnaissance to the extent that the correct route to the top of Hlobane was unknown to him. The proposed routes up and down the mountain were based on Wood's distant viewing and although he had roughly guessed their location, his fatal presumption that the connecting ridge between the two plateaus of Hlobane and Ntendeka presented an easy passage would prove to be a graveyard for many of Buller's men. The plan was for the two groups to attack the mountain from both ends after dark. Wood's plan was for Buller to advance from the east to take the higher plateau of Hlobane and then seize the Zulu cattle, while Russell's force simultaneously attacked from the west along Ntendeka's plateau to facilitate Buller's return. Wood believed the final stage of the plan was equally easy to execute – Russell would meet up with Buller and their combined force would then drive the captured cattle back to Khambula.

Buller's force consisted of about 400 mounted men, all local volunteer horsemen except for a few imperial officers. Russell's group amounted to 640 officers and men and a 200-strong detachment of disaffected Zulus led by King Cetshwayo's half-brother, Prince Hamu. Both groups left Khambula just after dawn on 27 March in high spirits and fully confident that this was going to be a straightforward raid with the possibility of a large bonus from seizing so many booty cattle. Zulu spies followed their every move.

At noon, Buller's men unsaddled for an hour to take lunch and then moved off to the south of Hlobane. Buller did not consider it necessary to reconnoitre Hlobane, which suggests a high level of overconfidence on his part. Due to this omission, his imminent expedition to capture Hlobane was doomed to failure; he would find the mountain top virtually inaccessible, and once there, it offered no escape route. The weather was hot and sunny and their presence was clearly seen by the Zulus guarding their cattle on Hlobane who lit a row of signal fires. The significance of the fires was not realized by Buller, who deliberately proceeded for several miles beyond Hlobane before making camp. Buller's intention was to give the watching Zulus the impression that the real target of his column was the Zulu army, its location still unknown to the British, who wrongly presumed it was far away near Ulundi or on its way to attack Pearson's column at Eshowe. For the Zulus watching events from the top of Hlobane, there was little doubt what Buller was intending by riding past Hlobane; watching Russell's column heading towards the western end of the mountain they correctly anticipated that their stronghold was to be attacked from both ends. Knowing that the main Zulu army was approaching, the Zulus on Hlobane prepared for the British attack with growing confidence. They then built up the rough stone barriers guarding the cattle paths at each end of Hlobane to a height of 3 feet.

Buller's colonial scouts proved incompetent and for a crucial few hours seriously neglected their duty by attending to their own welfare rather than observing events off to the south. Buller remained unaware of the close proximity of the approaching Zulu army that was now camped only 5 miles from Hlobane and alerted to Buller's presence by the Zulus' signal fires and their scouts' reports. Had Buller's force, during the last hour of daylight, looked in the direction of Ulundi rather than concentrating their attention on the possible routes up Hlobane, they would certainly have seen the distant Zulu army advancing across open country towards them. A campsite was found in sight of Hlobane and, as dusk approached, Buller's men lit a number of campfires. After dark the fires were stoked to give the watching

Zulus the impression that they were staying put. At about 8.00 pm, Buller gave the order to stoke the fires. His force then departed and under the cover of darkness he led his men back towards the western end of Hlobane, where they began the laborious task of following a cattle track that appeared to lead in the general direction of the plateau top.

Buller's black scouts should have been the eyes and ears of his expedition but they knew only too well that their words were never heeded. Indeed, they had understood the Zulus' signal fires but had chosen to keep the information to themselves rather than be ignored or ridiculed. Even when a scouting patrol from the column accidentally discovered the Zulu army during the night, Wood failed to make use of the information. Astonishingly, and worse, the information was disputed and an officer's word was publicly challenged. The incident arose when the Border Horse, which was supposed to be part of Buller's group, had left Khambula later than intended and had inadvertently become mixed with Russell's force. In the confusion, they and their commander, an experienced ex-cavalry lieutenant colonel named Weatherley, spent most of the night unsuccessfully trying to find Buller. Weatherley's second-in-command, Captain Dennison, and a party of scouts, inadvertently came across the encamped Zulu army. Undetected due to the darkness, they bravely crept to within several hundred yards of the Zulu camp to assess the situation before quietly withdrawing to report the fact to a startled Weatherley, who passed it to Wood, who rejected it.

While Wood was resting with Russell's column, the seemingly uneventful night of the 27th soon passed. Buller's attack against Hlobane had already begun under the cover of darkness. The route they chose was difficult to find; it was dark and the hillside was boulder-strewn and very steep in places. To make matters worse, their ascent was undertaken in a violent thunderstorm, which drenched the men and made their path slippery. Their ascent was virtually unopposed until the brilliant flashes of sheet lightning exposed the column of bedraggled men and horses to the Zulu guards patrolling the top of the path. The guards fired some shots and several large boulders were rolled down on the advancing force as it struggled up the steep cattle track, causing a number of casualties to both men and horses. As the British neared the rim of the flat-topped plateau, the defending warriors slipped away into the honeycomb of caves that link the top of Hlobane with its lower reaches. With the defending Zulus nowhere to be seen and with daylight breaking, the main British force set off across the rocky plateau gathering up Zulu cattle as they went. They were heading in the general direction of the far end of the mountain, where they expected to meet up with Russell's force later that morning. Unbeknown to Buller, Russell had already arrived at the bottom of the precipitous face known as the 'Devil's Pass' and found his route to the higher plateau of Hlobane virtually unclimbable, and certainly impossible for horses. The so-called pass was nothing of the sort; it was a steep and narrow ridge of hard rock, sheer on both sides, joining the two plateaus. Russell despatched a volunteer messenger to climb up the rocky ridge to find Buller and advise him not to attempt the descent by that route.

Meanwhile, the Zulus hiding in Hlobane's caves could clearly see the main Zulu army now less than 1 mile distant and steadily closing. They left their caves and were joined by an independent Zulu force of about 2,000 warriors that had just climbed onto Hlobane from the adjoining Ityentika plateau to the east. These Zulu reinforcements now prepared to attack Buller's men from the rear. They were from the abaQulusi tribe, supported by Mbilini's clan and the umCijo and inGobamakhosi regiments. Buller's men were soon alert to the dangerous situation developing and sped up. Probably because he was concentrating on protecting his retreating men with the looted cattle, it was several minutes before Buller became aware of the main Zulu army now approaching Hlobane. His first reaction was to rush the remaining unmounted black irregulars towards the pass so that they could escape to Khambula. He knew nothing of the precipitous cliff his men were approaching. As Buller's remaining force converged towards the top of the Devil's Pass, the emboldened and reinforced Zulus of Mbilini, who had been following them, closed in. It was only at the moment when unease turned into chaos that Buller first became aware of the enormity of the danger being created by the main Zulu army moving to encircle Hlobane.

In their attempt to join Buller on Hlobane, a group of Wood's men, under the command of Colonel Weatherley, had skirted the mountain but had inadvertently ridden towards the main Zulu army, who were now less than a quarter of a mile away and rapidly closing. They about-turned, only to discover that a force of abaQulusi Zulus, who had seen their predicament, had raced behind them off the mountain. Weatherley's men were swiftly being surrounded. To a man they successfully charged through the descending abaQulusi and rode with all speed towards the nearby *nek*, a saddle measuring some 200 yards across between Hlobane and Ityentika, in the mistaken belief that they could ride across the saddle and descend down the far side to the safety of the far valley. It was not to be. The Zulus knew only too well that the saddle ended abruptly at the head of a 300-foot precipice to the valley below. This sheer cliff face brought the charging troopers to a sudden halt. The Zulus rushed at Weatherley's trapped force, now in a state of panic, and drove them to the very edge of the cliff that ran along the northern side of Hlobane. In the fierce fighting that ensued, Weatherley, his son and sixty-six men were killed, either by being stabbed by the Zulus or from being thrown over the cliff edge. The terror of the rout and bloody slaughter caused some men and horses to jump off the cliff. The few who made it alive to the base were relentlessly chased by the fleet-of-foot Zulus and killed.

As at Isandlwana, the approaching Zulu army was large enough to surround the whole Hlobane Mountain and, as at Isandlwana, the Zulus advanced to block off the only escape route. The upshot amongst both Buller's and Wood's columns was panic and pandemonium. With the Zulus bearing down on them, both columns could clearly see that they were on the verge of being surrounded by an overpowering force of Zulus. Wood was unsure whether Buller and Russell had seen the approaching Zulus. From the safety of his position some 2 miles away, Wood tried to warn his two commanders and sent a written order to Russell mistakenly ordering him to move immediately to Zunguin Nek, 5 miles from the scene. By obeying Wood's order and departing this key position, Russell's force controversially abandoned Buller and his men to the encircling Zulus. With the abaQulusi now attacking Buller's panicking column from their rear, some of his men and horses attempted to climb down the precipitous ridge. Many simply slipped and fell to their deaths. For the few survivors, their ordeal was to become even more serious as the Zulus from the main force now reached the lower reaches of the ridge and began closing in on both sides of Buller's descending men. The Zulus began firing at point-blank range into the desperate soldiers while others darted among them, stabbing and spearing them to death. At the base of the pass there was little that Buller or his surviving officers could do other than to desperately try and hold their remaining men together and pour rapid fire into the attacking Zulus.[4]

With hundreds more Zulus converging on the Devil's Pass the fighting was soon over and only those riders who had reached the lower plateau with their horses had any chance of getting away. Those still struggling down the pass or on foot soon fell. The harrowing experience continued for the mounted survivors, who were chased for several miles by the jubilant Zulus. It was a long and frightening trek for those fleeing for their lives; many were caught and killed.

No one taking part in the attack knew the layout of Hlobane and, as at Isandlwana, accurate intelligence reports of a Zulu army camped only 5 miles distant had been completely disregarded. Collectively, Wood and Buller provoked the second greatest disaster of the war. Yet the news and implications of the defeat at Hlobane would be successfully screened the following day by the British victory at Khambula, just as the successful defence at Rorke's Drift screened the appalling defeat at Isandlwana.

Against all expectations, the action at Hlobane was a great victory for the Zulus but was the second most serious disaster for Chelmsford's invasion army, with Wood losing fifteen officers and nearly 200 of his men when they unexpectedly encountered the main Zulu army. Buller and his survivors were forced to retreat to Khambula. The following day the victorious Zulus anticipated a similar victory when they set off to attack Wood's headquarters on Khambula hill, which was well fortified.

Khambula

Earlier, on the afternoon of 28 March, the British troops remaining in the Khambula camp began to hear rumours of the unbelievable disaster that had befallen Buller's force at Hlobane. Until this point, the prevailing atmosphere throughout the camp was one of absolute confidence. Rumours had long since been circulating that the Zulu army might seek to attack the Northern Column and the men enthusiastically welcomed the prospect of avenging Isandlwana. That afternoon, the Hlobane survivors began arriving back at Khambula camp in their ones and twos; many were wounded, all were deeply shocked. These were men who had earlier set out with boundless confidence to attack the Zulu stronghold. Now the full extent of their loss was becoming abundantly clear.

With such a large Zulu force now so close to Khambula, Wood correctly expected that an attack on his position was imminent and that evening everyone in camp completed their preparations for the expected battle. All knew that the Zulu army would heavily outnumber them.

For the attack against the Northern Column, Cetshwayo again gave command to Ntshingwayo kaMahole, the victor of Isandlwana. He was supported by Chief Mnyamana kaNgqengelele of the Buthelezi. The brutal lesson learned by the Zulus at Rorke's Drift had convinced Cetshwayo that the British force should not be attacked in an entrenched position; rather, they should be attacked on the move or between camps. Cetshwayo was also aware that his warriors were supremely confident and would relish the opportunity of attacking the British, and perchance force the invaders to retreat to Natal. He accordingly warned his warriors: 'Do not put your faces into the lair of the wild beasts for you are sure to get clawed.'[5]

The British position at Khambula was on the highest point of a long ridge that itself was overlooked by a far-off range of surrounding hills, known locally as Nqaba kaHawana (Hawana's place of refuge). It was an ideal position to defend as it dominated the immediate and lower surrounding area for more than half a mile. Only 3 miles from the camp was a forested area with abundant wood for campfires, and a number of fresh water springs around the camp led into streams that formed the headwaters of the White Mfolozi River. A rocky cliff protected the camp to the south and the flat terrace leading from the camp to the cliff was used as a cattle pen. The main headquarters of the camp was built on a small knoll or natural rise in the ridge, which was fortified with an earthwork redoubt. Immediately next to the redoubt was the main camp area, which consisted of two strongly entrenched wagon laagers.

Hardly slowing from the battle at Hlobane, the Zulu army had continued its march towards Khambula and spent the night 10 miles from the British position along the banks of the White Mfolozi River. Early the following morning they began their advance towards Khambula in five well-spaced columns. Towards midday, the whole Zulu army stopped to undergo their pre-battle purification rituals followed by an address from Chief Mnyamana. He gave a timely reminder to the regiments that the king's order was not to attack the British in an entrenched position; they were to seize the camp cattle, which would lure the soldiers away from their wagons and tents.

As at Isandlwana, the Zulus initially advanced on a front estimated by Wood to be 6 miles wide and they maintained the formation until it divided into the classic horns formation. The right horn, consisting of the uVe and iNgobamakhosi regiments, moved towards the north of the camp. The left horn, the uKhandempemvu, uMbonambi and uNokhenke regiments, were advancing from the south, and the main chest of the Zulu army slowed to take up position about 1 mile west of the redoubt. It is still a mystery why the Zulu commanders permitted the attack to take place against such a strongly fortified British position as it flew in the face of the king's orders. Zulu oral history recalls that the enthusiasm of the mass of young warriors overruled the orders of the commanders. They also believe that the Zulus interpreted the collapsing of the camp tents to give the British a better field of fire as an indication that the British were about to abandon their position. It was a defensive military procedure unknown to the Zulus.

The right horn approached from the north across open ground but remained well out of rifle range and then swung round towards the British position. To the south, the left horn ran into unexpected difficulties. Their approach to the camp followed the course of a stream, which was wet and marshy to both sides. Within moments, the leading warriors became bogged down in knee-deep mud and their advance stalled less than a mile from the camp. Chief Ntshingwayo's intention was for both horns to join up on the ridge, where it was level ground, and with the British surrounded, attack simultaneously – but each horn was still out of sight of the other. The right horn to the north presumed the left horn to the south had made matching progress and, by 1.30 pm, the right horn had advanced to within 800 yards of the British position, where they paused to regroup before their final attack. Seizing the opportunity, Wood ordered Buller to take about 100 of his mounted men to fire point-blank volleys into the packed ranks of the waiting uVe and iNgobamakhosi. Notwithstanding the appalling disaster of the previous day, these riders were well practised in the tactic of provocation and rode out to within 100 yards of the Zulus and fired several fast and deadly volleys into the packed ranks of chanting and stamping warriors. This action was too much for the Zulus, who immediately charged.

With shouts of 'We are the boys from Isandlwana!' the right horn raced towards the camp and into a firestorm from the artillery and a rapid series of violent close-range volleys. Some Zulus even managed to reach the outer line of wagons but eventually they were forced into an urgent retreat. Many British soldiers later wrote home in admiration of the Zulus' bravery. The Zulus made several gallant attempts to breach the British line but each attack was driven back by further close-range volleys, causing an even greater great loss to the Zulus. About a half-mile to the north of the camp was a rocky dip in the ground. The attacking Zulus withdrew to the protection of this cover and, apart from some desultory and inaccurate fire, they took no further part in the battle.

Being out of sight of the British position, the Zulu left horn was still largely unaware of the course of the raging battle and by the time they had cleared the marsh, the right horn was in full retreat. Wood turned his men's attention, and that of the 7-pounder guns, in the anticipated direction of the approaching left horn, which was now clambering up the hillside towards the British. The attacking Zulus began to mass within 100 yards of the camp cattle laager. At this point some of the uNokhenke broke through the camp's outer defence, which resulted in a brief hand-to-hand skirmish. Wood ordered a series of volleys into the advancing Zulus followed by a full-scale bayonet charge, which steadily drove them back from the close proximity of the camp.

The chest (the main massed ranks of the Zulu formation) – the uThulwana, iNdlondlo, iNdluyngwe, uDloko, iMbube, iSangqu and uDududu regiments – now mounted its first attack. The warriors initially advanced in good order to the rhythm of spears being beaten against shields, but soon took serious casualties from the sustained volleys of rifle fire and, like the right horn, they too fell back. The uVe and iNgobamakhosi made one final determined attack towards the redoubt but, once again, they were beaten off and sustained further serious casualties. The whole Zulu attack was now stalled and their main force made no further attempt to advance on the British camp. The Zulus were exhausted and by late afternoon they affected a mass withdrawal. Wood seized the opportunity to turn their withdrawal into a rout. He ordered the guns to fire canister shot into the retreating Zulus and unleashed his several hundred mounted irregular troops, all imbued with the indiscriminate spirit of revenge, to harass their withdrawal. Every Zulu caught was killed. The killing went on until darkness fell; only then did the slaughter cease.

Wood lost three officers and twenty-six NCOs and men killed or seriously wounded. It is probable that more than 500 Zulus were killed in the immediate area around the camp but it is more likely that twice as many again were slain along their line of retreat.[6] The battle had been decisive. The growing chronicle of British disasters in Zululand had stopped. They had the victory they desperately needed to obscure their awful loss at Hlobane just twenty-four hours earlier. King Cetshwayo knew his kingdom was doomed.

Chapter 12

The Zulu Defence of Ulundi, and the Prince Imperial Louis Napoleon

Following the Battle of Khambula, the Zulu capacity to mount a serious offensive against the British was broken. At the opposite end of the country, the Zulus had also been defeated at Gingindlovu and their total casualties since Isandlwana now numbered well in excess of 5,000 dead, with countless numbers wounded. All the strategic advantages that King Cetshwayo had won at Isandlwana were irretrievably lost and the tide of war now turned decisively against him. The king desperately tried to reopen diplomatic contacts with the British in a final attempt to discover what terms they would accept for peace. It was a futile gesture as both Chelmsford and Sir Bartle Frere needed a decisive military victory at Ulundi to avenge Isandlwana.

All the while, Cetshwayo watched helplessly as the three British columns moved inexorably towards his Zulu capital. Chelmsford believed the Zulus were now openly reluctant to gather round the king as they realized that their defeat was inevitable; Zulu folklore confirms Chelmsford's belief. The initial attempt in May to regroup the Zulu army had met with only partial success, perhaps due to a rumour that swept across Zululand that those warriors surrendering to the British would be castrated and their wives given to the soldiers. As the British advanced ever closer, greater numbers rallied to the king's call to arms. A number of Zulu chiefs were disillusioned with war and in anticipation of defeat, Prince Makwendu kaMpande, one of Cetshwayo's junior brothers, had already surrendered himself and his family to the British. He was later followed by Prince Dabulamanzi, the commander at Rorke's Drift, who along with Mavumengwana kaGodide, a commander at Isandlwana, established a diplomatic relationship with Chelmsford. More defections along the coastal regions were rumoured and some chiefs declared that they were unable to fight as their *imizi* were overcrowded with wounded. Cetshwayo called an urgent meeting of chiefs and all agreed to commence negotiations with the British – only to have them thwarted by Chelmsford.

Meanwhile, the end of May saw the Second Division assemble along the banks of the Ncome River near Koppie Alleen. They were joined on 31 May by Chelmsford and crossed the border into Zululand, as did Wood to his north. The reinvasion of Zululand now began in earnest. On 1 June, a number of Zulu scouting parties were discreetly shadowing Chelmsford's advancing column when one of them observed an isolated mounted British patrol in the process of making a midday coffee stop. The party had off-saddled at an isolated and deserted homestead belonging to a headman named Sobhuza. Accompanying the British patrol was a recently appointed civilian observer to Chelmsford's staff, the 22-year-old Prince Imperial of France, Louis Napoleon. The prince's position, specifically as a non-combatant, had been made with Queen Victoria's permission. Until that year, Louis Napoleon and his deposed father, Napoleon III, were both living in England as exiles from France.

Back in January, when the appalling news of Isandlwana reached a stunned Britain, many of Louis' friends from Woolwich had already secured appointments among the reinforcements being hurried to South Africa. Louis immediately asked permission to join them. For him, the war offered an ideal opportunity to see real action, without any of the political repercussions that might attend his participation in a conflict in Europe. Prime Minister Disraeli was aghast; permission was refused. Louis shamelessly used his mother, the Empress Eugénie, to use her influence with Queen Victoria, and he was allowed to go. His role was officially that of an observer. However, while the commander-in-chief, the Duke of Cambridge, asked Lord Chelmsford to find Louis a position on his staff, it was made clear that there could be no question of his exercising any authority within the British Army. The decision to allow Louis to travel to Zululand as an observer was undoubtedly a further burden to Lord Chelmsford, who by April 1879 was still struggling to turn the war in his favour.

On arriving at Chelmsford's headquarters, the young prince quickly frustrated those charged with his care. Even when attached to Lord Chelmsford's staff, he soon exasperated his senior officers, including Colonel Buller. Against orders he displayed a penchant for overenthusiastically giving chase to lone Zulu scouts, putting his own life, and that of others, at unnecessary risk. Accordingly, he was confined to camp, a serious disciplinary matter for any young officer. On the morning of 1 June, he had deviously persuaded his supervisory officer, Major Harrison, to overlook the restriction on his movement and allow him to accompany a small party about to depart camp for a routine sketching mission. With Harrison's blessing the party set off and two hours later they came across a seemingly abandoned Zulu homestead, where the party off-saddled. Coffee was brewed and the men relaxed. The safety of the group was left to a single scout who was instructed to watch the surrounding area, and who failed to notice an approaching Zulu scouting party.

The Zulus consisted of some thirty warriors formed from a combination of the iNgobamakhosi, uMbonambi and uNokhenke regiments, which coincidentally included one of the king's personal attendants, the warrior Mnukwa. The watching Zulus realized the British patrol was several miles from the advancing column and therefore highly vulnerable to a Zulu attack, especially as the scouting group seemed uncharacteristically relaxed and unaware of their approach. Seeing the riders taking their ease among the huts the Zulus decide to seize the opportunity and, using the cover of the ground, stealthily approached the unsuspecting party through the *kraal's* head-high mealie crop until, unobserved, they were able to get to within 30 feet of the dismounted riders.

Within a matter of moments the still unsuspecting British decided to move on. With the horses saddled the prince gave the order to mount. At this critical moment the Zulus fired a close-range volley at the mounting soldiers before charging among them. The startled patrol panicked and was put to flight. In the confusion every man sought to protect himself as best he could; two fell, mortally wounded.

As the Zulus opened fire on the patrol the prince desperately tried to mount his horse, but something was seriously wrong. He had always been regarded as one of Europe's eminent horsemen but he now failed to perform this routine but life-saving action. He fell heavily to the ground. Dazed, he managed to regain his feet as the Zulus closed around him. He ran towards a dried riverbed and turned to face the Zulus. He drew his revolver and fired several shots before a spear struck him in the thigh. The Prince withdrew the spear to use it as a weapon but the Zulus quickly overwhelmed him before spearing him to death. The Zulus may have realized that they had killed an officer as several warriors took the opportunity to traditionally 'blood' their spear blades in the prince's body; the seventeen stab wounds subsequently gave rise to the myth that, in death, the prince had bravely 'faced his foe'. The Zulus disembowelled the bodies and Mnukwa took the prince's sword. It would later be returned to Chelmsford as a peace offering before the British made their final attack on Ulundi.

The death of the Prince Imperial came as a severe blow to Chelmsford and the whole invasion force was stunned. The immeasurable shock waves reverberated through both the British and French nations and across the British Empire; the news even overshadowed Chelmsford's earlier disaster at Isandlwana.

In the military context, the prince's death amounted to little more than a regrettable scandal. It was an insignificant incident and had no bearing on the conduct or outcome of the campaign. The prince's body was returned to England for burial, firstly at Chislehurst and then later at Farnborough Abbey in Hampshire.

During the morning of 5 June, Wood's Flying Column saw its first action when a reconnaissance patrol of irregular cavalry chanced upon a large Zulu force occupying the base of eZungeni hill overlooking the Upoko River. The irregulars approached the Zulus and commenced sporadic fire into the Zulu position, whereupon the Zulus, vastly outnumbering the irregulars, retaliated by advancing on them in their classic horns attack formation. Realizing they were in peril of being surrounded, the irregulars rapidly retreated. The sound of firing alerted a nearby troop of 17th Lancers, who rushed to the scene. This would be the very first engagement in Zululand for the Lancers and all were 'keen as mustard' to bring further honour to the regiment by routing the Zulus.[1] Like many before them, the Lancers did not understand Zulu tactics and deployed using the classic cavalry tactic of charging in line. The Zulus may have been impressed, but were not intimidated, as the cavalry repeatedly swept past them in extended line and it was impossible for the Lancers to engage the Zulus. The rocky terrain was totally unsuitable for cavalry and the Zulus held their ground, taking casual pot-shots at the riders as they swept by. The regiment then took its first casualty when a Zulu marksman, using a Martin-Henry rifle, shot and killed Lieutenant Frith, the regiment's adjutant. The sudden and unexpected loss of this popular young officer brought the action to an abrupt halt and, carrying Frith's body with them, they returned to camp.

The column marched on to Mthonjaneni, only 17 miles from Ulundi.

Here, Chelmsford formed a strongly entrenched base camp, then, leaving his cumbersome wagon train and spare animals, he took the remainder of his force and marched on towards Ulundi. Now only the Emakosini Valley, the 'place of kings' and burial sites of Cetshwayo's ancestors, lay between Chelmsford's invasion force and the king's royal *ikhanda* at Ulundi. The site was guarded by several hundred warriors of the uNokhenke regiment who set fire to the memorial huts to prevent them falling into the hands of the British. Cetshwayo tried repeatedly to call a halt to the invasion but all his attempts were deliberately ignored by Chelmsford; only the final battle at Ulundi would satisfy the British. Zulu homesteads along the route of advance were burnt to the ground and their cattle driven back to the army slaughterers. On 26 June, a British force attacked along the Emakosini Valley, destroying royal homesteads. At one, esiKlebheni, they destroyed the *inkatha ye sizwe ya'kwaZulu*, the sacred coil of rope bound in python skin, which was said to embody the unity of the old Zulu kingdom from the time of King Shaka. It had been closely guarded by successive Zulu kings and its destruction was a serious omen to the king. The British also burnt every hut and village in sight and destroyed vast amounts of mealies. This attack cleared the path to the Mthonjaneni heights overlooking the White Mfolozi River; Ulundi was now visible through the smoky haze in the middle distance.

Still optimistic that he could halt the British, King Cetshwayo sent two of his royal envoys, Nkisimane and Mfunzi, to treat with Chelmsford. As a gesture, they brought with them the Prince Imperial's sword taken as booty from his body on 1 June. The envoys sought terms required for a Zulu surrender; Chelmsford informed them that he required the surrender of all British arms captured at Isandlwana and gave them until 3 July for the king's reply. Chelmsford knew full well that the king could not possibly comply with this ultimatum because the Martini-Henry rifles seized by the Zulus were now spread across the Zulu kingdom. Chelmsford continued his advance to the White Mfolozi River, where he consolidated his army's position and prepared his troops for the defeat of the Zulus. Chelmsford was under no illusion. He desperately needed the vindication for Isandlwana that this final battle would bring. Only then could he return to Britain with his reputation intact – but knowing full well he still had to answer to Parliament, the press and the public for his previous defeats and losses. Chelmsford was acutely aware of his predicament; only a victory at Ulundi would enable him to retire home with honour.

THE ZULU DEFENCE OF ULUNDI

King Cetshwayo was also in a delicate position. When the envoys, Nkisimane and Mfunzi, returned to brief the king, they were prevented by the king's own advisers from reporting back to him. Like Chelmsford, Cetshwayo and his advisers needed this battle; surrender to the British was not an option for the Zulu king. He knew he must suffer a military defeat in order to retain his credibility and bargaining position after the battle.

Late on 3 July, Cetshwayo attempted one last call for peace. As a desperate gesture he sent a herd of his finest cattle towards Chelmsford's camp but the warriors guarding the river, the uKhandempemvu, indignantly sent them back. They wanted to fight the British invader.

Chapter 13

The Battle of kwaNodwengu–Ulundi, 4 July 1879

It was from King Cetshwayo's dusty and impoverished capital at Ulundi that Britain's sophisticated political and military domination across South Africa had been so suddenly and seriously challenged. Situated on the Mahlabatini Plain, just 55 miles from the site of the inconceivable Zulu victory over Lord Chelmsford's force at Isandlwana, Ulundi consisted of an estimated 1,500 huts spread over an area later measured to be no more than 90 acres in total, with the king's personal quarters, the *ikhanda*, located centrally. Another nine *amakhanda* were located within 2 miles of Ulundi. Movement through Ulundi was via a labyrinth of passageways radiating out from the royal household, which dominated the capital. During the three weeks leading up to 4 July, the population of Ulundi had swollen by the influx of some 20,000 warriors responding to the king's call to resist the British invasion. Now, most of the women, children and other non-combatants had begun to move away towards the protection of the surrounding hills to the north and east. Carrying their bundled possessions, they clogged the tracks through the bush in their desperation to escape the unknown consequences of the forthcoming battle. Cetshwayo was still at a loss to understand why his country had been invaded, and why his capital was being approached by a British force with the obvious intention of destroying everything he stood for. All his pleas to treat had been refused or ignored; he could only surrender or fight. He chose to fight, knowing it was the only option his people would understand and that, in the longer term, his defeat was necessary to rid his country of the British.

On 3 July, Chelmsford despatched Colonel Buller with a strong force of some 500 mounted men. His main objective was to reconnoitre the terrain and locate a suitable site for the final battle and to ascertain the Zulu dispositions. The Mahlabatini Plain, with Ulundi and its vastly sprawling conglomeration of hundreds of huts at its hub, stretched between two distant ranges of hills, and Buller was especially interested in a small rise just 2 miles from the king's homestead. It would make an ideal defensive position. As Buller approached the grassy plain he detached sixty men of the Transvaal Rangers under Commandant Raaf to serve as a rearguard.

The Zulus had already anticipated such a move. Buller was led into a carefully prepared ambush near the Mbilane stream when a party of concealed Zulu scouts suddenly appeared from the waist-high grass about 200 yards from Buller's riders and then ran off towards the king's homestead. True to form, Buller's men gave chase. Buller's ADC (*aide-de-camp*, or adjutant), Captain Sir Thomas Fermour-Hesketh, shouted out that he saw another body of Zulus hiding in the grass ahead. Buller ordered his men to halt and, as they reined in, some 4,000 Zulus, under the command of Chief Zibhebhu, rose up around them. The Zulu trap had been sprung, albeit prematurely. The Zulus had plaited and woven grass into a series of ropes specially designed to trip the horses when they were rapidly pulled tight. Buller's men managed to extricate themselves before the ropes could entrap them but the flanks of Zulus were already rushing to surround Buller's men. Another group of Zulus armed with captured Martini-Henry rifles then fired a volley from about 50 yards distance, which inflicted some casualties and panicked several of the horses.

Buller's men were forced to ride for their lives and near the kwaNodwengu homestead they were reinforced by Raaf's men who poured volleys into the pursuing Zulus. The fleeing riders managed to re-cross the river to the safety of Chelmsford's advance camp, later named Fort Nolela, and the Zulus withdrew. For the soldiers about to go into battle, the level of the Zulus' spirited attack left them in no doubt that the following day was not to be a foregone conclusion. That night, the Zulu army completed its noisy and ritual preparations for battle, which added to the anxiety of the British; few slept. It is known that King Cetshwayo departed from Ulundi just before dawn.

At 4.00 am on the morning of 4 July, Chelmsford's 5,000 sleeping men were roused from their fitful sleep and, as dawn broke at 6.00 am, they set off in one column to march the final 3 miles to Ulundi. It was the largest force deployed by Chelmsford for any battle during the Zulu War. At 6.45 am, and unopposed by the Zulus, this cumbersome force waded across the shallow White Mfolozi River and then, in a tightly packed column, marched towards the previously reconnoitred small rise in the middle of the Mahlabatini Plain. The unwieldy column enclosed Chelmsford's headquarters staff, the spare ammunition and entrenching tool carts, as well as the Royal Artillery's guns, although these were positioned so as to enable them to come into action on each face without delay. With the sprawl of huts that was Ulundi now in view less than 2 miles distant, the Zulus could be seen forming up in opposition to the advancing column. Visibility over the Zulu army's position was still partially obscured by drifting smoke from a thousand Zulu camp fires and from the early morning mist hanging over the Mbilane stream that wound its way between the two armies. Many thousands of Zulus could also be seen assembling on the more distant hilltops to the north. Chelmsford ordered the advancing British column to 'form square', which it did, turning slowly and menacingly to face the advancing Zulus. A few minutes later, the British gained the high ground they sought and settled down to await the expected Zulu attack.

The assembled Zulu army was to the north and east of the square and totalled more than 15,000 men, with another 5,000 along the hills in reserve. All were formed up in regimental order and began to advance steadily for their first attack. Just as Chelmsford had anticipated, the Zulus were relying on their traditional attack formation and their horns, or flanks, began to encircle the square. All the Zulu regiments that had fought the earlier battles of the war were present and command at Ulundi appears to have been shared between Chiefs Mnyamana, Buthelezi, Ziwedu and Ntshingwayo – the victor of Isandlwana – while the vigorous Chief Zibhebhu of the Mandlakazi commanded the left horn. A captured Zulu prisoner commented:

> All the army was present today. We had very sick hearts in
> the fight when we saw how strong the white army was, and
> we were startled by the number of horsemen.[1]

The Zulu advance slowed down as it approached the square. Chelmsford wrongly presumed that this indicated a reluctance to fight but, instead, the Zulus were manoeuvring from their traditional irregular lines into well-ordered formations, with just several hundred skirmishers in the lead. At 8.20 am, Buller and his mounted troops moved out of the square. Using Buller's proven tactic of provocation, they rode to within 100 yards of the massed Zulu force and raked its leading ranks with several volleys of rifle fire. This blatant and bloody taunt enraged the Zulus, who charged. Buller and his men rapidly withdrew into the relative safety of the square, which enabled the artillery and riflemen to commence volley fire. The men forming the square were prepared for the imminent onslaught and the infantry were lined up in four ranks, two kneeling and two standing, with the artillery pieces and Gatling guns sited at the corners of the square and in the centres of the four sides.

Battle commenced at about 8.45 am, with the mounted men on the right and left of the square the first to be committed. The most determined Zulu attack came from the left horn under the command of Chief Zibhebhu. For a period of twenty minutes the British rate of fire was so steady and accurate that the Zulus were unable to get close enough to inflict any serious damage upon the British line. Chelmsford was especially pleased with the behaviour of the infantry, who were mostly inexperienced replacements and until now relatively untried. The men were steady and their firing was well controlled on all sides of the square. Volley firing by sections was employed throughout the battle, although on several occasions it was necessary to wait between volleys for the volley smoke to clear. For their part, the Zulus were unable to inflict much damage to the British square even though they possessed several hundred Martini-Henry rifles taken from Isandlwana. Their usual firearms, a collection of antiquated flintlock and percussion rifles, were never a threat to the British, although Chelmsford was prepared and ready for considerable casualties.

At about 9.00 am, the Zulus were becoming disorganized by their severe and escalating losses and their enthusiasm to attack the British wall of fire began to wane. They nevertheless stood their ground in the face of overwhelming firepower; repeated Martini-Henry volleys, the barrage from the Royal Artillery's 7- and 9-pounder guns and from the column's two Gatling guns wreaked havoc. Most non-Zulu historians state that the Battle of Ulundi was a half-hearted resistance by the Zulu army. To the contrary, it was a fiercely fought battle with a number of Zulus managing to get to within 30 yards of the British line. But, under such a noisy barrage of rifle and machine gun fire, and bombarded by the artillery, they could not properly see the British line through the smoke and lost their cohesion as a fighting force. With the Zulu attack unable to break through the British line, the attack began to falter. It was evident to the British that the Zulus were being beaten. Under a hail of bullets many warriors took what cover they could in the long grass and some brave individuals crawled back towards the soldiers to return fire. Interestingly, even with controlled volleys, the Zulu casualty rate for fatalities was only 10 per cent effective at 250 yards, while at point-blank range it was less than 15 per cent.[1] Large numbers began to leave the battlefield and this only served to weaken the resolve of those further back and previously keen to engage the British. With the Zulu attack controlled, Chelmsford again sought to inflict the maximum number of casualties upon the Zulus and, as at Khambula and Gingindlovu, he ordered Buller and his mounted troops, along with the 17th Lancers, out of the square to harass the retreating Zulus.

The Lancers attacked with great enthusiasm. They were still smarting from their previous failed clash against the Zulus when they lost their adjutant, Lieutenant Frith. This time they could charge across open country and they fell upon the Zulus, showing no mercy as they speared and hacked at the fleeing and wounded warriors.

Chelmsford's mounted irregulars then joined the slaughter and, being mindful of the massacre of their colleagues at Isandlwana, trotted among the scattering Zulus, shooting them with impunity. One of the Edendale troop was seen to shoot and wound a warrior and then set about questioning him. Having got the answers he sought, the trooper shot the warrior dead.[2] Many warriors lay down in the grass in the hope of escape knowing that they would be out of range of the riders' swords but once the immediate area around the square was secured, the Native Contingent was released to kill any wounded or hiding Zulus. The horror of indiscriminate killing continued for another two hours and extended for several miles in all directions until the fleeing Zulus had either escaped or been killed. The Zulu reserves that had occupied the slopes of the surrounding hills were beyond the reach of the cavalry so the 9-pounder guns were moved from the rear and front faces of the square to shell them.

It was immediately clear to the men forming the square that the victory had been a decisive one. As soon as the last groups of Zulus had been forced back over the hills Chelmsford ordered the destruction by shellfire of King Cetshwayo's royal *ikhanda*. The final set piece battle of the Zulu war had lasted just forty minutes.

The wide-ranging patrols of Lancers began to set fire to the surrounding royal homesteads while others, including Bengough's NNC, continued to track down wounded and hiding Zulus. The ongoing sound of sporadic gunfire evidenced the hunt and execution. The British ransacked the king's huts and then set fire to Ulundi; those looking for treasure were disappointed for there was nothing of value to loot. All the while, the cavalry routed the fleeing Zulus for another hour, killing every warrior they could find. Only two Zulu prisoners were taken that day.[3]

All mounted troops were then recalled to the square, but not before they had killed about 1,500 Zulu warriors. As was usual following a successful battle, Chelmsford addressed his gathered men and thanked them for their efforts. The entire force then about-turned and with Ulundi now well ablaze, marched back towards the White Mfolozi River with the band playing *Rule Britannia*, followed by the *Royal Alliance March*. They passed the battlefield and its glinting heaps of expended ammunition cases – later estimated to have amounted to more than 35,000 rounds of Martini-Henry ammunition. By the evening, the might of the Zulu army had been shattered. As Bishop John William Colenso would later write, it was 'a bloody but barren victory'. W.E. Gladstone summed up the war as being 'the death of 10,000 Zulus … defending their hearths and homes'.[4]

Chapter 14

Beginning of the End

Although the British presumed the Zulu War was over, they were still seriously engaged in operations to the north of the country. Peace would not reach the Ncombe River Zulus for another two months. Even though the Zulu army remained a formidable force, the British troops that had invaded Zululand and destroyed Ulundi had finally made their point; Britain would always be victorious in the end. The troops then marched out of Zululand and left its people, particularly those whose wasted homes and livelihoods had the misfortune to have been along the invasion route, to their fate.

The war had cost the British seventy-six officers and 1,007 men killed, plus a similar number of black Natal auxiliaries. A further seventeen officers and 330 men had died of disease and ninety-nine officers and 1,286 men were invalided through injury away from the campaign. Exact figures for Zulu losses are impossible to assess; they certainly lost 10,000 warriors killed in action throughout the war and conservative estimates suggest a similar number died from their injuries.

Chelmsford had no intention of chasing after King Cetshwayo. Capturing the king and restoring normality to Zululand would be thankless tasks that would occupy Wolseley, his recently arrived successor, for many weeks, if not months. Chelmsford was fully aware that before Wolseley could report anything detrimental about him, he would already be back in London with Ulundi being portrayed by his staff as a brilliant victory. The glory would be his to enjoy. Chelmsford sailed home on the RMS *German* in the company of Wood and Buller, his most effective and reliable commanders, although both had earlier confided to Wolseley that they objected strongly to Chelmsford's strengthening suggestions that they bore much responsibility for the war.

At Ulundi there was no clearing of the battlefield and for many weeks only deserted and smouldering villages evidenced the once thriving heart of the Zulu nation. The dead bodies of slain Zulus remained where they had fallen and these were left to predators or to rot and shrivel in the sun. The

British roughly estimated that not less than 1,500 Zulus had died in the battle for Ulundi while Buller suggested that his mounted men increased the death toll by yet another 500 during the far-ranging Zulu rout.[1]

On 19 July, Wolseley addressed a gathering of some 250 Zulu chiefs and laid out his plan for the division of Zululand. It was with a degree of caution that Wolseley prepared to enforce a strict settlement on the defeated Zulus. He was fully aware that the British invasion force was exhausted and too widely spread out across Zululand to consider further hostilities. Shrewdly, he promised the Zulu chiefs that they could retain their positions, subject to their warriors surrendering any royal cattle in their care and laying down their weapons. Wolseley informed the chiefs that:

> I am glad to see them because their coming here shows that they wish for peace, as the great queen does in whose name I speak. We have been at war with Cetshwayo, not with his people. We have beaten the king and burned his *kraal*. He is a fugitive in the bush, and shall never again rule in this land.

The Zulu chiefs must have been mystified by the statement as, until they were attacked by the British, they had been at peace. Nevertheless, the chiefs accepted.

Wolseley wrote an illuminating but chilling entry in his diary that sums up his approach to the Zulus:

> Perhaps I am brutal but I think it important to punish these northern tribes severely as a warning to all others in South Africa as to what they may expect should they ever be fools enough to consider waging war on the English. Up to the present, beyond shooting and wounding 10,000 men, we have not punished the people as a nation, and our leniency in now allowing all the people to return to their *kraals*, retaining all their cattle, may possibly be mistaken for fear. I should like to let loose the Swazis [traditional enemy of the Zulus] upon these northern tribes at once, but I have to think of the howling societies at home who have sympathy with all black men.

But the main prize for Wolseley, King Cetshwayo, was still missing, although it could only be a matter of time before he was found and captured. To discourage the Zulus hiding their king, Wolseley gave orders for the searching troops to burn *kraals* and carry off cattle in any area where the king was suspected to be hiding. Parties of mounted troops had been sent into the furthest corners of Zululand to find the king with authority to freely engage in brutality to gain information. In one savage act, soldiers interrogated Chief Mpopha of the Hlabisa clan. He was first knocked to the ground and then questioned by soldiers using red-hot coals, a tactic that paid off.[2] It was not long before troops, led by Major Marter, discovered the king's former friend Mnyamana, who betrayed him by warning the British that the king was hiding at a location in the Ngome Forest. On 28 August, the king was tracked down to a remote village by Marter. There was little the king could do. After a few minutes' conversation, he quietly gave himself up. Marter treated his prisoner with dignity although two of the king's servants were shot when they tried to escape. A tent was provided for him and his wives, and the 60th Rifles mounted a guard over it. For two days he remained in camp while transport was arranged. Colonel Clarke gave responsibility for interpreting between himself and the royal party to Lieutenant Harford, a fluent Zulu speaker.

With so many bands of Zulus left wandering about the country, the potential for a resumption of conflict, albeit on a small scale, continued to smoulder. Indeed, neither the loss of the battle nor the burning of Ulundi was particularly significant to the Zulus. Ulundi could have been rebuilt quickly and the northern abaQulusi remained bitterly opposed to any suggestion of surrender. On 24 August, Wolseley learned that the abaQulusi intended to continue opposing the remaining British. While he was considering this new threat, the fugitive Cetshwayo ordered all Zulus, including the abaQulusi, to surrender. He knew that otherwise the war would have continued. Once the remaining groups of Zulus heard that the king had been captured, most sought to make peace. The remnants under Chief Manyanyoba also sought to give themselves up but their attempt to surrender coincided with an order from Wolseley to a local commander, The Hon. Colonel Villiers, that he should 'clear Manyanyoba out', and on Villiers' orders, troops under Colonel Black marched out to Manyanyoba's stronghold overlooking the Ntombe River, where a group of warriors promptly surrendered. The troops then advanced towards a number of caves where the remaining warriors, women, children and animals were hiding. Unfortunately, one of the warriors in a cave inadvertently discharged his rifle, whereupon the warriors who had just surrendered were immediately slaughtered by their guards, who suspected a trap. The surrender of Manyanyoba and his people came to a halt and the troops marched back to camp.

On 31 August, King Cetshwayo was brought by cart to Wolseley's camp overlooking the scarred remains of Ulundi. After Cetshwayo alighted from the cart, his terrified wives hung on to him believing he was doomed to immediate execution. He strode in with the aid of his long stick, with a proud and dignified air and grace, looking every inch a warrior. He wore his grand *umutcha* of leopard skin and tails, with lion's teeth and claw charms around his neck. Well over 6 feet, fat but not corpulent, with a stern air to him, he looked what he was – a proud ruler. Arrogant as ever, and not to be outdone, Wolseley declined to meet with the king, merely sending him a message that he would remain a captive of the British. At that, the king's resolve left him and he was seen to crumple dejectedly. After that, the royal party were driven in a mule wagon to the coast via kwaMagwaza and St Paul's. In charge of the party were Lieutenants Poole and Harford, with a mounted escort. From the coast he was embarked on the steamer *Natal* and exiled to the Cape.

On a very hot 1 September 1879, 200 of the most senior Zulu dignitaries and chiefs were summoned to the newly established British headquarters at Ulundi, where Wolseley addressed them concerning the fate of Zululand. Through his interpreter, John Shepstone, the gathered assembly was brusquely informed that their captured king was being sent into exile at the Cape and would never be permitted to return to Zululand. They were then informed that Zululand was to be divided into thirteen independent chiefdoms, each ruled by a Zulu chief selected and appointed by the British, with each chief to have command under the overall supervision of a British administrator.

Without exception, the thirteen new chiefs were men who had either fought for the British or had deserted Cetshwayo prior to his capture. Without the support of the people, none would be able to exercise much control. Chiefs were appointed with the deliberate intention of creating political disharmony and rivalry. One of the chiefs was a complete outsider, appointed in recognition of his service to the British by providing mercenaries for the Natal government. A Sotho chief, Faku, was appointed chief of the district near Rorke's Drift, previously dominated by Chief Sihayo. On appointment, Faku ordered Sihayo to leave his district, together with his son Mehlokazulu. Chief Mnyamana, Cetshwayo's senior councillor, was offered a territory but refused to accept it – whether out of loyalty to his exiled king or because he was going to be given a tract of country that, though amply large enough for his extensive following, did not include one-third of the section of land where his people were situated. Mnyamana knew that this extensive tract of his own northern area, the land of the abaQulusi, was to be allocated to Chief Hamu. This settlement was Hamu's reward for defecting to Colonel Wood's Northern Column during the campaign. For these reasons Mnyamana refused to sign the paper as he did not see his way to govern a people that were unlikely to respect him as their chief. The remainder of Mnyamana's chiefdom was therefore given to Ntshingwayo and, in consequence, the second most powerful man in Zululand after Cetshwayo was excluded from the settlement. Ntshingwayo in turn was reluctant to accept the district because it contained so many Buthelezi and Mdlalose people, as well as another chief's (Sekethwayo's) personal homestead. Sekethwayo was appointed over a district further to the west.

Only four of these carefully selected chiefs were present at the meeting. All those present signed an agreement that they would variously respect their new boundaries, abolish the formal Zulu military system, and not obstruct any of their people who might wish to work in neighbouring territories. As was generally expected, John Dunn was awarded the largest and most influential chieftainship in Zululand, along the border with Natal, in return for his loyal services to the British during the campaign. The Zulus were absolutely forbidden to import firearms or become involved in any form of trade that did not reach them through British-controlled Natal or the Transvaal. Capital punishment without trial was also forbidden, land could not be sold or purchased without British permission, and they were to keep the peace and apply the law according to the 'ancient laws and customs' of their people, as long as these laws did not offend the sensitivities of the British administrator.

Meanwhile, King Sekhukhuni of the Pedi people had proved to be an able and determined ruler whose domain lay just to the north of Zululand, south of the Limpopo River and near the Boer settlement at Lydenburg in the Transvaal. By the 1870s, Sekhukhuni possessed an army whose military strength was widely considered to be second only to that of the Zulus. Unaffected by the Zulu campaign, they remained a large and powerful independent African kingdom and had an unbroken record of resistance to both Boer and British intervention. Sekhukhuni was fiercely opposed to any

European settlement yet, unlike King Cetshwayo of the Zulus, he was pragmatic enough to take advantage of the economic changes that swept across southern Africa in the wake of the discovery of diamonds at Kimberley in the late 1860s. As recently as 1878, the Pedi had routed a full-scale British expedition against them led by Colonel Rowlands VC. Still nurturing his resentment for having missed the opportunity of defeating the Zulus at Ulundi, Wolseley remembered that an equally glittering prize was still there for the taking – defeating Sekhukhuni. Wolseley knew it was his overriding duty to impose order on British possessions in southern Africa without embarking on the expense or risk of another unnecessary war. Nevertheless, the resolution of the Pedi problem could now be elevated to one of major military significance, which would give Wolseley an easy victory to complete the war's 'unfinished business'. While Wolseley professed to hope that the utter humiliation vented upon Cetshwayo might have been enough to reduce Sekhukhuni into submission, the reverse seems to have been the case, with his Pedi people preparing instead for a last-ditch stand for fear that the fate of the Zulus might befall them. By the beginning of October the die was cast. Wolseley's excuse, if he needed one, was that the belligerent Sekhukhuni continued to threaten British interests and, better still, it was Chelmsford who had failed to remove him.

Wolseley marched his troops north from Zululand. Many of the soldiers were still recovering from their war against the Zulus so Wolseley called on the Swazi to assist. The end of the Zulu War had left the Swazi kingdom in a vulnerable position, its leaders having vacillated throughout the campaign. Wolseley now offered them the chance of redemption. Having been reassured of British power, and still nurturing his own long–standing grievances against the Pedi, their leader, Mbandzeni, was only too pleased to comply. In October 1879 he assembled an army of more than 8,000 men from the royal Swazi regiments and sent it north to join the British. The following month, and with considerable ease, Wolseley overran the Pedi capital at Tsate but there was no sign of Sekhukhuni, who had already retired to a stronghold on the flanks of the nearby Leolu Mountains. During the battle, the Swazi played a crucial part in his success and were rewarded with permission to pillage, plunder and seize Pedi cattle at will. The king was captured a few days later. He was taken under guard to Wolseley's camp, and for the second time in a few short months Wolseley witnessed the sight of a once-proud and powerful African monarch brought as a prisoner before him. Like King Cetshwayo, the power of King Sekhukhuni was now broken. Later accounts reveal that the Swazi army created a positive impression among the British, which they were able to exploit for years to come. As MacLeod himself put it, 'To the British mind in general, Russians and Zulus are friends, Turks and Swazis are angels.'[3]

Meanwhile, the British troops returned to deal with Manyanyoba and on 5 September attempted to smoke the Zulus from their caves, without success. On 8 September, the troops returned and destroyed the caves with dynamite, notwithstanding that they were still sheltering many Zulus. On 22 September, Manyanyoba, unprepared to take further losses, surrendered to the British. He and his surviving followers were escorted to the Batshe Valley near Rorke's Drift, where they sought to settle.

At home the British nation cheered. The public welcomed home the worn-out regiments that had suffered greatly during the mismanaged campaign. There were plenty of heroes to fête and their names became known in every household. Queen Victoria, after years of refusing to involve herself in the nation's affairs, was pleased to pin decorations and orders on the fresh tunics of her brave soldiers and for several weeks the country enjoyed being proud of its army, until memories faded and fresh news succeeded old.

Meanwhile, public opinion at home had polarized against the war. Disraeli refused to receive Chelmsford, who had cost the country so much and brought discredit to the British Government. Some newspapers continued to pillory Chelmsford, popular songs mocked him, and even some of his fellow peers were critical. But it was those who really mattered, the Horse Guards and Queen Victoria, who rallied to his support. Chelmsford was showered with honours. His rank of lieutenant general was confirmed and the queen used her influence to have him appointed Lieutenant of the Tower.[4]

Chapter 15

Closure of the Zulu War

The *raison d'être* for the British invasion of Zululand was to overthrow the perceived barbarism of King Cetshwayo in order to protect the European population of Natal against the threat of an imminent Zulu invasion. Immediately following the Zulu victory at Isandlwana, Sir Bartle Frere wrote in a despatch dated 12 February, later published as a Parliamentary Paper:

> It has become painfully evident that the Zulu king has an army at his command, which could almost any day unexpectedly invade Natal, and, owing to the great extent of frontier and utter helplessness of the undisciplined hordes of Natal natives to offer effectual resistance, the Zulus might march at will through the country, devastating and murdering ...
>
> From every part of South Africa outside the colony, where the native races predominate, come the same reports of uneasiness and intended rising of the native race against the white man.

In reality, this was not as singular, or to the point, as it seemed. Beneath the veneer of this apparently laudable crusade lay more practical and commercial causes. These included the subjugation of the Zulu people in order to facilitate the British policy of confederation in South Africa – itself a smokescreen to allow European commercial interests, both in Natal and the diamond fields, which needed access to the Zulu workforce. Almost as important, Frere considered the defeat of the Zulu army as vital to protect the growing number of Boers settling in Zululand while, at the same time, it would confirm Britain's military invincibility to any potential adversary. It would also ensure the vainglorious Frere and Chelmsford honourable places in history. Nevertheless, from the British position, the war had been successful, enabling Wolseley to report:

> Zululand, having been conquered by us, according to Zulu law,
> really belongs to Her Majesty the Queen.[1]

His conquest would prove a curse for the Zulu people.

It still remains difficult to identify any legitimate reason for Britain going to war against the Zulus. Indeed, it was soon evident to the British people and government that the war had been a ghastly mistake. It is therefore not surprising that by March 1881, nearly two years after the war, even the defeated Zulu king struggled to find any justification for the war and while held prisoner at the Cape he dictated a letter to the governor, Sir Hercules Robinson, in an attempt to understand recent events. In his inimitable way, King Cetshwayo poignantly wrote:

> Mpande did you no wrong, I have done you no wrong, therefore you must have some other object in view in invading my land.[2]

That 'other object' continues to elude the historians who study the Zulu War and who still rely heavily or exclusively on the Zulu refusal to comply with the British ultimatum of December 1878 as the justification for war. Many historians' sources are invariably based on contemporary accounts that were highly subjective, purely because it was inevitable that they were written by surviving senior British officials and officers with important reputations to preserve; and with regard to the unexpected defeats, sufficient scapegoats abounded, some obligingly killed by the Zulus while loyally following their commanders' orders. Apart from private letters and reports from those involved, official military accounts of the day tended to rely on the official *Narrative of Field Operation,* but that narrative refrained from any allusion to controversy. Perhaps the most honest explanation can be credited to Laband and Thompson in their *Field Guide to the War in Zululand,* in which they state, 'There is still no general agreement on the causes of the Anglo-Zulu War,' although the sustained Boer migration into Zululand was clearly the precipitate cause of the war.

In 1879, the British Government and its operatives in Natal had succeeded in defeating and dividing the Zulu nation. In retrospect, Frere's justification for the Zulu War was widely accepted by the white population of Natal. Initially, the overriding and terrifying assumption that a bloodthirsty Zulu invasion of Natal was imminent, falsely promulgated by

Frere, can today be seen as little more than an official excuse for going to war. Understandably, Natal's European settlers took their pre-war cue from the British, who directly influenced the Natal newspapers to regard war against the Zulus as inevitable, yet there is evidence that few actually considered it desirable. However, once the war began, support for the official British line strengthened immeasurably. Frere's propaganda had been successful and the white population believed they had been spared an appalling fate at the hands of invading Zulu *impis*. More importantly, much money was to be made from supplying Chelmsford's army.

With Britain having deployed its full power and not a little malice against the Zulus, there were a number of influential people who resolutely believed from the outset that the war had been an unnecessary evil. Among them was the Bishop of Natal, John William Colenso, known to the Zulus as *'Sobantu'* ('Father of the People'). He preached to packed congregations that the Zulu nation under King Cetshwayo had presented no real threat to Natal. Nevertheless, diaries of the High Commissioner, Sir Bartle Frere, and the Secretary of State for Native Affairs in Natal, Sir Theophilus Shepstone, reveal they had deliberately provoked the conflict to further their wider ambitions for South African confederation. There can be little doubt that Colenso was right in his damning assessment that Isandlwana and all the other defiant battles were nothing more sinister than brave acts of self-defence by the Zulu king and his army against the invading British.

Tragedies abound in any war. King Cetshwayo's crime appears to have been his alleged attempt to rouse his country in the face of ever-increasing threats of invasion by Britain. Perhaps the most obvious tragedy in this war was the absence of any intention by the British to pursue their policy of confederation once the war was won. Instead, they withdrew from Zululand, leaving it ravaged and leaderless. Not satisfied with their victory at Ulundi, and all the death and destruction this brought to the Zulus, their victorious invasion force deliberately wasted the land along their lines of withdrawal. Wolseley then divided the country into thirteen chiefdoms and exiled the Zulu monarch to remove any form of national leadership. He then departed from Zululand, leaving the impoverished Zulus to their fate. Cetshwayo's relatives were treated even more harshly. In retaliation for the war, Wolseley had given instructions that members of the royal house should abandon their homes and move into Dunn's territory; it was an order that was simply ignored. Nevertheless, Wolseley had very effectively subjugated the Zulu nation and his hurried and hard-headed settlement satisfied the immediate needs of the home government in a moment of crisis. In less than two years, the overall situation in Zululand was doomed to deteriorate to such an extent that the Colonial Office would have to abandon the arrangement.

The growing unrest between the various Zulu chiefs would shortly become so serious that uncontrollable and appalling violence across Zululand would soon threaten British interests as well as the very structure of Natal. With the conjunction of these elements, the inevitable spectre of rebellion began to fester throughout the nation. It would shortly erupt into a decade of violence and civil war that would more effectively destroy the basis of Zulu royal power than the 1879 British invasion. British officials claimed that the ordinary people had retained possession of most of their land but by losing their king and their ability to raise an army, they lost both their identity and the means by which to defend themselves.

By the end of 1879, British policy for Zululand became aimless. The reason for this lack of purpose was clear. Circumstances had changed since the first invasion in January. Mainly due to ongoing adverse press reporting at home, Disraeli's government was on the verge of collapse as a direct consequence of the war, and with it went Britain's political enthusiasm for further colonial development or military adventures in southern Africa. Worse still, the setbacks experienced by Britain in the Zulu War had sent a clear message to her brooding adversaries, especially to the Boers in the Transvaal and Orange Free State. Even the Russians had woken up to Britain's vulnerability to Russian naval vessels, which could 'stand off' her ports in South Africa.[3] The reason was clear to all: if the British lion could be seriously mauled by an ill-equipped force of part-time warriors, a well-prepared and trained European force would undoubtedly fare even better.

British policy in Zululand floundered on. Defeating the Zulus was one thing, holding them down was another, so new laws were promulgated. Across Zululand capital punishment without trial was forbidden, land could not be sold, traded or purchased without British permission and the chiefs were to keep the peace and apply the law according to the 'ancient laws and customs' of their people, so long as these laws did not offend the sensitivities of the British administrator, although, for some weeks, no one could be found to accept this poisoned chalice. In October, a Mr Wheelwright was appointed to the civilian position of British Resident in Zululand, a post that attracted an annual salary of £600, plus an expense account of £100. He was tasked with the role of being the 'eyes and ears' of the British Government and to monitor the thirteen chiefs. He had no voice or power, the position lacked any credibility and this thankless task soon proved impossible. He resigned.

Melmoth Osborn, the senior official in the Natal civil service and close friend of Theophilus Shepstone, was currently serving in the Transvaal and was persuaded to accept the task. He was duly appointed as the British Resident Administrator of Zululand. He too was soon to discover that the position lacked any real authority other than to offer advice to the new chiefs and to oversee them if it appeared that they were acting beyond the terms of their appointments. Wolseley endeavoured to clarify his policy when he wrote:

> I have been careful to make it clear that we intend to exercise no administrative authority over the country, and that we wish to disturb the existing conditions of life and government only where, as in the cases of the military system and the barbarous practices of witchcraft, these conditions were irreconcilable with the safety of British subjects of South Africa, or with the peace and prosperity of the country itself.[4]

The British invasion of Zululand had severely disrupted the Zulus' economic structure and caused massive loss of life. Now the post-war settlement was deliberately designed to keep the Zulu people in disarray while their military defeat would ensure the destruction of their political system. Wolseley knew only too well that over several decades, the Zulu royal house had inextricably penetrated all aspects of civilian social life to the extent that King Cetshwayo, through his previously loyal chiefs, had exercised total control over the Zulu people. Now there would be no control. By their military defeat and the removal of their king into exile, they also suffered total destruction of their political system, added to which, the population had to focus on more pressing problems of preventing starvation and re-planting for the coming season. The inevitable result of Wolseley's deliberately unreasonable settlement saw Zululand slip inexorably into chaos, the country lacking leadership, control and supplies. Within months, Zulu fought against Zulu as the new borders of the country and individual chiefdoms indiscriminately cut across both the social and political groupings that had developed during the previous fifty years.

To give his draconian plan the cloak of respectability and to remove any ambiguity, Wolseley appointed a second boundary commission in 1881 to clarify two outstanding issues. A new external border of Zululand was required, where possible following natural physical features, and to demarcate the thirteen internal boundaries or minor kingdoms. The northern boundary of Zululand was to be moved southwards to the Phongolo River to exclude the abaQulusi and Emagazini people, together with most of Hamu and Mnyamana's people. In the north-east the new boundary would follow the Lubombo Mountains, and the former territory that was now excluded from the new Zululand would be given back to the Tongas. The Zulus' western boundary was extended to the benefit of the Transvaal.

The commission was further instructed to ignore Wolseley's earlier assurances that the Zulus would be left in full possession of their land. Many Zulus objected to chiefs being imposed upon them from other clans and protested by adopting a policy of non-cooperation. When the matter of further unrest was brought to Wolseley's attention, he instructed the Boundary Commission to inform the growing number of disaffected Zulus that they were free to move to another chief's territory, but the Zulu people were not unlike any other people. They were bonded to the districts where they had been born and which their ancestors had won by farming or warring. The Zulu people would only move from their districts as a last resort and were not prepared to move merely to satisfy white attempts at political or economic manipulation.

The Boundary Commissioners soon realized the problem of new boundaries and the imposition of unpopular chiefs was more serious than previously thought. They informed Wolseley that many of the appointed chiefs were unsuitable and that many disaffected Zulus were ignoring or resisting the new chiefs. Wolseley responded by disregarding that portion of their report. In due course, some of the settlement's more severe problems came to light; Wolseley merely responded by claiming the fault lay not in the settlement itself, but in the Zulus' unwillingness to follow the settlement. In reality, the new borders of the country and the boundaries of the chiefdoms ensured that established clan groupings were now placed under unsympathetic clan chiefs, and long-standing rival groups found themselves collectively under the same appointed chief. Adding fuel to the growing fire, Wolseley instructed the appointed chiefs to collect all outstanding royal cattle and firearms and deliver them to the British Resident. Of all Wolseley's diktats, this most irritated the Zulus; after all, cattle were virtually the currency of the Zulu economy. The king owned most of Zululand's cattle, which made him the most powerful man in the kingdom. His royal herds were easily recognized by their whiteness, indicating their belonging to the king. Due to their large number they were distributed through many royal households and represented not only the king's wealth, but also the livelihood and sustenance of the many ordinary people who tended the herds. Wolseley's instructions merely gave those newly appointed chiefs who felt sufficiently confident the legal opportunity to seize Cetshwayo's cattle and plunder from those Zulus who had previously been loyal to the king. This disruption quickly developed into a crippling and very destructive civil war and more Zulus died during the immediate period following the Zulu War than in the war itself.

Wolseley's harsh treatment of the Zulus began to create concern across Natal and eventually caused questions to be asked in the home parliament. Had there been a blood-thirsty army sitting on the Natal border, then British policy might have been understandable. As it was, the Zulu army had only responded to Chelmsford's invasion, itself engineered by Wolseley. Not satisfied with his pyrrhic victory, Wolseley ignored repeated Zulu pleas for justice and laid down severe terms for the 'settlement' of the defeated nation.

One such settlement decision would soon result in an intractable problem at the most senior level of Zulu society that would have a devastating effect on the kingdom's subsequent struggle for survival. During the war, Chief Zibhebhu had kept British patrols away from the main army on the last stage of the march to Isandlwana and then played a prominent part in the battle. Zibhebhu also commanded the Zulus who harassed British scouting and watering parties on their final approach to Ulundi, and his *impi* had very nearly trapped Buller's mounted men in a skirmish the day before the Battle of Ulundi. In the aftermath of the British victory, Zibhebhu had been appointed to his own area at Bangonomo in the north, from where he offered sanctuary to the fugitive Cetshwayo. Whether this was a genuine offer or an attempt to enable the British to capture the king is unknown. Knowing how devious his chief was, Cetshwayo declined the offer, though he nevertheless sent his 11-year-old son, Dinizulu, into Zibhebhu's care, along with many of the royal women and 100 head of cattle. Cetshwayo was distraught to learn that, on the arrival of his wives, they had been forcibly taken into Zibhebhu's *isiGodlo* – the ultimate insult to the king.

Wolseley's determination and confidence increased further once King Cetshwayo was imprisoned at Cape Town. Wolseley had very effectively subjugated the Zulu nation and his hurried and hard-headed settlement satisfied the immediate needs of the home government in a moment of crisis but, in less than two years, the overall situation in Zululand was doomed to deteriorate to such an extent that the Colonial Office would have to abandon the arrangement. The growing unrest would become so serious that uncontrollable violence on a wide scale would threaten British interests as well as the very structure of Natal. With the conjunction of these elements, the inevitable spectre of rebellion began to fester throughout the nation. It would soon erupt into a decade of violence and civil war that would more effectively destroy the basis of Zulu royal power than the original British invasion had. British officials claimed that the ordinary people had retained possession of most of their land. This is possibly true, but by losing their king and their ability to raise an army, they lost the means to defend Zululand. Natal settlers now greedily looked at Zululand for its fertile farmland and abundant labour force; the old Zulu order had finally collapsed.

But, unbeknown to the British, the debacle of the earlier Zulu war had a hidden and lethal sting in the tail. The war had convinced the watching Boer politicians and generals that the British army was not invincible. Encouraged by growing discontent against British interests throughout the Transvaal, the Boer community made secret preparations to resist further British influence. Only six months later they commenced military action against the British at Majuba. It was a conflict that brought early disasters to the British and developed into even bloodier campaigns – the two Boer wars.

The inevitable result of Wolseley's settlement on the Zulus was a crippling and very destructive civil war, by which the Zulus lost what little they had left from their lengthy resistance to the invasion. With so many bands of hungry and leaderless Zulus left wandering about the country, the potential for a resumption of conflict, albeit on a small scale, nevertheless continued to smoulder on. The Zulu people now subsisted in some distress, which gave added impetus to those who favoured the Zulu cause, such as Bishop Colenso, who had learned through rumours spread by Sir Theophilus Shepstone that Cetshwayo and his principle adviser, Mkhosana, had died in captivity. Under pressure from the bishop, the rumour was negated and Mkhosana was exchanged from his exile with the king's hairdresser, Dambuka. Mkhosana's release and return to Zululand enabled him to proclaim that the king was alive and well, which brought much cheer to the hard-pressed Zulus. Due to the bishop's intervention, Cetshwayo was moved from prison to an isolated farm on the Cape Flats, Oude Moulen, where he was able to receive visitors. Ever the shrewd diplomat, Cetshwayo used his interpreter to write numerous letters complaining about his unjust treatment. By keeping up a barrage of correspondence he began to bring his plight to notice beyond the Cape.

The unrest continued; the British responded by levying a hut tax and demanding that chiefs kept their areas under control. The result was uproar throughout the nation, which resulted in a petition being served on the authorities to return Cetshwayo so that he could re-establish a central civil authority. But the request was rejected. Shattered by the rejection, Cetshwayo's companion, the hairdresser Dambuka, Chief Mkhosana's replacement with Cetshwayo, hung himself. The effect of this suicide on the king was to bring on a bout of serious depression. This news even alarmed the home government, who feared the king might follow suit. They informed the Cape authorities that they should consider the king's future – but it would prove to be a long process.

Under the determined guidance of Bishop Colenso, Cetshwayo set about formally requesting permission to meet with Queen Victoria in order to outline his claim for reinstatement as King of Zululand. On 14 September 1881, permission for the visit was telegraphed to Sir Hercules Robinson, the High Commissioner in South Africa. However, the king's visit would be deliberately delayed by British officials in South Africa who were worried by the implications of his return to Zululand. Ever determined to reduce the king's influence with Zulu affairs, Shepstone began agitating for the partition of Zululand and accordingly wrote as Secretary of State for Native Affairs in Natal to his superiors that the north of Natal was suffering from the pressure of Zulus who had migrated into Natal 'being afraid of the past barbarism' of Zulu rule, and that they should be required to return to Zululand. Official British consensus at the Cape was different. They chose instead to give Chief Zibhebhu control over a vast swathe of northern Zululand, as this would effectively eliminate Cetshwayo on his inevitable return to Zululand from having any influence in the north. Under pressure from his own officials, and not a little from Zibhebhu, Sir Henry Bulwer prepared a plan to dissolve the thirteen chiefdoms before re-partitioning Zululand prior to the king's return. In the partitioning declaration, Zibhebhu would be given the area to the north of Zululand, the centre of the country would be 'earmarked' for Cetshwayo, while the south of the country would become a 'reserve' for those Zulus not wishing to live under either Cetshwayo or Zibhebhu.

Information began reaching officials that civil unrest across Zululand was likely if matters were not resolved. Cetshwayo had used Bishop Colenso to send a message to the Zulu people to go to Maritzburg to 'pray' for him; his request was unambiguous. The authorities only began take the threat seriously when they learned that a 2,000-strong force, including more than 500 chiefs and *izinDuna*, was being assembled for the march. The march crossed into Natal, an 'illegal' act in itself, and slowly headed for Maritzburg. Seriously alarmed at the thought of such a huge force descending on the town, the British sent officials to negotiate in the hope that the Zulus could be persuaded to return home. After considerable argument and vague promises, the Zulu deputation agreed to retreat. But Cetshwayo's plan had worked.

At last, Cetshwayo was given the news for which he had so long awaited – he was to go to England to plead his case. On 12 July 1882, Cetshwayo embarked on RMS *Arab* for London. Shepstone's son, Henrique, accompanied the king's party as interpreter. Cetshwayo arrived in London in early August and was enthusiastically received by crowds of curious Londoners. On 14 August 1882, King Cetshwayo formally met Queen Victoria at Osborne House on the Isle of Wight and, after returning to London, had further discussions with her officials – a remarkable feat for an illiterate man who did not speak more than a few words of English.[6]

Although Queen Victoria was wary of interfering with her government, she nevertheless urged her ministers to facilitate Cetshwayo's repatriation. In due course the king was returned to South Africa, where he arrived at Cape Town on 24 September. He was returned to Oude Moulen but was required to wait until 7 December for British permission for his return to Zululand before regaining the Zulu monarchy. The Natal authorities did everything they could to delay the king's return. Disease in Zululand was one excuse, but the reality was that they needed more time to reduce the area over which Cetshwayo would have control.

Meanwhile, in mid-1882 the authorities brought in a further hut tax, which was levied across British-controlled Natal as a means of raising revenue from Zulu migrant workers. The levy was fixed at fourteen shillings per hut – an exorbitant figure at the time. Further rules were circulated across Natal, which included a ban on black people using public transport. They were also forbidden alcohol and a night curfew was imposed. Working Zulus were now without any rights. However, this resulted in a huge crime wave. Illegal drinking dens and prostitution flourished – concepts previously unknown to the Zulus.

CLOSURE OF THE ZULU WAR

In August 1882, Sir Henry Bulwer was asked by the home government for an overview on the success of the settlement arrangements as rumours of mismanagement of the country had reached Parliament. Bulwer replied that any unrest was caused by an insignificant minority and added:

> The Zulu people, there is little doubt, would have gladly come under the rule of the British Government. They would have accepted that rule without question or misgiving. They would have accepted it for all reasons, not only because it was the rule of the government that had conquered them, but because they knew it to be a just and merciful rule. They say, The government conquered us, we belong to the government.[5]

In a note to Shepstone on 20 September, Bulwer wrote about Zibhebhu:

> either he will accept the fate and become our bitterest enemy, in which case we can look out for trouble, or he will resist Cetshwayo and we will have civil war.

When the permission finally came it was tempered by news that shocked the king; two large swathes of Zululand had already been disposed of under the terms of the partition. One was an area bordering Natal to be known as the Zulu Native Reserve under the control of John Dunn and Chief Hlubi, while the other area had been allocated to Chief Zibhebhu, a former rival of the king who would have control of Zululand to the north of the White Umfolozi River. This was contrary to the terms the king had accepted in London. Cetshwayo reluctantly signed the agreement and the following January he was permitted to return to Ulundi with the intention of rebuilding his shattered nation. He was re-installed at Emtonjaneni, where even more conditions were put upon him. Many thought these additional conditions were a deliberate trap to cause his downfall.[7]

Cetshwayo was re-installed as King of the Zulus in February 1883. Following the ceremony, the king, his wives and retainers returned to the Mahlabatini Plain with the intention of re-establishing his former capital at Ulundi. Within days numerous chiefs flocked to re-affirm their allegiance to the king. Notable by his absence was Zibhebhu and those chiefs under his influence.

Zululand remained in turmoil. With Cetshwayo sandwiched between his enemies to the north and British Natal to the south, and with the northern AbaQulusi rising in his support by laying waste to their enemies, he was required by the terms of his restoration to maintain peace across Zululand, and to this effect he sought help from Natal. It was refused. Due to the division of the country, another civil war was tragically born. Amidst the confusion of Zulu clans raiding other Zulu clans, and with chief set against chief, Cetshwayo's former general and cousin, Zibhebhu, Chief of the Mandhlakazi Zulus, began raiding and evicting any clan from the northern area who he felt was opposed to him. Unsurprisingly, chiefs loyal to the king decided to fight back and at the end of March they set out from Ulundi with an army of some 5,000 loyal warriors, many from the Usuthu. In typical fashion, they laid waste to any village through which they advanced, while Zibhebhu's army retreated. But Zibhebhu was pulling the invaders into a trap. The Usuthu failed to realize their predicament until too late. Zibhebhu's army closed in and swung behind the Usuthu, trapping them. A mass slaughter then commenced. Worse was to follow: Zibhebhu immediately pushed on into Cetshwayo's territory, with his warriors taking revenge by killing and plundering until, having forced marched for 40 miles, they were just a few miles from Ulundi. As dawn broke on 20 July, Zibhebhu's warriors could see the first movements stirring in the king's *ikhanda*. The only army expected at Ulundi was that of their own returning warriors. As reality dawned the alarm rang out and the remaining Usuthu rushed to form up in a defensive arc to protect the royal *ikhanda*. With their people fleeing for their lives, and without any direct orders, the Usuthu moved forward to the attack but were soon brought to a halt when it was realized Zibhebhu's force was overwhelming. The Usuthu turned and ran.

The Mandhlakazi routed Cetshwayo's force and destroyed the king's *ikhanda* by firing the huts and indiscriminately killing anyone left behind. The royalists were heavily defeated, losing more than 500 warriors. Some sixty of the most important chiefs loyal to King Cetshwayo were killed. They were gathered together and driven into a cattle *kraal* where, regardless of their stature, they were all slaughtered. Those killed included Ntshingwayo, who had commanded at Isandlwana and Khambula. Sihayo, whose sons had precipitated the British ultimatum, also died. Apart from firing the royal *ikhanda*, all of the king's property, including presents from Queen Victoria, flamboyant uniforms and trinkets, was seized and removed by Zibhebhu's men. The surviving Usuthu women and children were rounded up to be absorbed into the Mandhlakazi. Cetshwayo was just able to escape but was wounded when two of Zibhebhu's men threw spears at him without realizing who he was. Cetshwayo managed to bluff his way out of the predicament and, although wounded, was able to take refuge in a forest near the White Umfolozi River. Rumours soon began to spread across the Zulu nation that the king had been killed at Ulundi. Cetshwayo sought assistance from the British, who ignored his plight. Fearful of being captured by the Mandhlakazi search parties, Cetshwayo was forced to flee to Eshowe, where, on 17 October 1883, he sought protection from the British Resident Commissioner. Without doubt, the routing of King Cetshwayo by previously loyal Zulus at Ulundi on 21 July marked the final stages of the demise of the Zulu nation. In essence, a Zulu chief achieved everything that Lord Chelmsford had failed to achieve when he invaded Zululand in 1879.

King Cetshwayo died following a meal on 8 February 1884, probably poisoned by his own people. He had earlier been seen on a walk and appeared fit and well. Zulus were familiar with numerous form of poison that could be administered in beer or snuff, both of which were to the king's liking. Curiously, the king's staff on the day failed to raise the alarm for four hours. When the British doctor examined the body, he requested a post mortem, which was refused by the Zulu officials present – and there the matter closed.[8] To prevent his grave from becoming a future rallying point for Zulu dissenters, the king was buried in an isolated and beautiful part of the Nkandla Forest at Nkunzana, near the Mome Gorge.

Several months later, *The Medical Times* published a letter from a British doctor who had examined the king during his captivity:

> As ex-King Cetshwayo is stated to have died suddenly of fatty degeneration of the heart, it may interest readers to know what the state of his heart was in August 1882. In auscultation the heart sounds were absolutely normal and the appended sphymographic tracing will show the healthy state of the arterial system.

Both then and now, and without doubt, the Zulu people regarded Cetshwayo as a great king. Certainly he was highly intelligent and, following his capture by the British, he had impressed all those who met him, including Queen Victoria. It was his personal tragedy that his reign became enmeshed with white men's politics. History shows that he sought to live in peace with the whites. Cetshwayo's heir was his youngest son, Prince Dinizulu. His inheritance was a people riven by civil war, a country in ruins, villages and homesteads burnt to the ground and cattle and crops destroyed or plundered.

Poetically, when he returned to England Wolseley fared no better. Both the people and the government were by now unconvinced by his treatment of the Zulu people. *The Broad Arrow* journal publicly noted his quiet return and wondered whether to praise or condemn him. The usual public trimmings of glory were conspicuously absent although he received the Companion of the Bath, a decoration he had rejected four years earlier. It is most likely that this very public rebuff was due to the influence of those in high places who had actively protected Lord Chelmsford.

Chapter 16

Long Live the King

With King Cetshwayo dead, and with British encouragement, the two main Zulu chiefs in the northern part of Zululand, the hated Chief Zibhebhu of the Mandlakazi and Chief Hamu of the Ngenetsheni, set about trying to finally destroy their historical enemy, the Usutho. They commenced a series of vicious attacks, and on 30 March 1883, the two armies met in a full-scale battle. The Usutho were utterly defeated, and worse, they lost their leading ranks, which were slaughtered to a man. Even with the battle won, Zibhebhu never achieved total victory over the Usutho as the greater proportion of the tribe were able to retreat ahead of Zibhebhu's warriors to the safety of their caves, but were then subjected to siege tactics by Zibhebhu and a group of well-armed white bounty hunters and adventurers. Natal was unaffected by the human tragedy unfurling, being conveniently distant; the Usutho were soon starving. The disinterested British watched but did nothing to prevent the situation worsening. With the Zulu nation in deepest chaos, Natal and Boer settlers looked greedily at Zululand for its fertile farmland and abundant labour force. Not only had the old Zulu order finally collapsed, it was now open to plunder. Two Usutho chiefs, Mehlokazulu and Ndanankulu, cut off relations with the British in Natal and sought help from the Boers, who, seeing their opportunity, readily agreed. The Boers brought the young successor to King Cetshwayo, Prince Dinizulu, to safety in the Transvaal and on 21 May 1883, pronounced him King of the Zulus. The effect on the Usutho was dramatic: they abandoned their refuges and poured across the Transvaal border to offer allegiance to their new king. Refreshed and now backed by Boer firepower, the Usutho re-entered Zululand and advanced on the Mandlakazi of Zibhebhu, who retreated into the Lubombo hills.

With Boer assistance, the Usutho were about to reverse their fortunes and now had the Mandlakazi at their mercy; they were not to receive any. After a ferocious battle in which Boer firepower shattered the Mandlakazi, the victorious Usutho rounded up Mandlakazi survivors, including their

185

women and children, and banished them to the lands around Eshowe. The victory for the Usutho was sweet, until they were required to pay the Boers the high price they had been coerced to agree. The Boers required Dinizulu and his senior advisers, by threat of hangings or of being shot, to sign away a vast swathe of Zulu territory extending from the old 'disputed territory' of the 1870s into the heart of Zululand north of the Reserve, which included Chief Hamu's Ngenetsheni people. Dinizulu was appalled but was powerless to stop them. The Boers declared the area the Nieuwe Republiek (the New Republic). The site lay between the old 1879 battlefields of Hlobane and Khambula. The Boers immediately set about building a suitable capital for their government, calling it Vryheid (Freedom). Having totally reduced the Ngenetsheni to abject poverty, these starving people subjected themselves to the Boers as workers and tenants. With the Boers and British still acting malevolently towards them, the remaining Zulus were now trapped between two aggressive white powers.

Following a contrived scuffle in 1886, the Boers murdered Prince Dabulamanzi, the Zulu chief who had commanded at the Battle of Rorke's Drift. Negotiations between the British and Boers began and in 1887 the Cape Government took full control of Zululand and its affairs by annexing Zululand. One probable reason was British concern that Boer expansion towards the Indian Ocean would give the Boers a sea port that could threaten British interests in Natal. The proclamation was read to the Zulus at Eshowe. King Dinizulu and his chiefs were horrified and astonished by the proclamation's requirements. Dinizulu had never accepted the invasion of 1879 as an absolute defeat because, following Ulundi, the British had abandoned Zululand and its people to their fate. He now found that, not only had the British and the Boers stolen his country from under him, but the British – who now proclaimed jurisdiction over him – refused to accept his rightful status as Cetshwayo's heir. They preferred to lend their support to rival groups within the Zulu kingdom with the sole intention of undermining the residual influence of the Zulu royal house. In November 1887, the British allowed Prince Zibhebhu and his followers to return to northern Zululand from their exile in the Eshowe district in what can only be seen as a deliberate attempt to counterbalance support for Dinizulu.

Either by accident or design, Zibhebhu's homestead at Bangonomo was not far from Dinizulu's own settlement at Nongomo. Dinizulu was understandably furious at finding himself living so close to the man he considered responsible for the death of his father. Dinizulu assembled a large force of warriors at the stronghold of Ceza Mountain and, when the British sent armed police to order him to disperse, he chased them off. In fear of Dinizulu's army, Zibhebhu moved his own followers close to a British outpost at iVuna Hill, but on 23 June 1888, Dinizulu attacked them. Riding ahead of his men on horseback, Dinizulu, still only twenty years old, led a ferocious charge that scattered the Mandlakazi, all within sight of the British fort. Zibhebhu and the survivors fled. In an attempt to restore some order, the British immediately hurried troops into Zululand to confront the victorious Dinizulu, but then they suppressed him.

The policy of 'divide and rule' had fatally damaged Dinizulu's ability to resist, and where once the kingdom had presented a united front against the invasion of 1879, many influential Zulu figures now held back or sided with the British. Although the fighting spluttered on for several months, Dinizulu was never in a position to inflict the sort of defeats upon the British his father had done at Isandlwana and Hlobane, and after the dispersal of a royalist force at Hlopekhulu Mountain, near Ulundi, on 2 July 1888, Dinizulu and his uncles, Ndabuko and Shingana, fled to the Transvaal Republic. Worried the British might take retributive action against them, the Boers denied them sanctuary and instead the weary fugitives crossed into Natal and surrendered to the British colonial authorities.

Prince Dinizulu was detained on the grounds of causing 'public violence' and charges of high treason were eventually brought against him for allegedly supporting armed resistance against the British. Although no evidence was produced, the charge was 'determined resistance and attacks against Her Majesty's Forces led in person by Dinizulu'. Dinizulu and his uncles were tried for High Treason, found guilty, and all three were sentenced to varying periods of exile on the island of St Helena, which served as a British political prison. The royal party was allowed to take several wives with them; Dinizulu took with him two wives, Silomo and Zihlazile, and the British Government allowed a stipend for their maintenance. For the first time, apart from King Cetshwayo's brief time in England, members of the Zulu royal family were exposed to British culture, and Dinizulu in particular was still young enough to enjoy the experience. He learned to speak and write English, to wear Western clothes, and to play the piano. Queen Silomo bore him two sons on the island, Prince Solomon Nkayishana Maphumuza and Prince Arthur Edward Mshiyeni, while Queen Zihlazile bore him two sons, David Nyawana and Samuel Bhekelendaba, and a daughter, Victoria Mphaphu. For a second time in ten years, a Zulu king had to endure the humiliation of capture and exile. Meanwhile, unrest among the Zulu people stirred, even though they remained fully exposed to the consequences of conquest. The worst excesses they suffered were a complete lack of influence in their own administrative affairs, the denigration of their customs and beliefs, the expropriation of their lands and their enforced involvement at the lowest levels in the burgeoning settler industrial economy.

Again, but too late, the British tried to control the unrest spreading from Zululand. The native population across Natal was becoming increasingly unsettled so the authorities reacted by imposing another hut tax of fourteen shillings – or cattle in lieu. The Usutho let it be known that they would refuse to pay, and furthermore, severed the remaining ties with the British Resident Administrator of Zululand, Melmoth Osborn. When the dispirited Usutho began cattle-raiding those clans subservient to Osborn, he responded by dispatching British and local units of Natal Police. The result was a stalemate as the troops were unable to penetrate the thick bush country occupied by the Usutho and a truce resulted. The British responded by putting a track through the forest to prevent a reoccurrence of the Usutho protests and then strengthened their control by conducting retributive public hangings and savage thrashings, worsened by carrying out the thrashings in instalments.[1]

Under such British domination, the Zulu social structure virtually collapsed. Disease and a six-year famine severely damaged their ability to feed or re-establish themselves and by 1889 the forceful collection of the hated hut tax had left young men with no option but to take up six-month work contracts in the growing towns and cities of Natal. This again had a powerful negative effect on Zulu social life. This ongoing crisis was followed in 1897 by the rinderpest epidemic, a fatal cattle disease that had spread from Cape farms virtually destroying the Zulus' remaining cattle. And then, just as they began the long process of restocking, the deadly East Coast fever obliterated their fledgling herds. To compound Zulu woes, Natal's new governor, Sir Arthur Havelock, established a fresh committee to consider the opening up of Zululand to white settlers. They collectively agreed that nearly half of Zululand was to be taken from the Zulus. At the same time, a £1 tax was levied on all migrant workers who had previously evaded the hated hut tax.

The colonial government then brought in the Code of Native Law, which governed all Zulus, both in Natal and Zululand. Offences were itemized along with fixed penalties, and *lobola* rates were standardized. But in trying to control the Zulus, the authorities had overstretched their patience. Talk of rebellion fanned through the people. For the rural Zulus unaffected by the war, little changed; they maintained their traditional homesteads and customs and continued to respect their local chiefs.

In 1898, Dinizulu, widely accepted by the people as the Zulu king, was returned to Zululand but without any official standing; the British even refused to acknowledge his claim to being king. To suppress his authority further, the British appointed him to the position of regional adviser. This gave him a reasonable salary but subjected him to official control. Dinizulu then created a new homestead at Nongoma, in northern Zululand, called oSuthu – named after his fathers' loyal followers.

This move coincided with the outbreak across swathes of northern Natal of the Anglo-Boer War, yet the war had little impact on the Zulus who sought to maintain a degree of neutrality. In late 1899 and early 1900, the Boers put considerable pressure on both the British and Zulu leaders by advancing into Zululand to both Nquthu and Nkandla. Knowing they lacked the resources to deter the Boers, the British quietly and successfully encouraged Dinizulu to monitor Boer movements and report such activities to the British. The British gave tacit agreement to allowing Zulu chiefs in the areas involved to re-arm their warriors and on departing Zululand towards the end of 1900, the Zulus were further encouraged to enter the old New Republic to raid deserted farms; this activity met with some success though small guerrilla bands of Boers continued to raid into Zululand, looting Zulu livestock and attacking small British outposts.

In 1902, the authorities, probably due to the rise in warnings of a widespread Zulu rebellion in protest at so many public measures, created a land commission that divided Zululand into tracts of land. About half the country, nearly 4 million acres, was nominated specifically as reserves for use by the Zulus, but this half was the most unproductive and susceptible to cattle disease. The remaining 3 million acres was productive farmland and nominated for white use only. Much of this was then given over to recently introduced sugar cane plantations. The authorities swiftly moved the Zulu population into these unproductive areas but many resisted. Such people were classified as squatters and were duly evicted to the reserves. The Secretary of Native Affairs declared, rather flippantly, that the authorities could congratulate themselves as their natives were 'the best mannered and the best behaved, and the most law-abiding in South

Africa'.[2] Giving the best land to the white settlers seriously stunned the whole Zulu nation; the first murmurings of a peasant revolt began to spread. Rebellion was in the air.

In 1905, the authorities levied and enforced a new and prohibitive 'poll tax' on the native population across Zululand and Natal. The tax coincided with a total crop failure, caused by aphids, which was followed by a violent and destructive hailstorm – Zulu folklore recalls that these events were 'signs' that action must be taken against the white people's laws. The Zulus resisted paying the tax in increasing numbers until the authorities became alarmed. Matters came to a head on 7 February, when men of the Fuze clan demonstrated against tax collectors and killed two officials. The authorities reacted immediately by proclaiming martial law and dispatched a column under Colonel Duncan McKenzie to quell the disturbance with permission to use whatever force he deemed necessary. McKenzie's men raided the Fuze homestead and killed a number of Zulus deemed to be 'resisting', and captured another thirty. Following their trial, Whitehall confirmed the sentences. Twelve were shot by firing squad and three were hanged. McKenzie then toured northern Natal, middle and southern Zululand, raiding and destroying any *umutzi* suspected of supporting the rebels. His subordinate, Colonel Lechers, ordered the surrender of hundreds of men who had earlier demonstrated. When the surrendering process stalled, Lechers ordered their homestead be shelled. He was later to receive a knighthood.

The feared rebellion now took hold north of the Tugela River. The Zondi clan under their chief, Bambatha kaMancinza, attacked a police post at Kate's Drift, leaving four police dead, including their sergeant. Many hundreds of Zulus flocked to support Bambatha. They wore their tribal war accoutrements and more than a thousand warriors gathered in full war regalia, something the British has presumed was now a memory. Surrounding chiefs rallied to Bambatha's call and, using their local knowledge and King Cetshwayo's grave as a rallying point, attacked McKenzie's force. In a fit of pique, McKenzie ordered Cetshwayo's grave to be disturbed and burnt along with a number of neighbouring homesteads. McKenzie had numerous spies 'loyal' to the administration who reported that Bambatha would shortly be moving his force through the remote and densely wooded gorge at Mome. The gorge is several miles long, overlooked by rolling hills and, even today, thick with dense vegetation. Nevertheless, it could hide a number of *impis*. McKenzie closed in on the unsuspecting

Bambatha and positioned his artillery so that it could fire directly into the gorge. On McKenzie's order, the artillery opened fire causing huge casualties among the Zulus. Many tried to flee but ran into the prepared positions, where they were shot down in their hundreds. McKenzie's men had been issued with dum-dum bullets, which caused horrendous injuries to the fleeing Zulus, of which a total of 1,500 were killed, including Bambatha.[3] The fire of rebellion spread and more chiefs rallied to the protest. On instructions, McKenzie and his men undertook a murderous campaign killing anyone they chose, rebel or otherwise.

The campaign lasted nearly six months and involved 20,000 soldiers and men from police and militia units. By the end of the action, some 2,500 Zulus had been killed, with another 5,000 put in prison; the authorities lost twenty-five of their men. This time, no death sentences were issued but the alleged ringleaders were banished to St Helena. The remainder were given short sentences, which included flogging or mutilation. Dinizulu had been powerless and inactive throughout the rebellion. Although viewed by the Zulus as their king, to the British he was a mere *inDuna* and therefore insignificant. The authorities arrested him anyway and charged him with high treason – for allegedly harbouring the fugitive Bambatha – which carried the death sentence. His trial took place in November 1908 at Greytown, where most of the evidence against him came from Bambatha's wife, who admitted she had lived near Dinizulu. He was found 'not guilty' of the more serious charges but convicted of harbouring Bambatha during the rebellion, which he strenuously denied. He was taken to Pietermaritzburg Prison to serve a four-year term. In 1909, Louis Botha, a former Boer general, became prime minister of the new Union of South Africa, and in 1910, the colony of Natal became a province. Botha ordered Dinizulu's release. On leaving prison Dinizulu built himself a new homestead at oSuthu. Supplied with copious amounts of alcohol, he died in 1913.

In the same year, the Union Government passed the Natives' Land Act, which consolidated ownership of the best farmland in white hands and enforced the removal of those Africans already living on those lands who were surplus to the owner's labour requirements. The objectives of the Act were to officially segregate land ownership; it also had the effect of undermining the ability of rural Africans to be self-sufficient, leaving many of them with no alternative but to seek work in the burgeoning industries beyond Zululand.

Dinizulu was succeeded by his 20-year-old son, Solomon, who was the first Zulu king to have been raised a Christian. He was a quiet and easy-going man who preferred to dress in European clothes and enjoy the comforts of a Westernized lifestyle, although he remained deeply committed to his people and to the concept of the royal house. His position as king was officially denied by the government, which continued its long-established policy of hostility towards the royal house but would nonetheless continue to exploit it when it suited. Solomon was therefore required to conduct a delicate balancing act throughout his reign, attempting to assert a degree of autonomy in the face of an administration upon which he was dependent for both recognition and the paid stipend that went with it.

In order to restore order throughout Zululand, and to emphasize the controlling influence of the Zulu royal family, Solomon created new *amabutho* to strengthen his army, and married off his sisters and daughters to influential chiefs across the land. This was a shrewd political move as power was again focused onto Solomon, forcing the Union government to acknowledge his role as the rightful leader of the Zulu people. When Africa agreed to support Britain in the First World War, Solomon agreed to supply Zulu troops but, although a Native Labour Corps was sent to France, fighting troops were not. In return for Solomon's support, the Union government finally recognized him in 1917 as the formal head of the Zulu royal house.

With powerful political influence restored to Solomon, the black Natalians, the *amakholwa*, began to swing their allegiance towards the Zulu royal house. Formally loyal to colonial rule, many had fought for the British in 1879; they had become as marginalized from power and property ownership as their Zulu neighbours had been due to the 1913 Act, and all sought greater equality with their white neighbours. In 1923, the newly-formed African National Congress (ANC) joined forces with the *amakholwa* under the leadership of John Langalibalele Dube, and the Inkatha kaZulu party was formed with Solomon at its head. The hope of all concerned was that the Zulu kingdom would survive and flourish.

Without doubt, Solomon's greatest achievement was his exploitation of a meeting with the British heir apparent, Edward, Prince of Wales, in June 1925. The meeting greatly enhanced his claim to the Zulu throne. The prince – the future Edward VIII – was on a royal tour of the Union and was scheduled to visit Eshowe. Despite the reservations of the Native Affairs

Department, permission was granted for Solomon to meet the prince. Solomon recognized the political opportunity and orchestrated an extraordinary display of Zulu unity, perhaps the last true gathering of the 'old Zulu order', and some 60,000 Zulus attended, many of them in traditional dress. Solomon carefully and publicly included among his entourage representatives of groups who had fought against the royal house in the bitter years since 1879, notably Bokwe, the son of Zibhebhu of the Mandlakazi. Solomon, wearing a British-style uniform trimmed with leopard skin, formally presented Prince Edward with gifts before the two retired for a private meeting. The contents of that meeting were never officially revealed but it was firmly believed among Solomon's supporters that Solomon and Edward had met king to king. Privately, Prince Edward had acknowledged Solomon's position as the hereditary ruler of his people.

At the time of his death on 4 March 1933, Solomon's sons were all minors. His senior son, Cyprian, by his first wife, Chistina Sibiya, had been born in August 1924 and was just nine years old. A regent, Dinizulu's son, Prince Arthur Edward Mshiyeni, was appointed until Cyprian and other princes came of age. Under Mshiyeni's strict eye Cyprian grew up among companions of his own age – including Prince Mangosuthu Buthelezi, whose mother, Princess Magogo, was a daughter of Dinizulu, and whose father, Mathole, was chief of the Buthelezi.

In 1952, Cyprian was finally officially recognized as king by the government – the first of his family since Cetshwayo to be so. In 1953, a young university-educated Zulu, Mangosuthu Buthelezi, a 25-year-old cousin of King Cyprian, became seriously involved in politics and was elected to the tribal constituency of Mahlabatini, which included Ulundi, with its 30,000 people.[4] In October 1955, the territory of Zululand was re-established and its lands returned to the Zulus. At the same time, the Zulu monarchy was re-established and King Cyprian resumed the position as king with Prince Buthelezi as his Traditional Prime Minister of the Zulu People, a position he still enjoys.

Although King Cyprian continued to support the ideals of Zulu tradition and customs, he was little more than a figurehead due to ongoing poor health, exacerbated by cirrhosis of the liver and diabetes. He died of liver failure in September 1968. His successor, Goodwill Zwelithini, was eighteen years old when his father died; a regent was appointed until his traditional Zulu coronation, attended by 20,000 Zulu people, took place on 4 December 1971.

In 1975, inspired by King Solomon's attempts to focus Zulu unity in the face of outside intimidation, Prime Minister Buthelezi founded a new version of Inkatha – later the Inkatha Freedom Party (IFP). King Goodwill himself has moved between supporting the IFP and distancing himself from it, but has always claimed to be king of all Zulus, whatever their political allegiance.

After seventy-six years of vicious turmoil, Zululand was again ruled by its own leaders. It has to be a total triumph of mankind that today, of all the visitors to Zululand and its battlefields, it is the British who are the most numerous and popular with the local people. After everything the Zulu people have endured in the name of Christianity, modernization, socialization and progress, the rural Zulus continue to live in their timeless way, in their same *umuzi* and in dwellings that have not changed since the invasion of 1879. Yet they seem to hold no grudge against the British, as Harry Escombe, who became the second Prime Minister of Natal in 1897, had written in June 1889:

> There is not in the whole of Her Majesty's possessions a race more loyal and more wronged than the Zulus.[5]

Appendix A

The *Mfecane*

Two significant factors were responsible for the *Mfecane* tribal migrations across the area known as Zululand and Natal. The first was the slave trade run by the Portuguese through their trading station at Delagoa Bay, whose facilities were discovered by Lourenco Marques and Antonio Caldeira in 1554 and lay north of the area where the *Mfecane* originally occurred. The second was the pressure of expanding populations competing for limited resources. By 1590, Portuguese traders based at Delagoa Bay began trading with these local tribes and soon extended their interest in trading ivory for copper beads as far as the Tugela River to the south. In 1593, Portuguese shipwrecked survivors trying to reach the safety of the north reported passing through nine groups of settled natives, all of which referred to their chief as *inkosi*, indicating a common language even though these settlements were up to 20 miles apart. Among the larger groupings were the Bhele, the Zizi and the Dlamini. It was the structure of such large groups that eventually heralded their downfall; succession rivalries and schisms between the more powerful members simmered, especially among the subjugated *inkosi*, whose clan had been assimilated into a more powerful clan. Following the death of Bhungane of the Hlubi, his sons commenced a dispute that fractured their clan. Trade was also responsible for internecine dispute, with local *inkosi* protecting their trading sources, usually by defending their river boundaries.

In 1824, the slavers moved towards the Nguni. This unsettling and inhuman practice set in motion a progressive exodus of formerly untroubled people into already occupied territory, which, in turn, resulted in additional pressure of overcrowding and overgrazing on progressively dwindling resources, thereby outstripping the capacity of the land to support them. Conversely, there is evidence that the *Mfecane* was already under way well before ivory and slaves had been traded from the region, probably since the 1750s. Therefore it seems unlikely that slaving or trading were prime factors leading to the *Mfecane*; undisputedly they made it worse. Whatever the cause of this pernicious *Mfecane* process, it was a process of disintegration and extermination, which commenced relatively slowly, but as the effect rippled outwards, it escalated with violence hitherto unseen in southern Africa.

When the effects and consequences of the economic *Mfecane* reached the coastal Nguni, the process of expansion by force began when the Ndwandwe, under Zwide, forcibly and violently drove the Ngwane, under their chief Sobhuza, from their tribal area. They, in turn, fell upon their less militant neighbours in an explosive pattern that was to wreak havoc and cause further misery across southern Africa, killing male warriors of the vanquished and absorbing their women and children in the process. In a relatively short space of time, the *Mfecane*, with its multiple causes, forced tens of thousands of refugees into the unknown area of Pondoland between the Umzimkulu and Umzimvubu rivers. This area was originally named No-Man's-Land by the first explorers, who described the countryside as populated by starving and despairing skeletal people. Nevertheless, the *Mfecane* brought famous leaders to the fore, who, in turn, created strong societies. Pre-*Mfecane*, no southern Bantu people possessed a permanent standing army with specialized military training or a military hierarchy.

Appendix B

Boer Account: Blood River

The mist gradually cleared and Sunday dawned bright and clear. Pretorius gave the order to shoot as soon as sights and targets could be distinguished. With a total disregard for danger, the Zulus charged, but within a quarter of an hour they were forced to withdraw to a position 500 yards away. When they launched the second attack they were fired upon with deadly accuracy. Once again, the Zulu attack was repulsed and they retreated to a distance of 400 yards. Pretorius now directed the copper cannon towards the hill where the leaders of the Zulu force congregated. The second and third rounds burst among the *izinDuna* and led to a third fierce attack lasting nearly an hour.

Soon after the Zulus had retreated, once again a mounted commando of a few hundred men led by Field Cornet Bart Pretorius launched an attack upon them. Twice the commando was driven back, but at the third attempt, they managed to split the Zulu force in two. The greater part of the commando force now emerged from the laager and deployed from the north and south along the river, where hundreds of fleeing Zulus were shot amongst the reeds and in the river until the river ran red. At this point Ndlela's 3,000 crack *impis* went into action. They attempted to cross the river at the drifts above and below the hippo pool but were swept along by the hordes of fleeing warriors being shot down by the Boers. At last the entire Zulu army took flight in all directions. The pursuit lasted until midday, when the commando returned to the laager, where 3,000 Zulus lay dead.

Information sheet given to visitors at the Blood River Visitor Centre.

Appendix C

Chelmsford's Orders to the Five Invasion Columns

No. 1 Chelmsford's Coastal Column
Chelmsford's orders to Colonel Pearson were:

> Cross the Tugela at Fort Pearson and encamp on the Zulu side;
> when ordered to advance, to move on to Eshowe, and there,
> or in its neighbourhood, to form a depot, well entrenched.

No. 2 Reserve Column
Chelmsford's orders to Colonel Durnford were:

> To form a portion of No. 1 Column, but act separately,
> reporting to Colonel Pearson; to remain on the middle Tugela
> frontier until an advance is ordered, and Colonel Pearson has
> reached Eshowe.

Later that day, Durnford was instructed to cross the Buffalo River, await
further orders and make camp on the Zulu side. He was then ordered to
move to the camp at Isandlwana.

No. 3 Centre Column
Chelmsford's orders to Colonel Glyn read:

> No. 3 Column to cross at Rorke's Drift when the thirty days
> expired; to move forward and form an advanced depot,
> strongly entrenched, as found advisable from the nature of
> the country, etc. To assist in clearing the border south-east
> of Rorke's Drift, and to keep up communication with the
> columns on left and right.

APPENDIX C

No. 4 Northern Column
Chelmsford's orders to Colonel Wood VC were:

> To advance to the Blood River. In the event of a further advance, the advance depot of this column to be near the intersection of the roads from Utrecht to Ulundi, and Rorke's Drift to Swaziland; but to delay its advance towards the Umvolosi River until the border is cleared, and to move in a southerly direction towards Colonel Glyn's column to assist it against Sihayo.

No. 5 Reserve Column
Chelmsford's orders to Colonel Rowlands VC were:

> To observe any Boer military activity whilst maintaining a state of readiness in northern Zululand.

In terms of the proposed invasion of Zululand, Chelmsford's main invasion force was remarkably small when the magnitude of the undertaking is considered. His force of regular troops consisted of the two battalions of the 24th (2nd Warwickshire Regiment), the 90th, single battalions of the 2/3rd, 1/13th, and a battalion of the 80th held in reserve at Luneburg, all supported by detachments of the Royal Engineers and Royal Artillery. This force was initially divided between four columns, and apart from the No. 2 Column under Colonel Durnford, which consisted only of locally-raised troops, amounted to a total of nearly 6,000 highly professional and well-armed soldiers. In support of the column were a similar number of native troops, known disparagingly as the 'untrained untrainables', who were divided into seven battalions and led by white officers and NCOs, not necessarily with any military training or command of the English or native language. To this force were added irregular units based on the quasi-military Natal Police, together with frontier guards and local defence groups with grand names such as the Natal Hussars, Natal Carbineers and Durban Rangers.

Enthused with their general's optimism, the main British force crossed the Buffalo River into Zululand on 11 January; everyone's fervent hope was that the Zulus would stand and fight. Regardless of the validity or otherwise of the stated causes, Britain was about to engage the Zulus in a number of vicious battles. They were battles that would be fought to the bitter end, with enormous losses on both sides; battles in which neither the British nor the Zulus would take prisoners.

199

Appendix D

The Ultimatum

Matters again came to a head during early 1878, when a number of Boer and displaced native settlers joined those already illicitly farming a particularly sensitive Zulu area, the same area that was generally becoming known as the 'disputed territory', directly to the north of Rorke's Drift.

In the British tradition of apparent compromise, Frere deferred the problem by reluctantly constituting an independent boundary commission. This was at the persistent request of the Governor of Natal, Sir Henry Bulwer, a long-time friend of the Zulu people. The commission was instructed to adjudicate on title to the disputed territory. Cetshwayo was consulted and he agreed to abide by the commission's decision on condition he could nominate three senior chiefs, *izinDuna*, to participate. The commission's principle members consisted of three highly respected officials led by Michael Gallwey, a barrister who had become the Attorney General of Natal in 1857 at the age of thirty-one, Lieutenant Colonel Anthony Durnford RE, who had served in South Africa for many years and knew the area and the Zulus thoroughly, and John Shepstone, brother and deputy of the Secretary for Native Affairs. The Boers sent Piet Uys, a farmer who had lost relatives to Dingane's *impis*, together with Adrian Rudolph, the Boer Landdrost[3] of Utrecht, and Henrique Shepstone, who served on his father's staff in Pretoria.

The commission sat for nearly five weeks, during which time they considered voluminous verbal and written representations. Gallwey utilized all his legal training to impartially evaluate the material, a task made especially difficult because several unsigned Boer documents proved to be outrageously fraudulent, with many worthless claims put forward as evidence. In fact, the picture became a confused tangle of spurious claims and counter-claims. Boundaries defined on paper simply could not be followed on the terrain. There were a great number of contradictions not only in the documents but also by witnesses called before the commission. Gallwey concentrated the commission's attention on two main issues: who owned the land prior to the dispute and whether any land under dispute had been properly purchased or ceded.

No boundary line had ever been agreed between the Zulus and Boers and for many years the local Zulu chiefs had repeatedly implored the British governor in Natal for advice and help in dealing with incidents involving aggressive land-hungry Boers. It had long been Boer policy, if policy it may be called, to force the Zulus gradually to edge further and further from their rich pasturelands. Hitherto, little notice had been taken of their petitions. The Boundary Commissioners concluded:

> that no cession of territory was ever made by the Zulu people, and that even had such a cession been made by either Panda or Cetywayo [sic] it would have been null and void, unless confirmed by the voice of the nation according to the custom of the Zulus.[4]

The right conferred to the Boers was, the commissioners maintained, simply a grazing right, and that any such right was conferred only in respect of land within the Utrecht district, west of the Blood River. The commissioners held that the Boers never acquired, and the Zulus never lost, dominion over the disputed territory, and that it was still properly a portion of Zululand and, furthermore, the developing Boer settlement at Utrecht must also be surrendered. The Boundary Commission eventually delivered their unexpected verdict in July 1878 to an astonished Sir Bartle Frere, who determinedly sought to coerce the commissioners to amend their findings, without success.

On 4 June, Durnford wrote home that the report of the commission was nearly ready 'and will please no one except perhaps Cetewayo [sic].' Durnford drafted the report, which was completed on 20 June 1878. The commissioners were not permitted to divulge the result to anybody until the high commissioner had decided to make it public. However, Durnford could not resist hinting to his family at the satisfactory conclusion the commission had reached. He wrote on 24 June 1878:

> I think our views will be maintained – at least I hope so. You see we have gone in for fair play.

On 28 July, an incident occurred that Frere used to agitate widespread anti-Zulu sentiment. Two sons of Sihayo, a local but important chief, crossed the river border to restrain two of their father's absconding wives on suspicion of their adultery. The terrified women were duly apprehended and marched back across the border at Rorke's Drift, only to be clubbed to death in accordance with established Zulu tradition. Throughout Natal, the incident received officially orchestrated publicity out of all proportion to the event in order to further inflame public antagonism against Cetshwayo. Shepstone had commenced this policy of subversion against Cetshwayo in a report to Lord Carnarvon dated 11 December 1877, in which he wrote:

> The sooner the root of the evil, which I consider the Zulu power and military organization, is dealt with, the easier our task will be.

Even the pro-Zulu Bulwer was forced to agree that the danger of collision with the Zulu was growing and wrote to Frere that:

> the system of government in the Zulu country is so bad that any improvement was hopeless – we should, if necessary, be justified in deposing Cetshwayo.

Rebuffed by Durnford and the Boundary Commission, Frere knew that publication of the commission's findings could unleash powerful forces against Britain. Native nations would believe their campaign against progressive European settlement was vindicated and the furious Boers faced surrendering their land and farms in Zululand. Frere knew the Boers could well retaliate against Britain by resorting to military action against British-controlled Natal – which, in turn, might provoke additional antagonism from a number of the Boers' European allies, especially Holland and Germany. This possible complication would be most inconvenient as Britain was becoming seriously engaged in war against Afghanistan, and relationships with Russia were deteriorating.

To Frere, the invasion of Zululand remained the single option; after all, British victory was a certainty. A Zulu defeat would facilitate British progress to the north and confederation could proceed. It would also placate the Boers, and such a display of British military force would certainly impress any African leader who might well have contemplated making a stand against British expansion. Invasion would also overturn the Zulu king by eradicating his military potential and unshackle a valuable source of labour for British and Boer commercial activities. Frere ordered his General Commanding British Forces in South Africa, Sir Frederic Thesiger (shortly to become Lord Chelmsford), to proceed to Natal to secretly prepare his forces for an immediate and brief war against the Zulus. For the previous ten years, he had been concerned with administration, as Adjutant General in India. The pedantic Chelmsford would have well understood the theory of British Army tactics being the basis of every military operation undertaken anywhere in the world. Tactics involved meticulous planning, rather like contemplating a game of chess, but nevertheless sticking to rigid rules and using equipment totally unsuitable outside Europe. This attitude would inextricably lead Chelmsford's invading army into defeat. His army would wear red jackets in heat of 35°C, use tactics better suited to the previous century and ignore intelligence reports of his enemy's intentions and movements. This attitude would give King Cetshwayo and his commanders the advantage of perfect knowledge of British positions in Zululand's difficult terrain, provide them easy and accurate intelligence of British action and inaction, and enable Zulu subterfuge and decoys to mislead Chelmsford.

In blissful ignorance of such implications, there were important personal considerations for both Frere and Chelmsford; success for Frere would strengthen his already glittering career and for Chelmsford an early defeat of the Zulu army would be popular and ensure him a heroic return to England. Meanwhile, Frere pondered the Boundary Commission's findings and decided that inactivity was the best, albeit temporary, solution.

Frere gained more time by forwarding the report to Hicks Beach, the new Colonial Secretary in London (who had succeeded Lord Carnarvon). He also requested additional imperial troops, ostensibly to protect Natal and the Boer families still within the disputed area. Frere knew full well that Hicks Beach's official reply would take several months to reach him, by which time the Zulus would be defeated.

On 9 October, an incident occurred that precipitated action by Frere. A local chief, Mbilini, led his warriors through the Pongola Valley in the area under dispute attacking immigrant Boers and natives and stealing their cattle. Frere was already in the process of devising an ultimatum that he and his advisers knew would be impossible for Cetshwayo to accept. It would also negate the Boundary Commission's report and justify war against the Zulus. The raid by Mbilini formed the basis of the first item in the draft ultimatum.

APPENDIX D

The ultimatum

Eventually, on 11 December 1878, Zulu representatives were summoned to the site of an enormous shady fig tree on the Natal bank of the Tugela River to learn the result of the Boundary Commission's deliberations. Today, the stump of the tree, a national monument, languishes in the shade of a motorway. John Shepstone represented the British officials, while Cetshwayo sent three of his senior *izinDuna* together with eleven chieftains and their retainers to report back the findings.

John Shepstone was an insensitive choice for several reasons. He was the brother and deputy of the Secretary for Native Affairs, Sir Theophilus Shepstone. He was actually working for the Boers at the time of the commission, and whilst it could be argued that he could therefore represent the Boers, he caused confusion among the Zulus by announcing the findings on behalf of the British. He was also infamous among the Zulus, having once led a party that tracked down, shot and wounded a wanted Zulu, Chief Matyana. Matyana escaped; John Shepstone lost both his captive and his reputation.

Writing was unknown to the Zulus, who were nevertheless accomplished at memorizing even lengthy speeches. This probably accounts for the number of senior Zulu representatives who would have to corroborate each other when they reported back to Cetshwayo. At the first meeting, the findings of the Boundary Commission were announced, though couched in heavily worded terms designed to cause the Zulus confusion. Mr Fynney, Border Agent, carefully translated these to the Zulu deputies. The meeting adjourned for a roast beef lunch and reassembled in the afternoon, when the ultimatum was read and translated, sentence by sentence, again by Mr Fynney, and was listened to with the utmost attention by the deputies with increasing indications of concern and apprehension. The astonished Zulus then anxiously set off to report the terms of the ultimatum to their king; Cetshwayo had a reputation for executing the messengers of bad news and therefore, understandably, his emissaries tarried. A white resident, John Dunn, duly learned of the ultimatum and sent his own messenger to Cetshwayo with advance warning.

The main requirements of the ultimatum were twofold:

1. Conditions to be fully met within twenty days
a. The surrender to the British of the Swazi chief, Mbilini (for cattle raiding)

b. The surrender of Chief Sihayo's two sons (for crossing the river border into Natal, abducting and then murdering two of Sihayo'a adulterous wives) plus a fine of 500 cattle
c. A fine of 100 cattle for having molested two British surveyors, Deighton and Smith, at a border crossing.

2. Conditions to be fully met within thirty days

a. A number of prominent Zulus were to be surrendered for trial (no names were specified)
b. Summary executions were forbidden
c. The Zulu army was to disband
d. The Zulu military system was to be abandoned
e. Every Zulu was to be free to marry
f. Missionaries were to be re-admitted to Zululand without let or hindrance
g. A British resident official was to oversee Zulu affairs
h. Any dispute involving a European was to be dealt with under British jurisdiction.

In the meantime, the British invasion force was already advancing on three fronts towards the border of Zululand in total confidence that Cetshwayo could not comply with the British ultimatum.

Appendix E

King Cetshwayo in London

On Monday, 30 October 2006, English Heritage fixed one of its famous blue plaques – which mark the residence of a significant historical figure – to the imposing front of a Victorian townhouse at 18 Melbury Road, Kensington, London. The plaque commemorates the fact that, for two weeks in August 1882, the house was the home of the Zulu king, Cetshwayo kaMpande, and his entourage during his brief but highly significant visit to London.

In the aftermath of the British invasion of 1879, the king had, of course, been taken into captivity, lodged firstly in the old Dutch castle in Cape Town, and then at the farm Oude Moulen on the Cape Flats. Once he had recovered from the shock of defeat and exile, he had campaigned tirelessly to be allowed a voice in Zulu affairs. While British and colonial politicians who had supported the invasion remained reluctant to allow him any direct influence, his plight attracted the attention of a number of well-connected tourists, for whom a visit to the king became an essential part of a visit to the Cape, and who took up his cause on their return to England. Several times Cetshwayo asked to be allowed to visit London to put his case in person and each time he was refused but, as the post-war settlement imposed on Zululand slid into anarchy, he came increasingly to be seen as a viable solution to an increasingly volatile problem. The government in London began to consider an extraordinary *volte-face* in policy – the restoration of a man whom British troops had waged a six-month war to depose. It was argued that Cetshwayo was the only man with sufficient authority to impose order in Zululand and that, since he would be entirely dependent on the British for his return, he would no longer be a threat to British interests.

The king was finally granted permission to visit London in 1882. He left Cape Town for London on 12 July, accompanied by three of his *izinDuna* who had accompanied him in exile, as well as an interpreter, Robert Dunn, and – to keep a close eye on him – Henrique Shepstone, a member of the powerful dynasty who largely shaped colonial Natal's policies. The king arrived off Plymouth on 5 August, and was greeted by a throng of journalists, all keen to interview the man who had humbled British troops in the field. Throughout his trip, King Cetshwayo played the role of a consummate diplomat, receiving visitors with quiet dignity, always publicly regretting the war and apparently marvelling at the power and benevolence of his hosts.

From Plymouth he was taken to the house in Melbury Road, where a suite had been made available to him. News soon spread of his arrival, and curious crowds gathered outside in the hope of catching a glimpse of him. Cetshwayo was obliged to make frequent appearances at the window. He was nervous, at first; uncertain of his reaction. But when his appearance was greeted with enthusiastic cheers he accepted the obligation with good humour. Crowds, indeed, soon dogged his every move as Londoners became enchanted by the man whom they found very different in person to the scowling savage portrayed in the illustrated press in 1879. Although a large man, the king cut a considerable dash in a smart outfit of European clothes and carried himself with considerable majesty. When Cetshwayo and his attendants were photographed by the fashionable society photographers Bassanos, such a crowd gathered outside that one young boy was heard to comment, 'He ain't Ceta-wayo, for he can't get-away!' Shown a statue of Achilles in Hyde Park, the king observed quietly, 'You see, it was not so long ago that they fought as we do – without clothes.' Taken to the Royal Arsenal at Woolwich, he was impressed – as his hosts intended – by the display of imperial might. 'I feel that I have grown up, so to speak, in a day; that from the childhood of understanding I have suddenly sprung to manhood.'

From London, on 14 August the king was taken by special train and yacht for a brief audience with Queen Victoria at Osborne House on the Isle of Wight. According to the press, a 'large crowd assembled to witness the departure,' and the king and his attendants 'were greeted with hearty cheering.' In the event, the royal audience lasted scarcely fifteen minutes and was apparently cool – the queen was, after all, one of Lord Chelmsford's most loyal supporters – but polite enough. The queen presented Cetshwayo with a silver cup as a souvenir (it is now in the KwaZulu Cultural Museum at oNdini). Later, the queen commissioned her portrait painter, Carl Sohn, to paint Cetshwayo's picture.

More importantly, the king had several meetings at the Colonial Office to discuss his political future. To his delight, it was agreed that he would be restored to Zululand – although the full conditions limiting his authority were not made clear until after his return to the Cape.

The king and his entourage left England at the end of the month. The mission had been a huge political and diplomatic success and, indeed, the impression Cetshwayo had created in the minds of the British public did much to alter their opinion of the Zulu people. In the years since the invasion many had become uneasy about the justice of the war, and the king's apparent dignity in defeat helped to change the image of the Zulus from one of ruthless savages to noble warriors – a view that has continued to colour popular perception to this day.

Sadly, the king's restoration proved disastrous. He returned to Zululand in early 1883, but such were the deep divisions engendered by the British invasion that he was unable to contain the existing rivalries and a spiralling cycle of violence. His return polarized opinion within Zululand – between royalists and anti-royalists – and a civil war broke out, which led first to a crushing military defeat and then to Cetshwayo's death.

The prime mover behind the efforts to secure a blue plaque to recognize the king's visit to London was archaeologist Dr Tony Pollard, who in 2000 directed the battlefield survey at Isandlwana. He said:

> While in Africa I was told a story by a Zulu about the king's meeting with Queen Victoria in England, about how his magic was greater than hers. It struck me that if these events are still talked about in Zululand today we should certainly be remembering them here in Britain. People tend to think of events like the Zulu War taking place in some exotic, far-off place but they also had an incredible impact in Britain and this plaque will hopefully remind people of that.

Notes

Introduction

1. Quoted by British Prime Minister Disraeli in *The Life of Benjamin Disraeli, Earl of Beaconsfield*, by W.E. Gladstone, London, 1920. His full quote reads:

   > A very remarkable people the Zulu. They defeat our generals; they convert our bishops; they have settled the fate of a great European Dynasty.

   As a direct consequence of the defeat, Queen Victoria was about to preside over the inexorable process of degeneration of both her government and the furthest fringes of her empire. For example, on hearing news of Isandlwana, the King of Burma 'wanted to order a march on Rangoon forthwith', quoted in *The Lords of Human Kind*, by V. Kiernan, London, 1972.

2. *Ibid.*
3. Bryant, A.T., *Olden Times in Zululand and Natal*, Shuter & Shooter, London, 1929.
4. Rattray D, & Greaves, A, *David Rattray's Guidebook to the Anglo-Zulu War Battlefields*, Pen & Sword, Barnsley, 2002.
5. Stringer, Prof C., *African Exodus*, Henry Holt & Co., New York, 1998.
6. Malthus, Rev T.R. (1766-1834). Every species will expand exponentially until it exhausts its food supply.
7. At the time of the Anglo-Zulu War of 1879, the Zulu language was oral and not written. Written accounts by Zulus of military action do not therefore exist. Zulu accounts would have been recorded post-event by British officials, who would not note anything that discredited British interests. Furthermore, based on their bitter experience of white people, such Zulus would have been either appreciative of a reward or apprehensive for their safety (while under questioning) and match their answers accordingly. See *Zulu Thought-patterns*, by Axel Ivar Berglund, Indiana University Publishing, Johannesburg, 1989.
8. Omer-Cooper, J., *The Zulu Aftermath*, Longmans, London, 1966.
9. Wilson & Thompson, *The Oxford History of South Africa*, Oxford, 1971.
10. Voight, J.C., *Fifty Years of the History of the Republic in South Africa 1795-1845* Vol. 2, Struik, Cape Town, 1969.

Chapter 1

1. Omer-Cooper, J.D., *The Zulu Aftermath*, Longman, London, 1966.
2. Kay, Dr S., *Travels and Researches in Caffraria*, Waugh & Mason, New York, 1834.

Chapter 2

1. Omer-Cooper, J.D., *The Zulu Aftermath*, Longman, London, 1966, a term first used by E. Walker in 1928. See also Appendix A.

NOTES

2-5. AZWHS Journal 17.

6. Bulpin, T.V., *Shaka's Country*, Howard Timms, Cape Town, 1952, quoting Fynn's diary.

7. *Ibid*.

8. James Stuart Archive Vol. 1; these archives are the collective oral accounts of several hundred Zulus.

9. Gray, S., *The Natal Papers of John Ross*, University of Natal Press, 1992.

10. The custom continued until more recent times, and is believed still to be practised in remote parts of Zululand where the elderly or terminally sick can only anticipate the ending of their life by being 'taken for a walk'.

11. Wilmot, A., *History of the Zulu War*, Richardson & Best, London, 1880.

12. The location is just north-west, under the dam overlooked by the tourist village of Shakaland.

13. Bryant, A.T., *The Zulu People*, Schuter & Shooter, Pietermaritzburg, 1949.

14. Etherington, N., 'Two million had perished', quoted in *George Theal, the father of African Historiography*, Monash University Press, Australia, 2008.

15. Kay, Dr S., *Travels and Researches in Caffraria*, Waugh & Mason, New York, 1834.

16. Bryant, A.T., *History of the Zulu War*, Shuter & Shooter, London, 1929.

17. The Natal Papers of John Ross.

Chapter 3

1.a. White South Africans are known to use the skills of *sangomas* when conventional medicine fails. The *sangoma's* skills are not to be ignored; if a Zulu believes he will be cured, then he stands a good chance of making a good recovery – the practice closely mirrors the Western use of placebo medicine to achieve similar results. See also *The Social System of the Zulus*, Eileen Krige, Shuter & Shooter, 1950, for a full review of Zulu medicine.

1.b. All the items described can still commonly be seen for sale at markets across KwaZulu Natal.

2. Pre-battle rituals were vital to Zulu *impis* and army. These rituals had to be conducted by specially trained *sangomas* in a set pattern using special medicine, or *muti*.

3. *Natal Mercury*, 27 September 1879.

4. *Natal Colonist*, 17 April 1879.

5. The practice of modern white armies pre-battle, where they are joined in prayer by army chaplains, could be described as a similar ritual.

6. Today, the favoured tool for retribution is the handgun or the ubiquitous AK47.

Chapter 4

1. Marshall, H.E., *South Africa*, Cassell, London, 1915, referring to Drake's secret circumnavigation from east to west after having discovered the Cape Horn passage to the Pacific Ocean. By 1879, a total of sixty-three European vessels were lost between the Cape and Durban – see also Smail, J., *With Shield and Assegai*, Howard Timmins, Cape Town, 1969.

2. Voigt, J.C., *Fifty Years of the History of the Republic in South Africa*, C. Struik, Cape Town, 1969.

NOTES

3. Van der Post, L., *The Heart of the Hunter*, Penguin, London, 1923.
4. Voigt, J.C., *Fifty Years of the History of the Republic in South Africa*.
5. Greaves, A., *Crossing the Buffalo*, Weidenfeld & Nicolson, London, 2005.
6. Peires, *House of Phalo, Journal of South African Studies*, Johannesburg, 1981.
7. Meinjes, J., *The Voortrekkers*, Corgi, Transworld Publishers, London, 1973
8. *Ibid.*
9. See Appendix A for details.
10. From Zulu accounts held at the Zulu Museum, Ncome River.
11. In 1999, a new Zulu museum was built on the Zulu bank of the Ncome River overlooking the battle site, and as visitors there discover, claims of any Boer victory are strongly rebutted. Disregarding the cross-river interpretation of events, it is certainly curious that the Boers, armed with antiquated firearms, claim they accounted for 3,000 Zulu fatalities in the same time span that the British defenders at Rorke's Drift in 1879 – armed with sophisticated breech-loading Martini-Henry rifles, also used at point-blank range – accounted for only 351 Zulus. On the same day at Isandlwana, the Zulus faced 1,000 experienced troops armed with identical rifles, and supported by artillery; British volley fire accounted for 1,000 Zulus before the British camp was overwhelmed. Nevertheless, at Blood River the Zulus avoided a tightly compacted enemy in possession of firearms. They also discovered that the rounds fired by the Boers had a limited effective range. Over a distance of more than 100 yards, the Boer low-velocity rounds would bounce off a sun-hardened shield held at about 45 degrees. This knowledge resulted in the Zulu belief that their shields were magical, especially when doctored with magic *muti*, a belief strongly held and maintained for the next sixty years until the Zulus met the British at the battle of Isandlwana.
12. See Professor Hattersley, quoted in *The Zulu War*, by Alan Lloyd, Granada Publishing, London, 1974.

Chapter 5
1. Greaves, A., *Crossing the Buffalo*, Weidenfeld & Nicolson, London, 2005.
2. Voigt, J.C., *Fifty Years of the History of the Republic in South Africa*, C. Struik, Cape Town, 1969. For details of Shaka's attack on his mother, see JSA v.1. Account supported by modern Zulu folklore.
3. Many years later, the site of King Shaka's burial was purchased by a farmer and today Shaka's grave lies somewhere under Cooper Street in the small town of Stanger, north of Durban.
4. Voigt, J.C., *Fifty Years of the History of the Republic in South Africa*.
5. Van Jaarsveld, F.A., *The Afrikaner's Interpretation of South African History*, Simondium, Cape Town, 1964.
6. Taylor, S., opinion supported by Zulu historian Magema kaMagwaza, quoted in *Shaka's Children*, HarperCollins, London, 1995.
7. JSA v.1 p.247.
8. See map *The Vassal State*, courtesy Voigt, J.C., *Fifty Years of the History of the Republic in South Africa*.
9. Binns, C.T., *The Last Zulu King*, Longmans, London, 1963.

NOTES

Chapter 6

1. JSA v.1 p.247.
2. Duminy and Guest, *Natal and Zululand from Earliest Times*, Shuter & Shooter, Pietermaritzburg, 1989.
3. Taylor, S., *Shaka's Children*, HarperCollins, London, 1944.
4. Greaves, A, *Crossing the Buffalo*, Weidenfeld & Nicolson, 2005. For the reference to the legend being supported by H. Rider Haggard – see *Child of Storm*, by Haggard.
5. In 1857, an incident occurred that had a direct bearing on Zulu perception of British officials. Chief Sidoi, a resident in southern Natal, embarked upon a mass raid into the land of a neighbouring chief. When challenged by the British authorities, rather than face any punishment, Sidoi went into hiding and fled Natal along with many of his followers. Shepstone responded by seizing their property and burning their villages, even of those who remained in Natal. Almost immediately, Chief Matshana, a northern Natal chief, refused a magistrate's order to surrender a number of men who had killed a person widely believed to be a devil. Matshana refused so Shepstone sent his younger brother, John Shepstone, to arrest Matshana. John Shepstone deceived Matshana into attending a meeting to discuss matters on the promise that the British party would be unarmed. This ploy collapsed when Shepstone's men produced their concealed weapons and fired at Matshana. Although wounded, Matshana and most of his retinue escaped.
6. Ballard, C., *The Historical Image of King Cetshwayo*, *Natalia* magazine, 1983.
7. Formerly the highly respected Governor of Bombay.
8. Etherington, N., *The Shepstone System. Natal and Zululand*, in Duminy and Guest, *Natal and Zululand from Earliest Times*, Shuter & Shooter, Pietermaritzburg, 1989.
9. *Ibid.*
10. Clammer, D., *The Last Zulu Warrior*, Purnell & Sons, Cape Town, 1977.
11. Chadwick, G., *The Zulu War of 1879*, Natal Education Activities, undated.
12. Binns, C.T., *The Last Zulu King*, Camelot Press, London, 1963.
13. Colenso, F., *History of the Zulu War*, 1880, letter dated 11 December 1877, Chapman & Hall Ltd., London, 1881.
14. Rider-Haggard, H., *The Days of My Life*, Longmans, London, 1926.
15. Wilmot, A., *History of the Zulu War*, Richardson & Best, London, 1880.
16. Anglo Zulu War Historical Society Journal 1.
17. O'Connell, D., *The Zulu War and the Raj*, Able Publishing, London, 2002.
18. Anglo Zulu War Historical Society Journal 1.
19. Droogleever, R.W.F., *The Road to Isandlwana*, Greenhill, London, 1992.
20. British Parliamentary Papers, C 2000.
21. British Parliamentary Papers, C 2079:39, dated 5 January 1878.
22. British Parliamentary Papers, C 2252, dated 24 January 1879.
23. AZWHS Journal 1.
24. Droogleever, R.W.F., *The Road to Isandlwana*, Greenhill, London, 1992.
25. Coupland, Sir R., *Zulu Battle Piece Isandhlwana*, Collins, London, 1948.
26. *Ibid.*
27. *Functions and duties of High Commissioner*, British Parliamentary Papers, C 2242).
28. Droogleever, R.W.F., *The Road to Isandlwana*, Greenhill, London, 1992
29. *Ibid.*

30. Colenso, Frances, *History of the Zulu War*, 1880, letter dated 11 December 1877, Chapman & Hall Ltd., London, 1881.
31. British Parliamentary Papers, C 2222, p. 176.
32. See Appendix C.
33. Blue Books, C 2308, p. 62.
34. Martineau, J., *Life and Letters of Sir Bartle-Frere*, Murray, London, 1895.

Chapter 7
1. British Parliamentary Papers, C 2308.
2. Although mainly armed with the stabbing spear and shield, the Zulu army possessed a large number of antiquated firearms. An English trader trusted by the Zulus, John Dunn, is often blamed for this trade but he only ever obtained permits to import 250 guns for King Cetshwayo. During the 1870s, as many as 20,000 guns entered southern Africa through Mozambique alone, most of them intended for the Zulu market. The majority of these firearms were obsolete military muskets, dumped on the unsophisticated 'native market'. This mass importation of firearms also contributed greatly to the destruction by Zulu hunters of remaining big game. More modern types were available, particularly the percussion Enfield, and a number of Zulu chiefs had collections of quality sporting guns. Individuals like Prince Dabulamanzi and Chief Sihayo of Rorke's Drift were recognized as good shots but most Zulus were untrained and highly inaccurate; numerous accounts of Zulu War battles note both the indiscriminate use of their firepower and their general inaccuracy.
3. Guy, J., *Destruction of the Zulu Kingdom, the Civil War in Zululand 1879-1884*, Longman, London, 1979.
4. Dunn, J., *Cetschwayo and the Three Generals*, Knox Publishing, Durban, 1886.
5. Greaves, A. & Best, B., *The Curling Letters of the Zulu War*, Pen & Sword, Barnsley, 2004.
6. Laband, J., *Lord Chelmsford's Zululand Campaign*, 1994, Army Records Society letter to Colonel Wood VC, 4 January 1879.
7. Hamilton Browne, G., *A Lost Legionary in South Africa*, London, 1912.
8. Public Records Office WO 33/44 S 6333.
9. Later confirmed by The Honourable Lieutenant Vereker. See Higginson WO 33/34 S6333.

Chapter 8
1. Greaves, A., *Isandlwana*, Pen & Sword, Barnsley, 2012.
2. Hattersley, A. F., *The Annuls of Natal*, Longmans, Johannesburg, 1938.
3. Laband, J., *Rise and Fall of the Zulu Nation*, Cassell, London, 1997.
4. Greaves, A., *Isandlwana*, Pen & Sword, Barnsley, 2012.
5. Laband, J., *Rise and Fall*, Cassell, London, 1997.
6. Laband, J., *Fight us in the Open*, Shuter & Shooter, Johannesburg, 1985.
7. An examination of some of the contemporary paintings of the time, often painted from descriptions given by actual combatants, clearly reveal palls of smoke on various Zulu War battlefields. This effect can be seen in, amongst others, C.E. Fripp's painting of *Isandlwana*, De Neuville's *Rorke's Drift*, Lt Evelyn's two sketches

of *Nyezane*, Crealock's *Final Repulse* of Gingindlovu, Orlando Norie's watercolour of *Kambula* and the equally famous *Illustrated London News'* Square at Ulundi.

8–10. Hallam-Parr, H., *Reasons of Defeat at Isandlwana 1879*, reviewed by Ian Knight, 1986.
11. Greaves, A., *Curling Letters of the Zulu War*, Pen & Sword, Barnsley, 2001.
12. A hole was made just wide enough for a man's body. The earth was then gradually excavated on every side until the cavity was large enough for the purpose. Before the corn was poured in, the interior was thoroughly plastered with fresh cow dung and the pit finally being closed with a thick covering of dung to make it impermeable to both air and water.
13. Ammunition was much prized by the victorious Zulus; they would snap off the rounds and pour the powder into their powder horns to be used with their ancient muskets.
14. The reserve of Zulus that had moved off towards Natal or had given chase to British fugitives later made their own way back to their homesteads.
15. Fynn, H.F., papers, *My Recollections of a Famous Campaign and a Great Disaster*, confirmed by JSA, p. 125.

Chapter 9
1. Greaves, A., and Best, B., *The Curling Letters of the Zulu War*, Pen & Sword, Barnsley, 2001. Letter to his mother, 2 February 1879. Smith-Dorrien jumped off a cliff into the Buffalo River and survived.
2. *Ibid.*
3. For the written accounts of August Hammar and Lieutenant Harford on the subject, see the AZWHS Journal, No. 24, December 2008, *The pre-defence of Rorke's Drift*.
4. His chief's heavy brass armlet, complete with a Martini-Henry bullet hole, was recovered the following morning and taken from the chief's body as a trophy by one of the defenders, Harry Lugg. It forms part of the author's collection.
5. *Pall Mall Gazette, The Defence of Rorke's Drift*, reprinted in the AZWHS Journal 13, June 2003.
6. *The Curling Letters of the Zulu War*, Pen & Sword, Barnsley, 2001.
7. See Frances Colenso's and Commandant Hamilton Brown's accounts as quoted in *Rorke's Drift*, Greaves, A., Cassell, London, 2002. It is for this reason that Hamilton-Brown never received his South Africa Campaign medal; he later relieved one of his men of his medal and had it re-engraved with his details. For sight of this and his other medals, contact the author.
8. Knight, I., *The Zulu War Then and Now*, Plaistow Press, London, 1993.
9. *The Curling Letters of the Zulu War*, Clery letter, 16 May 1879. For a full consideration of this aspect of the engagement at Rorke's Drift, see *Rorke's Drift*, Greaves, A.
10. Laband, J., *Rope of Sand*, Jonathan Ball, Johannesburg, 1995. Jim refers to James Rorke, after whom the drift was named.
11. Webb, C., *Zulu Boy's Recollections*, University of Natal Press, Durban, 1987, confirms the widespread Zulu population's feelings.
12. Laband, J., *Kingdom in Crisis*, University of Natal Press, 1992.

NOTES

Chapter 10
1. Zulu folklore confirms that showing one's force to the enemy was a traditional tactic; they hoped their size and presence would be sufficient to deter an invader.
2. Wynne, L., *A Widow-making War*, 1880. Produced for private circulation only.
3. Laband, J., *Fight Us in the Open*, University of Natal, 1985.
4. *Ibid.*
5. A retired British soldier serving with the NNC as a sergeant major then led another attack up the hill and somehow drove the Zulus out of the *umuzi* – the action so impressed Colonel Hart that the soldier, Jenkins, was granted a field promotion to lieutenant and an enhanced pension – both highly unusual for that time.
6. Knight, I., and Castle, I., *Fearful Hard Times*, Greenhill, London, 1994.
7. AZWHS Journal No. 4, December 1998.

Chapter 11
1. AZWHS Journal No. 5, June 1999.
2. Rattray, D., *Guidebook to the Zulu War*, Pen & Sword, Barnsley, 2002. Knowing they were a formidable foe, Wood was uncertain how to neutralize such a powerful and growing force ensconced only 25 miles from his Khambula base.
3. Laband, J., *Lord Chelmsford's Zululand Campaign 1878-1879*, Army Records Society.
4. Even today, only a few hardy souls have ever tackled this rocky ridge and it remains best viewed from the top of Hlobane.
5. Laband, J., *Rope of Sand*, Jonathan Ball, Johannesburg, 1995.
6. Laband, J., and Thompson, P., *The Field Guide to the War in Zululand 1879*, University of Natal Press, 1979.

Chapter 12
1. Mustard proved to be very popular with the troops in South Africa; it was supplied by Keens of London.

Chapter 13
1. Laband, J., *Kingdom in Crisis*, University of Natal Press, Durban, 1979.
2. Melton Prior, *Campaigns of a War Correspondent*, from *The Illustrated London News*, London, 1912.
3. Alinson collection, Bathurst Press, as quoted in *Kingdom in Crisis*.
4. O'Connor, D., *The Life of Sir Bartle Frere*, Able Publishing, London, 2002.

Chapter 14
1. Even after natural scavengers had done their work, skeletons and human bones littered the battlefield for many years. Curiously, the only attempt to clear the area occurred when an enterprising Natal trader arranged to collect sacks of bones for onward shipment to Durban. They were then sorted for grinding into bonemeal but the project came to a halt when the citizens of Durban realized what was happening and strongly opposed this commercial use of human remains.
2. Colenso Papers – see also Vijn's *Cetshwayo's Dutchman*, reprint of 1880 edition by Greenhill Books, London, 1988.
3. MacLeod Papers, quoted in Bonner, P., *Kings, Commoners and Concessionaires*, Cambridge University Press, 1983. The story of King Sekhukhuni and Britain's

military campaigns against him in 1878 and 1879 is a fascinating and dramatic one. It is not generally known that it was King Sekhukhuni, not King Cetshwayo, who was the original target for British military attention in South Africa during 1878. The Boers had undertaken their own campaign against Sekhukhuniland in 1876, but that had ended in disaster and defeat.

4. On 29 May 1884, he died, probably of influenza. He was buried in St Paul's Cathedral, though no politician was invited to accompany the procession. His coffin was led into the cathedral by two dukes, one field marshal and three major generals. Queen Victoria was represented, along with an array of lords, knights and ordinary soldiers. Later, a statue of Frere was erected on Thames Embankment, paid for by public subscription.

Chapter 15
1. Colonial Office Papers 879/16,204, No. 151.
2. *Ibid.*
3. O'Connor, D., *The Life of Sir Bartle Frere*, Able Publishing, London, 2002, for a full account of British vulnerability at sea.
4. Greaves, A., *Crossing the Buffalo*, Cassell, London, 2005.
5. Blue Books, C3616, p. 54.
6. See Appendix E.
7. Marks, S., *Reluctant Rebellion, the 1906-9 Disturbances in Natal*, Clarendon Press, Oxford, 1970.
8. Various accounts: see *The Last Zulu King* by Binns, C.T. Longmans, London, 1963 for a summary. For an overview of a number of conspiracy theories relating to the king's death, see *The Natal Witness* articles printed in June 1886.

Chapter 16
1. See CO 879/25 Havelock to Granville 15 March 1886 – quoted in *The Destruction of the Zulu Kingdom*, by Prof Guy, J., Longmans, Bristol, 1979.
2. Rider Haggard, H., *Cetshwayo and his White Neighbours*, London, 1882, and *Story of the Zulus* Gibson, J.Y., Longmans, London, 1911, for agreement with this theory.
3. A body was produced to the authorities as being that of Bambatha, although folklore holds that he duped McKenzie's men and escaped. The British medical officer removed the head, which was shown to a number of chiefs, who readily confirmed it was that of Bambatha. The head was then buried with the body.
4. He remains a powerful and popular Zulu leader and acclaimed worldwide for his astute leadership.
5. He was the defence lawyer for Dinizulu at his trial. See *A Remonstrance on Behalf of the Zulu Chiefs 1889*, Pietermaritzburg, 1908.

Bibliography

Journals and Newspapers
Army Medical Reports 1878.
Journal of African History (4):557-570.Guy, J.J., 1971. *A note on firearms in the Zulu kingdom with special reference to the Anglo-Zulu War 1879.*
Journals 1-33 of the Anglo Zulu War Historical Society.
Punch, London.
The Daily News, London.
The Graphic, London.
The Illustrated London News, London.
The Natal Colonist, South Africa.
The Natal Mercury, South Africa.
The Natal Times, South Africa.
The Natal Witness, South Africa.
The Times, London.

Books
Adams, J., *The South Wales Borderers*, Cambridge University Press, 1968.
Atkinson, C.T., *The South Wales Borderers 24th Foot 1689-1937*, Cambridge University Press, 1937.
Bancroft, J.W., *The Zulu War, 1879: Rorke's Drift*, Spellmount, Tunbridge Wells, 1991.
British Battles on Land and Sea, Cassell, London, 1898.
Bryant, A.T., *The Zulu People*, Shuter & Shooter, Johannesburg, 1949.
    Olden Times in Zululand and Natal, Cassell, London, 1929.
Bulpin, T.V., *Shaka's Country*, Howard Timms, Cape Town, 1952.
Castle & Knight, *Fearful Hard Times*, Greenhill, London, 1994.
Chadwick, G.A., *The Zulu War of 1879*, The Natal Educational Activities Association, undated.
Clarke, S., *Invasion of Zululand*, Brenthurst, South Africa, 1979.
Colenso, F., *History of the Zulu War and its Origins*, Chapman & Hall Ltd., London, 1880.
Colenso, J. W., Colenso Papers, 25 July 1879.
Cope, R., *The Ploughshare of War*, University of Natal Press, 1999.
Cory, G. (Ed), *The Diaries of the Rev. Francis Owen*, private printing, Cape Town, 1926.
Coupland, Sir R., *Zulu Battle Piece Isandlwana*, Collins, London, 1948.
Creswicke, L., *The Zulu War*, E.C. Jack, Edinburgh, 1900.
Crook, M.J., *The Evolution of the Victoria Cross*, Midas Books, London, 1975.
Cunynghame, Sir A., *My Command in South Africa*, Macmillan, London, 1879.
Dodds, G., *The Zulus and Matabele*, Arms and Armour, London, 1998.
Emery, F., *The Red Soldier*, Hodder & Stoughton, London, 1977.
Etherington, Norman, *Anglo Zulu Relations 1856-1878 – New Perspectives*, University of Natal Press, 1981.

BIBLIOGRAPHY

French, The Hon Gerald, *Lord Chelmsford and the Zulu War*, Unwin, London, 1939.

Gon, Philip, *The Road to Isandlwana*, Greenhill, London, 1979.

Greaves, A. & Best, B., *The Curling Letters of the Zulu War*, Pen & Sword, Barnsley, 2001.

Greaves, Adrian, *Fields of Battle – Isandlwana*, Cassell, London, 2001.

Greaves, A. & Knight, I., *A Review of the South African Campaign of 1879*, Debinair, Tenterden, 2000.

Guy, Jeff, *The Destruction of the Zulu Kingdom*, Longmans, London, 1979.

Hamilton-Browne, George, *A Lost Legionary in South Africa*, Werner Laurie, London, 1890.

Hayward, J. B. & Son, *Medal Rolls 1793-1889 of the 24th Foot, South Wales Borderers*, private publication, London, 1990.

Hodder, E., *Heroes of Britain*, Cassell, London, 1880.

Holme, N., *The Silver Wreath*, Samson Books, London, 1979.

Hope, R., *The 80th Regiment of Foot*, Churnet Valley Books, Gloucester, 1997.

Hurst, G.Y., *The Volunteer Regiments of Natal and East Griqualand*, Knox Publishing, Durban, 1945.

Kay, Dr S., *Travels and Researches in Caffraria*, Waugh & Mason, New York, 1834.

Kiernan, V., *The Lords of Human Kind*, Samson Books, London, 1972.

Knight, I., *With his Face to the Foe*, Spellmount, London, 2001.

The Sun Turned Black, Watermans, Windrow and Greene, London, 1995.

The Zulu War Then and Now, Plaistow Press, London, 1993.

There Will be an Awful Row at Home about This, West Valley Press, Shoreham, 1987.

Krige, Eileen, *The Social System of the Zulus*, Shuter & Shooter, Johannesburg, 1950.

Laband, John, *Lord Chelmsford's Zululand Campaign*, Alan Sutton Publishing, Jeppestown, 1996.

Rope of Sand, Jonathan Ball, Johannesburg, 1995.

The Field Guide to the War in Zululand, University of Natal Press, Pietermaritzberg, 1983.

Laband, J. & Thompson, P., *Kingdom in Crisis. The Zulu Response to the British Invasion of 1879*, University of Natal Press, Pietermaritzburg, 1983.

Laband, J., & Thompson, P., with Sheila Henderson, *The Buffalo Border*, University of Natal, 1983.

Laband, J., Thompson, P., & Henderson, S., *The Buffalo Border 1879*, University of Durban, 1983.

Leach, Graham, *The Afrikaners*, Mandarin, Johannesburg, 1989.

Lloyd, W.G., *John Williams VC*, Three Arch Press, Glamorgan, 1993.

Lummis, M., MC, *Padre George Smith of Rorke's Drift*, Wensome, Norwich, 1978.

Meintjes, Johannes, *The Voortrekkers*, Corgi, London, 1973.

Milton, John, *The Edges of War: A History of Frontier Wars 1702-1878*, Juta & Co., Cape Town, 1983.

Montague, C.E., *Campaigning in South Africa*, Blackwood, London, 1880.

Morris & Arthur, *The Life of Lord Wolseley*, Thomas Morris, London, 1924.

Morris, Donald, *The Washing of the Spears* (First Edition), Simon & Shuster, New York, 1965.

Mossop, George, *Running the Gauntlet*, Thomas Nelson, London, 1937.

Narrative of Operations Connected with the Zulu War of 1879, HMSO, London, 1881.

Newman-Norris, Charles, *In Zululand with the British throughout the War of 1879*, Allen, London, 1880.

BIBLIOGRAPHY

O'Connor, Damian, *The Life of Sir Bartle Frere*, Able Publishing, Knebworth, 2002.
The Zulu and the Raj, Able Publishing, Knebworth, 2002.
Omer-Cooper, J., *The Zulu Aftermath*, Longmans, London, 1966.
Paton, Glennie & Penn Symons, *Records of the 24th Regiment*, A.H. Swiss, London, 1892.
Peires, J.B., *House of Phalo*, Shuter & Shooter, Johannesburg, 1981.
Précis of Information 1879, Intelligence Division of the War Office, 1894.
Preston, A., *The South African Journal of Sir Garnet Wolseley*, A.A. Balkema, Cape Town, 1973.
Prior, Melton, *Campaigns of a War Correspondent*, Cassell, London, 1912.
Rattray D. & Greaves A., *David Rattray's Guidebook to the Anglo-Zulu War Battlefields*, Pen & Sword, Barnsley, 2002.
Reyburn, Lindsay, *The 1879 Zulu War Diaries of RSM F.W. Cheffins*, private printing, Pretoria, 2001.
Reynolds, Charles, *A Civil Surgeon*, diary entry dated 27 January 1879, private publication, 2003.
Smail, J., *With Shield and Assegai*, Shuter & Shooter, Cape Town, 1969.
Stalker, John, *The Natal Carbineers*, Davis & Son, Pietermaritzburg, 1912.
Stringer, Prof C., *African Exodus*, Mackie, London, 1998.
Swiss, A.H., *Records of the 24th Regiment*, Bremner, Devonport, 1882.
Van der Post, L., *The Heart of the Hunter*, Penguin, London, 1923.
Voight, J.C., *Fifty Years of the History of the Republic in South Africa 1795-1845* Vol. 2., Struik, Cape Town, 1969.
War Office, *Precis of Information Concerning Zululand*, London, 1895.
Whitehouse, Howard (Ed), *A Widow-making War –The Diaries of Capt Warren Wynne*, Paddy Griffiths Associates, Warwick, 1995.
Wilmot. A., *The Zulu War*, Cassell, London, 1880.
Wilson M. & Thompson L., *The Oxford History of South Africa*, Oxford University Press, 1971.
Wood, Sir Evelyn, *From Midshipman to Field Marshal*, Methuen, London, 1906.
Worsfold, W.B., *Sir Bartle Frere: a Footnote to the History of the British Empire*, Cassell, London, 1923.

Newspapers, Journals and Periodicals of 1878/79
Parliamentary Papers 1878-1906 (C 2222-2295).
Blue Books, 1878-83.
Mechanick, F., 'Firepower and Firearms in the Zulu War of 1879', *Military History Journal* 4 (6), 1979.
'Reasons of Defeat at Isandlwana 1879', *Military Illustrated*, London, 1986.
Trollope, Anthony, *South Africa*, quoted in *The Illustrated London News*, November, 1878.

Index

INDEX

INDEX